WILLIAMSTOWN BRANCH

WILLIAMSTOWN BRANCH

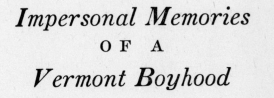

Impersonal Memories
OF A
Vermont Boyhood

BY

R. L. DUFFUS

W · W · NORTON & COMPANY · INC ·
NEW YORK

Contents

———◄••►———

———◄••►———

Fair Warning

———◆◈◆———

*N*ONE of these sketches is wholly true. None is entirely
untrue. In each case a remembered incident, personality
or remark inspired what followed. I have tried to keep
within the framework of the town of which I write, at the time
of which I write, as seen through the eyes and heard through
the ears of a boy of ten. If anyone questions what goes on in the
mind of a boy of ten, I can only say that this is the way it looked
to me then, as I recall it now. Let us remember that inside every
mature man there is of necessity the boy of ten as well as the
young man of eighteen and so on up the ladder of the years.

I have used some real names and some fictitious ones, with
no rule or system about it except an effort not to cause embarrassment to any living person.

I have written out of love for the village and town I knew,
and for the people who lived there. Life was better there in
some respects than it is in most parts of the world today. It was
worse in other respects. I do not try to pass judgment on where
the balance lies; but I do not wish to be listed among those
ancient parties who nostalgically worship an impossible past.

In those days, as now, I held my older brother and younger
sister in deep affection. Their stories of the year 1898 would be
far different from mine. They are not responsible for my story
and may be surprised when they read it. They may in fact wonder
if I am not in fact somebody else from some other town. Maybe
I am. But still, I hope they will not disown me.

WILLIAMSTOWN BRANCH

CHAPTER ONE

I'm Sorry, Miss Fillmore

*W*E LIVED, when I was ten years old, in a house just
outside of the village of Williamstown, Vermont, a
house that had once been a tavern on the stage route
which ran from White River Junction up the wild stream of the
White River to the divide, and then down the grade to Barre,
Montpelier, Burlington, and all the romance of the unvisited
north country. The road came out of something strange and
far-away, and it went to something a long way off.

The house belonged to an elderly gentleman named George
Ainsworth, who lived in one part of it while we rented the other
part for, I believe, seven dollars a month.

Since I have refrained from studious research in libraries and
am depending on the memories of a ten-year-old, carefully preserved somewhere inside the framework of a person infinitely
older, I know nothing of Mr. Ainsworth's ancestry. I am convinced, however, that he had ancestors. How he came into
possession of the General E. Bass house, which was where we
lived, I cannot tell. Perhaps he married it. Gentlemen of pre-
possessing exteriors have often married thrones and fortunes.
Why not houses?

Not that Mr. Ainsworth had the kind of smooth exterior that
would have won him a fortune in a then nonexistent motion
picture industry. He was not beautiful. Women could not have
fallen at his feet, even when he was young. By the time I knew
him he was bald-headed and offset this deficiency as many men
did in those times by wearing a beard. The beard turned white.

Mr. Ainsworth was a nervous man; there were then no fancy names for this infirmity. He was so nervous that he could not bear to have anybody sitting behind him in church—that is to say, the Congregational Church, which was the only one, according to his convictions, that was completely correct in its doctrines and administration.

So Mr. Ainsworth, belonging, as he was sure he did, to the only right church in Williamstown, sat in a special chair of his own in the rear left corner as you came in. My impression is that during services he tilted this chair back and enjoyed a solid comfort denied to those who were not too nervous to sit in pews. Mr. Ainsworth, from his rear chair, sang as loud as three choirs and as unmelodiously as a swamp full of bullfrogs in spring.

My father did not go to church at all, except on Easter, Christmas, and possibly Children's Day; he did not go to church in spite of the fact that he had met my mother while he sang in the Waterbury Congregational Church's choir. My father, sinful man that he was, sometimes went out in season to pick raspberries or blackberries on Sunday, or butternuts, or just for the exercise. He said that if God existed, and of this he never pretended to be sure, God was as likely to be up in Mr. Ainsworth's pasture as He was to be in the Congregational Church.

My poor father, as I now think. And, as I now also think, poor Mr. Ainsworth. In a way, they liked each other, and had some grand arguments. My father loved to tell of the evening they had a long set-to about the relative advantages of heaven and hell; my father said he didn't care to go to heaven if he had to meet the conditions laid down by Mr. Ainsworth and his friends, and Mr. Ainsworth replied, "Every man to his taste, Duffus, every man to his taste."

Mr. Ainsworth wouldn't have sent my father to hell if he could have done this by pressing a button. What he wanted was to win his argument, and on that occasion I think he did.

At all events, there was Mr. Ainsworth, living in a house that had once been important, in a village that might have been important if only the railroad had been built that way instead of by way of Northfield. Williamstown people had labored, lobbied and sweated to get the railroad, but all they got was a branch line from Barre, and there was no glory in a branch line.

The old stage road was, in my early time, an affair of dirt, mud or dust, depending on the season. I liked it best in summer, when it was mud or dust. We children could then run barefoot in it, cooling our toes in its sensual softness. When I had been even younger, but this I do not remember, except as I have been told, I made mud pies in the middle of it after a rain, and the horsedrawn traffic of that day detoured thoughtfully around me.

The stage coaches disappeared, and so, as a through passage-way, did the road. There was a sort of waiting period while somebody invented the automobile and somebody else invented the concrete-surfaced express way. We didn't plan to have this happen, and if we had been asked—as we were not—I am not sure we would have voted to have it happen.

The future couldn't be wiped out, not yet having arrived. Neither could the past, being dead and immortal.

The past was a room that Mr. Ainsworth had to own, in his capacity of owner of the house in which he lived and part of which he rented to us. Mr. Ainsworth was a pious man who didn't drink, dance, or chew tobacco. His wife had died a few years before my memories began, and therefore belonged with the ages. Mr. Ainsworth locked up a part of the house he didn't use and we didn't need. He locked up what I then thought of as mystery, but which I now know was history. We children saw it only once in a while, as he stood cautiously by with the key in his hand.

It was a fairly sizable hall, upstairs, on the eastern side, toward the hay barn; it had, I think, a broad-planked hardwood floor, perhaps of white pine or even oak; and it had a platform at the eastern end, with four or five steps leading up to it on each side.

This we knew, and perhaps we shuddered a little at the thought, must have been a place of mirth when our house was a tavern on the old stage route. There wasn't any such mirth among steady, church-going people in Williamstown in my day. Some of the wilder young folks danced, but not the very good of any age. Sometimes I wished I were bad, and could enjoy life to the full; but as a rule I felt safer being good.

However, the musicians must have sat on that platform, playing fiddles and other sinful instruments. I can see them now—in my mind's eye, if not my memory's—and the light-minded and light-footed people of Williamstown, and the passengers from the coaches that passed through, must have danced to their fiddling.

Who came through, in what stage coaches and what chaises, riding what horses, bound from where to where? I wondered about this then, and I wonder about it, with a greater store of worldly knowledge if not more wisdom, now. I see now, and perhaps I confusedly felt then, that something lovely may have passed that way—something wicked, too, something of the joy and fierceness of life that later generations tried to exclude.

But I never could have imagined Miss Fillmore, the school mistress, dancing there, in the wildness of her lost youth, and then being whirled off to an unknown, a beautiful, a tragic destination.

What a house this was, so solid, so built to stand! If the old dance hall was mysterious so, too, was the attic, with trunks in it that were never opened and furniture so out of date in the years of my youth that it must be worth a fortune now; and so, too, was the cellar. Down cellar the bark was still on all but one side of the beams that supported the floors. What trees, I asked myself even then, growing in what forests and cut by what sort of men?

The General E. Bass House, as it was called even after George Ainsworth owned it, was within easy running distance of the center of town. Let's say a mile in boy language, a quarter of a mile today. The center of town was the school house, the town hall, three churches, J. K. Linton's general store and postoffice, two drugstores, Seaver's drygoods store, the hotel, the livery stable, a blacksmith shop, the railroad station, the feed store, the creamery, and a sprinkling of residences. A little further along,

and to the right as you sprinted up from where we lived, were
the granite-cutting sheds—the stonesheds, as we called them—
in which my father and some hundreds of other fathers, mostly
Scottish, Italian, and French Canadian, spent six days a week
cutting or otherwise handling granite.

Houses were places in which to live, but I think many homes
in Williamstown were also beautiful; I think the General E.
Bass house was such, with its simple design of a colonial or
early republican front facing the road, and a wing behind.

Such a house was not cluttered by machinery of any kind.
It was heated, if this word is correct, by a series of coal stoves;
it was lighted by kerosene lamps; all its drinking water had to
be brought from outdoors, although washing water, with an
occasional modest and self-effacing white worm in it, could be
had at the kitchen pump inside; its privy was reached by walking out through the woodshed, which was much better than
wading through snow or dashing through the rain to the older-
fashioned, really outdoors variety; its bathing facilities were a
wash-tub luxuriously placed, in winter, in front of the kitchen
stove.

Mr. Ainsworth washed his face and hands every fine morning
in a tub of rain water under an eavespout just outside my bedroom window, spluttering like a whale coming up from a mile-
deep dive. He thought this did him good, and I don't doubt it
did.

The electric light, the telephone, and the natural ice re-
frigerator had been invented, and the automobile was just around
the corner; but we didn't have any.

If we had been rich we would have had a horse. I always
wanted a horse. Once I was a good boy for nearly a year, under
the impression that I might thus deserve a horse, a riding horse;
I believed then that being good was tangibly rewarded. But
good though I was for limited periods, and the period of which
I am now writing was not one of them, we did not have a horse.
Mr. Ainsworth had one at one time, and there had been a great
day when he hitched it up to the buggy and took the children
riding. Roswell Linton, younger son of the storekeeper, fell off

and was run over, but this did not harm him. Later Roswell got a horse, or pony, of his own. I could have killed him.

2

The day Miss Fillmore lost her pants was in January, 1898. I approach this date with misgivings, for it is hard now to realize that anybody was alive that long ago. Yet the biological fact is that somebody must have been alive then or nobody would be alive now; and I can prove, if required, that one of those who actually were alive was me.

In some ways the year 1898 had its advantages. I could see veterans of the Civil War walking around at their daily businesses, or parading with big flags on Memorial Day, just as though they were not embalmed in history. My maternal grandmother, the one who lived in Waterbury and the only one I knew, could have talked with someone who had talked with George Washington.

Some persons, also, were young in 1898, although it did not occur to them in my part of the country to start a youth movement, or proclaim themselves a lost generation, or look back with anger.

On the morning of the day Miss Fillmore lost her pants, I woke to a sense of winter and a disinclination to get up. It was not so much that I minded *being* up, even though school would be in session that day; it was *getting* up that I minded.

All night long the house had been making noises, as though somebody were drawing all the nails out. Something was, I believe; but the men who had driven the nails in had allowed for give and take. The house made noises, but kept on holding together, as it had done at all times for something like a hundred years.

The thermometer on this particular morning might have been a little above zero, or a little below, or quite a lot below. A really good thermometer in Williamstown, which was about a thousand feet above sea level, could get to twenty below without straining itself. There were farmers on the East Hill or the West Hill or down toward Williamstown Gulf who took thermometers seriously and with real competitive spirit; these people would sometimes get forty below in January and a hundred above in July, and from the airs they put on they might as well have been millionaires or foreign nobility.

There was snow outside the day Miss Fillmore lost her pants. I suppose this was the reason that though they did have ruffles they were made of flannel—cream-colored flannel, as I remember.

Nobody thought it wrong for snow to be outside in January, and on the other hand nobody had any money invested in the idea, as they did later when skiing came to Vermont. If the snow was too deep for wheeled vehicles, farmers got out their sleighs. The roads were not ploughed. They were smoothed down with snow-rollers. These were weighted wooden cylinders about fifteen feet in diameter, drawn by eighteen or twenty horses.

Very well, let us say five feet in diameter and drawn by two to four horses, depending on the depth and texture of the snow.

Such was the outdoors, although, since the windows were thick with frost, it was not clearly visible when I woke up. I lay for a while and brooded over the situation. I was certainly in for some chilly moments. Fortunately, as I now realize, I did not then have to take a bath in the morning.

I had once tried the experiment of taking my woolen underwear to bed with me. Not on me, I should add, but under the bedclothes. Thus these intimate garments were warm in the morning, and I started with a slight advantage over the Vermont climate; but I felt that this subterfuge was sinful. Indeed, almost anything that added to the comfort of life was sinful, among truly respectable people, in Vermont in 1898. I worried a good deal in those days about dying and going to hell.

Therefore, the clothes I was about to put on were on a chair beside the bed, and at room temperature. I do not know what room temperature was; but I suppose that when it was zero outside it was at least thirty-five above zero inside. The reason I believe it was above freezing is that in my grandmother's house in Waterbury, twenty-four miles downhill from Williamstown, there was a guest room with a pitcher full of water standing in a washbasin with a cake of transparent purplish amber

Pear's soap in a dish beside it, and I do not believe this water ever froze. On the other hand, my grandmother had what we didn't have, a coal-burning furnace.

If you stepped out of bed in our house in Williamstown in 1898 on a cold morning, or, indeed, any morning, you made sure that the chamber pot was where it ought to be, under the bed. Otherwise a person was in danger of stepping into it when he stepped out of bed. In one house in which we lived it was the family custom to gather up these utensils every morning and leave them on the back kitchen stairs for later disposal. Once, one of my sometimes diffident elderly collateral male relatives, who hated to make trouble for anybody, came down these back stairs without realizing the situation. He was in time for breakfast; but everybody who was present agreed that his arrival with one foot in a chamber pot and the other pots following him cast a damper over the occasion.

When it was cold enough, as it was on this particular morning, we three children—my older brother, my younger sister, and myself—were allowed to gather up our clothing and make a shivering dash for the kitchen, where we could dress by the stove. Somehow my mother managed to cook our breakfasts while we were doing this. She had already made my father's breakfast and fixed his lunch in his dinner-pail, and he had gone off to the stonesheds.

This was at seven o'clock in the morning. Employers at that time were extremely solicitous about their employees, and believed that it was better for the worker's character to be on the job at least sixty hours a week; this kept him out of mischief during those hours and sometimes made him tired enough to stay home and behave himself during the remaining one-hundred-and-eight hours of the week.

In the General E. Bass house, in January, 1898, we had, beside the kitchen stove, a stove in the sitting room, and perhaps a stove, not always kept going, in the upstairs bedroom. The kitchen stove was, of course, kept in commission all the year round. The others were put up and taken down, with their connecting pipes, at the proper seasons. I suppose some of my adult command of language comes from listening to my father when a stovepipe would unjoint itself when he was taking it down and let the soot get into his eyes and down the back of his neck.

The kitchen stove was like any kitchen stove of its time, with perhaps two very hot griddles, two lukewarm griddles, and a water tank or "reservoir," as we called it, at the back. The heating stoves were more ornamental. One parlor stove that I remember had a molding in front showing two or three chilly-looking individuals warming their hands over an open fire. The caption was *"En hiver,"* and it wasn't until I had three years of high-school French that I realized what this meant.

We burned anthracite coal and let the fires die down at night, banking them over with ashes. It might, I judge, take an hour to get the kitchen stove going well in the morning. The sitting room or parlor stove was such a slow starter that by the time it had got the room comfortably warm, the hour had come to choke it off for the night.

My mother was a good cook, although she did not have to be to get us children to eat. It was a Vermont custom for a person of any age to eat what was placed before him, and to eat all that was placed before him; this rule applied especially to the young. We had our preferences, but we were not supposed to actively dislike any food offered us.

Over quite a number of years, we had oatmeal, farina in various forms, Grape Nuts, and other pre-cooked breakfast foods, then just bursting on an astonished world (it was believed that if you ate too many Grape Nuts you really would swell up and burst), fried salt pork rather than bacon, toast, muffins, rolls, doughnuts, popovers (these my Aunt Alice in Waterbury made in a form never since equalled), griddle cakes, either wheat or buckwheat, with maple syrup, fried corn meal, eggs in various forms, and fruits—apples, apple sauce, dried prunes, dried apricots, preserves of various sorts, and once in a while, though usually not for breakfast, plums or berries put up at home. We had bananas occasionally and oranges at Christmas and New Year's, but not very often at other times, and then never for breakfast. I can't recall that we ever had orange juice.

I have probably left some things out. We did not have pie or beefsteak for breakfast, but we didn't come anywhere near starving. The people who did have pie and beefsteak for breakfast were farmers, who by breakfast time had already done as much work, out around the barns, as most city people then or now do in a week.

In 1898 it was thought that growing children would be better off without coffee, and for a year or so we youngsters were put off with cereal substitutes. But everybody meant well. I believed this in 1898, and I believe it now. It was just that some persons, including the manufacturers of Grano, contrived to mean well and still make a good profit out of it.

But I must not forget Miss Fillmore's pants, which, even at the moment of which I write, she may have been taking out of a bureau drawer in which dried rose leaves had been strewn.

Our ways were about to cross, as my brother, sister, and I sat in the warm, pleasant kitchen of the General E. Bass House on this winter morning in January, 1898. The kitchen got especially warm and pleasant when it was time to go to school. For this we put on more clothes: leggings or felt stockings with rubber shoes buckled over them; a reefer, or short overcoat; a woolen muffler; some kind of knit headgear. A Scottish relative once sent tam-o'-shanters to my brother and myself. They were perfect for our winter climate, but no other boys had them; we were free and independent and didn't care about public opinion, but we didn't want to look peculiar; and, quietly and firmly, we discarded them.

We put on what we had and started off, my brother and I. My sister was too young at this time, or it may have been after her illness which lasted so long and scared us all so much.

We did not especially mind going to school. For one thing, school was where our friends were, and we would have been lonely without them. School enclosed our small social life. It made us feel wanted, and secure.

We were lucky in one respect, or so we thought, during our school days in Williamstown. The Williamstown school board always felt poor, and judged that twenty-eight weeks of school a year was all it could afford. We therefore had plenty of vacations, which we couldn't have had if there had been no school, because there is no use in a vacation if it is not a vacation from something; and we couldn't have had them in such abundance if the town had been more extravagant in its educational largess.

This reminds me that one year, though maybe not 1898, my brother and I were janitors of the grammar school for one winter term of possibly eight weeks. This meant getting up before sunrise, starting fires, and sweeping up. I do not like to think of this episode even now. For these exertions we received, if I remember correctly, four dollars for the term, each, or approximately fifty cents a week. I still remember how pleasantly hefty the four dollars felt in my hand, in silver, with the goddess on one side, as the chairman of the school board handed them out. I can't remember what became of them, though I often wonder.

This day, however, we were merely going to school. We hadn't joined the working class. The school, which still stands, with some additions and afterthoughts, was of the early Grover Cleveland type: a box with windows and doors. Like our homes, it lacked plumbing. Drinking water was carried in a brown composition pail from, I believe, a nearby house. In the pail was a dipper. On the edge of the dipper, as I now know, were the micro-organisms that produce most of the diseases that children were accustomed to have—and were, indeed, almost encouraged to have—at that date.

My brother and I had almost none of them, and my sister didn't have all of them, though she did her best; but this was because our parents didn't believe that it was wise to have them and get them over with. When an epidemic of scarlet fever was running around town we stayed out of school. The result was that my brother and I had measles when we were in college, and I had mumps when I was working on a San Francisco newspaper and interested in other and higher things. On the other hand, if our parents had been of the democratic sort who believed that all children had a right to have all available children's diseases, we might not be here now.

Some of the young friends of those days have remained forever young: names carved on granite markers in the cemetery. I think of Richard Linton, son of a brother of the proprietor of the village store. We once spent a happy day on Richard's father's farm. I remember an extremely busy horse, operating what was rightly called a "horse-power"; I was sorry for the horse, because it walked uphill all the long working day, and never got anywhere. But Richard died.

I also think of Archie Staples. Archie and I were friends, as I hope, but once in a while he would prove that he could out-wrestle me. I presume he could have outslugged me, too. Archie got some ailment that reduced him to sitting, wrapped in a blanket, outdoors in front of the Staples' farmhouse in July; and then he, too, died.

I have no doubt Richard and Archie could have been saved by a miracle drug, if such had been handy. They might have done something in the world.

3

On this January day, 1898, school was keeping, and there were no known epidemic diseases as an excuse for staying home. So my brother and I stepped out into the snow in the front yard of the General E. Bass house. There was a hemlock in the front yard. We knew that spring was coming when the snow melted away from its exposed roots. Once it was struck by lightning, but the only resulting damage was that for years and years afterward nobody could mention lightning in the presence of any member of the Duffus family without being told how the hemlock tree was struck by lightning; how brave we all were; how some of us, myself especially, resisted the temptation to crawl under a bed; how the house might have burned down, but didn't—not until long after our time, in fact, when the east wing burned off.

Across the road was a row of maple trees. Behind these, to the right, was the Sibley house, a brick structure with pendant barns. A little girl lived there, and this little girl figured pleasantly in my thoughts, then and later.

On our side of the road, to the right, was a barn—one of two on the place; the other was back under the lee of the hill. The front barn had some value, even though Mr. Ainsworth no longer worked the farm; he could get a dollar or two or a circus ticket or two by letting somebody paint or affix an advertisement where passersby could see it.

The rear barn was still used to store hay, which I presume Mr. Ainsworth sold as opportunity offered; he didn't eat hay himself, and neither did we, except in packages and under brand names. My brother and I used to jump into the hay loft from the high platform in the center of the barn. This did us good, or so we thought; but as I learned later, from Mr. Ainsworth, it was not good for the hay.

Back of the rear barn was a hill which rose rather steeply for a few hundred feet. At one side, nearest the house, was a small gorge through which tumbled or trickled our branch of Stevens Brook. It was frozen now, and you could not hear its voice; but as it flowed it went into the Winooski, then into Lake Champlain, then into the Richelieu, then into the St. Lawrence, where all men and all waters spoke French and life was romantic, and finally into the North Atlantic Ocean.

I sometimes looked at our brook with envy. It went where I would have liked to go.

Across the road, behind the Sibley house and barns, were other and somewhat lower hills. They rose, beyond the immediate foreground, to sufficient heights to form the watershed that separated us from Northfield and from the main line of the Central Vermont Railroad.

At the foot of one of these slopes, not far from the Sibley house, was the overgrown beginning of a gravel pit. I say beginning, for it never did become a gravel pit. The reason was that a long time ago—and I suppose this meant four or five years ago—Mr. Sibley had started to excavate this slope, and one afternoon he had left his hired man there to work on it. A huge boulder came down when the hired man wasn't looking; we could see the boulder. We skirted this scene of tragedy, especially toward sundown, when the hired man might be coming back to study the situation, and perhaps decide how he might have acted differently.

I don't think he ever did come back, but if he did, if he cursed his luck and wondered who had taken his girl, we never knew.

However, my brother and I were about to go to school, and I don't know that we thought of the dead hired man at that moment. To go to school we turned right and trotted the quarter mile or so to the Pool Bridge, crossed it, and then, a little further on, turned left off the road. The Pool Bridge spanned our brook, which had taken a loop through Mr. Sibley's meadow, found the going not quite satisfactory, and slid around again toward the base of the East Hill. A brook, like a boy, kept trying one plan after another, and had its whims and no logic behind them.

My brother and I took our sleds with us, as an old man might take his cane or a stylish young man his gloves. They were, in a way, part of our winter costumes. Not to have a sled along was to be, or seem, undressed and impoverished. These sleds were low-slung. You lay flat and steered with your weight or with your toes. If you steered too much with your toes you not only showed a lack of skill, but you also wore out your shoes or rubbers, and this led to a paternal discussion.

Girls were not exposed to this temptation. How could a girl go, as we used to say, belly-bump? Girls, in that epoch, didn't have bellies. Girls sat up on tall sleds, and steered with a sort of rudder, squealing with a mixture of joy and, as I now think, pretended fear as they slid at possibly two miles an hour down slight declivities. This was long before the modern girl was invented. That came later: after the first World War, I believe.

I haven't the least doubt that almost any of these girls could have taken the Nose Dive on Mansfield without a quiver, if they had been expected to do so and had had six weeks' preliminary ski training. But they had been taught to believe that being timid, or seeming to be timid, made them more marriageable; and since that was the game, they played it.

I did not figure this out at that time, however.

I didn't figure out much at all about girls. In Williamstown in 1898 a boy was considered effeminate if he had too much to do with girls. On the other hand, there were mixed Sunday school classes, which went on mixed picnics, and sometimes there were mixed birthday parties, and the beginnings of pairing off.

I was a shy boy. Girls scared me. But I was the more reconciled to be going to school this morning because Millicent Byrnes, a wild and lovely Gaelic type whose memory hasn't left me all these years, was going to be there. One day, not long before, Millicent had abandoned her tall sled at the schoolhouse and asked me to take her for a ride on my own sled.

There comes back, too, the memory of the evening when Millicent and her sister Doreen came down to play innocent card games with my brother and myself, walking in unexpectedly when I, for one, had about decided that life was hopelessly dull. I was embarrassed and completely happy. Nothing whatever came of this, but somehow I believe it was worth while.

But girls at school flocked by themselves during recesses, and very often before and after school. Except when I drew Millicent on my sled on that one memorable day, I don't think I ever walked home from school with a girl. Girls giggled and tittered. Girls were believed to play with paper dolls. Girls laughed at awkward boys. How was I to know that girls had similar delusions about boys? How was I to know that they might even be attracted by boys? Nobody told me.

Boys had their own austere lives at school in Williamstown in January, 1898. They built snow forts and fought desperate battles. Some among us considered it ethical to dip snowballs in water the night before, and let them freeze before using them, but most of us didn't do this; and I don't recall that any of us were ever seriously mangled in these conflicts. I remember once capturing a snow fort under heavy fire. At least that was what I claimed. The enemy argued that I was either dead or a prisoner.

Some of us—fortunately for the safety of the Republic, not me—fought in real wars later, and found that these points did not have to be debated.

At times we went wild. Maybe it was on this January day, the day on which Miss Fillmore lost her pants, that I and others ran all over the school yard in the snow with our rubbers off, and I, at least, caught a terrific cold. Maybe it was this day that I climbed on the railing of the little balcony and tied up the bell cord by which the teacher, that is to say, Miss Fillmore, called us in from recess. This gave my classmates ten extra minutes of leisure, but perhaps it was one more of the events leading inexorably to the ultimate tragedy—for such I am convinced the thing that happened was.

4

Our teachers changed frequently because, as I now see, nobody could make a career out of teaching in that school.

One young man taught us for a term or two in order to make enough money to go to divinity school. I don't know what happened to him afterward, but he learned about sinners—a certain kind of sinner—from us.

Not that we were in any way vicious. I often marvel at our essential goodness—not my own goodness, but the fairly high morality of the group. If it were treated as a game, we would steal. I stole some lead pipe from Mr. Ainsworth's cellar, sold it for ten cents, and bought ten cents' worth of dates, which was then more than my brother and I could safely eat. We ate them, just the same.

I have committed much greater sins since then, but almost none that worried me so much. I was for some years afraid that Mr. Ainsworth would find me out and have me arrested; I am convinced now he did find me out, and smiled a little in his beard, and wouldn't have scared me about it for a ton of lead pipe. He knew I would grow up to be a good man, and, technically speaking, I did.

And yet, as long as four years after this crime, when I was going to high school in Waterbury and living with my grandmother and aunt, I saw a stranger coming down Main Street on a Sunday afternoon—of course on a Sunday I was especially sensitive to thoughts of sin and punishment—and wasn't at all sure he wasn't a detective looking for me.

My maternal grandmother gave me a certain amount of comfort. She didn't know what my trouble was, and I wouldn't have told her for anything less than a million dollars, but she did have her doubts about the relationship between being good and being fortunate. She said that if God looked after the godly, why had He allowed so many of them to perish in the train wreck at Ashtabula, Ohio. She was on firm ground. A lot of deacons and other pious persons who had been attending some sort of church convention had been killed at Ashtabula. Pious people said God's ways were not our ways, and perhaps He wanted these deacons elsewhere. But I never heard of anybody asking to be cremated in a railroad wreck because God might want him elsewhere; I got this thought from my grandmother, who was a wise and lovable woman.

However, Mr. Balfour, the teacher to whom I am now referring, was very much younger than my grandmother and hence more set in his views. Mr. Balfour worried me, not so much by anything he did as by his unsmiling attitude toward life. He was never unkind or cruel; he was dourly good. He had patience but no humor, conscience but no clear idea as to what conscience was for.

He honestly, and sadly, tried to educate us, and to some extent he did. I recall how he tried to teach us cube root with the aid of an actual wooden cube broken down in some instructive way into lesser cubes. There was one small final cube that proved the point, but I cannot now remember what the point was. In adult life I never tried to extract any cube roots. If the number to be dealt with was of a reasonably small size, I arrived at the solution by multiplying a few still smaller numbers two times. If the original number was a large one I simply gave up.

Another teacher was Mrs. Frankum, not young but still giving evidence of the warmth and charm that must have attracted the late Mr. Frankum. Mrs. Frankum had humor. She understood small boys—and, I suppose, small girls as well. I think she left her mark for good on every child who came under her care in that school, and in any other school in which she ever taught.

Her gift to my brother and myself was to stir our ambitions. It was fatally easy in Williamstown at the turn of the century for a boy to apprentice himself to the deadly trade of granite-cutting, which took intelligence but not much academic education. Mrs.

Frankum said fiddlesticks to any such proposal for us—and I imagine for most Williamstown boys she knew. She thought, and said, we ought to go to college.

We did, in fact, go to college, my brother and myself. It was impossible, by any reasonable standards, to do this, but—which is another story—we did. Williamstown could help us only just so far, for it had no high school.

I recall, over all the years, a dream I had in Mrs. Frankum's time. In the dream the familiar two-story school building had grown into a building of countless stories, reaching up toward the clouds. In doing this it had kept all its original characteristics. Each story represented a new step in education, and at the top was college. My brother and I were up there, in my dream, attending college.

I wish I could tell Mrs. Frankum how much we thought of her. Let the words I can't say to her go to other teachers, including some I never met.

But even Mrs. Frankum couldn't work miracles. Why do some ambitions, within limits and usually not in the form first projected and imagined—why do some of them work out, and others, just as real and shining, fail? It was while Mrs. Frankum was teaching us, I believe, that we were asked to write down the number of books each of us had read. My brother could remember two hundred or so, and so could I. And so also could Jim Nutting—whose real name I don't use here. Jim had a good mind and just as much interest in the world of books and of thought as we had.

The last I heard of Jim, years and years ago, was that he had been working as a brakeman on the Central Vermont Railroad. He had slipped while coupling cars by hand, in the old wicked way, and had lost a leg. He wanted as much as any of us, and that was what he got.

While I am still talking about school teachers, I must say a word or two about one whose name I do not remember, whose teaching left on me an aesthetic rather than an intellectual mark. This pretty young woman used to stand in front of the roomful of children, at the beginning of each session, and tie her apron.

She made a careful knot in the fresh white fabric. She did this by tying a bow in front and then switching it neatly around to the small of her back. Then she smiled back at us, and there wasn't anything within reason that we boys, at least, wouldn't have done to please her. However, she did not, unlike Mrs. Frankum, make us want to go to college; she made us want to stay in the seventh grade, or whatever grade it was she was teaching.

It was altogether a pure and unselfish love we boys felt for that teacher (or so we thought until we grew up and read modern psychology); I have wondered since then if in later years we did not in some instances fall in love with women of approximately our own age who resembled her; if we had not, in a sense, acquired a teacher fixation.

Still another young woman teacher lingers with an unforgettable pathos in my mind and heart. I do not know how to explain what I am about to say, but the reason we did not let ourselves fall in love with her, however purely, was that everybody knew she belonged to Willie Stone. Willie Stone, a neat and cheery young man of about this teacher's own age—I may as well call her Miss Miller—worked in J. K. Linton's store. If there had been a popularity contest I suppose he would have won it. There wasn't anybody in town who didn't like Willie Stone.

Even boys liked Willie Stone, who never pretended to be old and wise just because he had passed twenty-one. Boys skylarking around a country store could be troublesome to a clerk, who had no authority, yet was expected to keep the stock in good shape. Willie could do that without making enemies. I stole a chocolate once out of the candy counter, carelessly left open—one of the big one-cent chocolates. If Willie saw me, as I have since believed he did, he said nothing. He merely sauntered purposefully back to that end of the store and closed the sliding glass cover that protected the remaining chocolates.

For some reason this larceny never worried me, the way the theft of Mr. Ainsworth's lead pipe did. On the contrary, I felt rather proud of it. Still, I would return that chocolate if I could; I can't, because the store was long ago turned into a cooperative, and after that, burned down. In its place is a filling station, and I don't imagine the present proprietor would understand if I gave him a chocolate.

Willie Stone was then living at home, in a house that bordered on the schoolyard. He must have been living with his father and mother, though of them I have no present memory. Miss Miller, a lovely, pink, full-blooming blonde, full of sweetness and the laughing joy of life, lived a few miles out of town on a farm, over the hill, and it was inconvenient for her to go back and forth every day. So she roomed and boarded with the Stones. That was the way she and Willie met, and more than one young man about town must have envied Willie's opportunities.

But nobody, not even the young men who hung around the livery stable, made jeering remarks about Willie and Miss Miller. They wouldn't have dared make remarks about Miss Miller in such a way that Willie would hear of them. They wouldn't have wanted to, not even the young men who hung around the livery stable, ripe with derision and obscenities.

This was true romance, the love of Willie Stone for Jessamine Miller, the love of Jessamine Miller for Willie Stone. It was a thing beautiful to watch, and full of goodness, as even the children in Miss Miller's classes knew. Willie and Jessamine were going to be married in the spring.

I don't know how Jessamine got to and fro. Perhaps her father brought her on Monday morning and returned for her on Friday afternoon. At any rate, it was a horse-and-buggy trip, and would have taken an hour or more.

Willie wasn't able to go for her on Monday morning, because he had to open the store. He wasn't able to take her home on Friday, because Friday was a big night at the store, and Saturday even bigger. So Willie, being duly engaged to Jessamine, got a rig at the livery stable and drove out to the Miller farm every Sunday. He probably paid little or nothing for the rig, since his employer also owned the livery stable. He would stay as late as the parental Millers would let him and then drive back. Since he had to get up early six mornings in the week, and since the horse he drove was sure-footed, Willie formed the habit of tying the reins around his shoulders and dozing during the drive home.

One Sunday night a farmer living between the Miller place and Williamstown heard the swift passing clatter of hoofs and wheels, and then something moaning near his door, beside the road. He did not open it for some time. He believed somebody was drunk and he did not believe in drunkenness.

It was, however, Willie Stone. How the accident happened Willie was never able to explain. The way of it, most people thought, was that Willie had gone too sound asleep after saying good-bye to Jessamine; the buggy had hit a ridge of rock in the road; the horse had taken alarm and started to run, and Willie had been thrown forward under the wheels. He might have escaped with slight injuries, but he became entangled in the reins.

Dr. Watson did all he could for Willie Stone, and that was as much as any doctor in Vermont could have done at that time. But infections set in, and the torn flesh and broken bones wouldn't mend.

Willie lay in his bedroom in the Stone house for a long, terrible week, with the curtains drawn and the doctor coming and going every hour or so. I marvel now at Jessamine Miller, for she taught school all that week. We went up to the front row of desks, as the custom was, and recited our lessons, then went back and studied, or pretended to, while another group came up. Miss Miller gently asked her questions, as her way was, and told us when we were wrong, or called on somebody else to correct us.

One day, just before recess, she asked us to play as quietly as we could, so as not to disturb Willie. We did play quietly, too. The shades in the Stone house stayed drawn. Miss Miller went over during recess and at noon and after school. We went soberly home, not yelling until we were well away from the schoolhouse. We didn't argue or fight, not while Willie Stone was arguing so hard and deliriously for life and love.

The next morning, I think it was, Miss Miller said the prayer and read the Scripture with which school opened in that mainly

Protestant community. We didn't notice any change in her manner. We wouldn't have, under any circumstances: a teacher was a teacher, and we were too young to imagine what, or whom, she might be thinking about when she wasn't teaching.

But she paused at the end of the Bible reading, and we sat still and looked at her, because at last we sensed, I think, her trouble.

"Willie has just died," she said. Those were her very words, remembered after all the years.

Then she called the first class that was to come forward and recite. She didn't cry, or I would have remembered that, too. And I know why. Underneath her lovely femininity, her tenderness, her lost hopes, there was a consciousness of obligation. She had taken the school board's silver dollars to teach us, and though Willie Stone was dead she would do what she had undertaken to do.

I hope she was happy afterward. I don't know. I believe she left at the end of the term.

5

The case of Miss Fillmore was different—whether more tragic or less tragic I don't know.

She had come from out of town, from Waitsfield as I recall, or perhaps Randolph. This was, at any rate, too far away, as distances went then, for her to go back and forth on weekends. She stayed in Williamstown, boarded at Miss Jenkins' place, went to the Congregational Church, and didn't have any beau.

She may have been young and tremulous, but to us boys, and to some of the fun-loving characters who hung around the livery stable, she seemed an old maid. I wonder now, was she in her late twenties, or was it her early thirties? Was it her fault that she was unmarried at her age, whatever it was, or was the offence, rather, that nature had not made her pretty or physically warm toward men? I cannot make an image of her across the wilderness of years. The old maid was a figure of fun in our society of that date. There was even a game called Old Maid. I suppose the assumption was that an old maid was a woman who wanted a man and couldn't get him. Girls often married in their teens. At thirty a woman might begin to give up.

I don't know about Miss Fillmore. I never will know. I just feel guilty about her, for I sometimes imagine that it was I who gave her the final dagger stroke. I didn't mean to—but now I realize how little good this lack of evil intentions did Miss Fillmore.

I now assume that she was shy, and frightfully lonesome. I seem to know that she was teaching to earn money for some extraordinarily good purpose—not for her own delight, I imagine, but to help her parents or to send a younger brother or sister to high school or college. Let us imagine her moving in the friendly but possibly stiff society of Williamstown, going to church, attending church sociables and oyster suppers, looking wistfully for something—or someone—to happen, but still left too often to herself. She may have had some minor eccentricities—a flutter of embarrassment when she had to go past J. K. Linton's store on Saturday night, with the farmers and granite cutters sitting on the front porch if the weather were fine; a prissy manner of dressing, an affected laugh or accent, a sad effort to make a slightly superior education compensate for being so far along in years and unmarried and in a way homeless.

We were not a vicious community. We didn't mean to be cruel. But every village, then as now, had its loafers; and ours tended to hang around the livery stable. They didn't work there. They didn't work anywhere. They didn't work, as long as they could help it. The men who worked there had to have some knowledge and skill, or the horses wouldn't have lasted long. The loafers just hung around; maybe they liked the smell of horses and of stables.

It is now customary to regard a livery stable as romantic. It was not romantic; it was merely inefficient and not as noisy as a garage. In due season, I am sure, somebody will invent something noisier than a garage and more dangerous than an automobile—maybe the Wright brothers will invent the airplane—and then today's garage will be thought romantic. It isn't: it is merely more efficient than a livery stable, and less efficient than a jet-plane hangar.

What the livery stable had that no garage and no hangar will

ever have was horses. I don't know what the livery stable in
Williamstown lived on. The horses, of course, lived on hay,
barley, oats, and such delicacies; but how Mr. Linton managed
to make out on renting horses and rigs I can't imagine. A traveling salesman might take a rig, but I don't know where he
would have gone with it; a young man in love might save two
dollars for a long Sunday drive with his adored one. Beyond that
I am mystified.

When my father's rich brother, our Uncle Willie, came on a
visit to Williamstown, he threw money around liberally; he had
an iron foundry in Brooklyn and lived in an apartment which
cost him, as I recall, forty dollars a month, and if he hired a rig
at two or three dollars for the day he gave the livery stable
helper—the man who hitched him up—five dollars and never
asked for change.

But persons such as Uncle Willie were scarce. They wouldn't
keep a livery stable in the black.

However, livery stables did exist in every Vermont town at
that epoch, and they attracted characters who liked to sit around
in the sun in summer, or around the warm stove in the so-called
office in winter, and consider the facts of life. And their code,
such as it was, did not bind them not to talk about women.

I don't believe they talked much about respectable middle-
aged married ladies. You couldn't and wouldn't, not even in a
livery stable, in 1898, in Vermont, not even if you were a livery
stable loafer and never worked when you could help it. For one
thing, a woman who had been married ten years, who was up in
her middle thirties and had children, didn't then suggest romance, not to say scandal. A well-preserved widow might be
interesting to the gossips, male and female, but these were scarce.

Most interesting of all, of course, were the young women who
went wrong, as the saying was. Or who were suspected of having gone wrong. In a separate but somehow fascinating class were
young women who did not go wrong, or had not yet gone wrong,
but who had a warmth, an allure, a figure, a way of walking, a
voice, a glint in the eye, they could not or would not conceal or
moderate. The livery stable had these girls classified, and when

they went by, or even when they didn't go by, it talked about them. Anatomy was a livery stable specialty.

Yet the boys around the livery stable were not dangerous to unwilling women. Their extramarital or premarital relationships, I believe, were by purchase or other forms of consent. I never heard of what we now call sex crimes during my boyhood in Williamstown; and a boy was likely to hear of almost anything that happened, though usually not from his parents.

The livery stable boys talked, and it was clear by later events that they talked about Miss Fillmore. They talked about her for reasons just opposite from the ones that led them to speculate about a high-bosomed, swinging-gaited, ruddy-cheeked farmer's daughter of nineteen. They talked about her not because they judged she was having a romance or could have one, but because it was their opinion she could not and would not have a romance.

She could not have been of much interest to them, even so, until the day she lost her drawers. It was that event that brought her, in all her pathetic maidenhood, to the livery stable's attention.

It was that day, also, that left me with what I now recognize as a sense of guilt. This was not so much because I was then in one of my misbehaving phases; it was because I misbehaved in such a way and at such a time as to do Miss Fillmore an injury. My misbehavior reached its climax on the day Miss Fillmore lost her pants—and this was, for her, the wrong day, the unforgivable day.

Why Miss Fillmore lost her pants I can't clearly say, since I do not understand how women's drawers at that time were attached. My own dourly masculine apparel included what we called a waist, to which was buttoned whatever other underwear we wore. The union suit either had not been invented, or we did not know about it, or it was considered too advanced for us; when it was finally, and with a triumphant flourish, placed on the market, many persons thought civilization had reached its golden age.

Women did wear drawers, however, in January, 1898. Nobody saw these drawers, except, perhaps, their husbands, if they had husbands; but if a woman had a pair of drawers with lace on them I imagined she felt delicate and refined. And Miss Fillmore's drawers did have lace on them; I saw them and can so testify.

I have since believed that if we children had been behaving a little better, and specifically if I had been behaving a little better, Miss Fillmore might not have become sufficiently nervous and agitated to lose her drawers. I think there may have been some crucial button that responded to some swift and indecisive movement—and gave way.

At any rate, it did happen, and like so many fatal things that happen, it seemed commonplace at the moment. Miss Fillmore, conducting a class in grammar, was up at the blackboard making trouble about the way a girl from West Hill—a lovely girl, with sparkling black eyes that grew indignant and lurid under reproof—had diagrammed a sentence. This process consisted in picking out the subject, the principal verb, the leading adjectives and other modifiers, and so on, down to words that might as well not have been there at all, and indicating their relationships by horizontal lines with slanting branches. If I have preserved any interest in the English language it is because I resisted this sort of thing. Sallie Grainger didn't do anything to get herself into trouble; but when Miss Fillmore attacked her diagram Sallie lit up like a roman candle on the Fourth of July.

Miss Fillmore bit her lip and gave a little stamp, and as she did so the thing happened: her drawers fetched loose, her pants came off. With shamefaced presence of mind, she quickly drew back behind her desk, which happily for her was open behind but closed off in front. She kicked the offending garment under the desk, eyed us suspiciously, watching for the laugh that did not come, looked down at the watch pinned to the front of her shirtwaist, and declared a recess.

This was a historic moment. But we didn't know it at the time, and I don't suppose Miss Fillmore did either. We boys didn't even talk much about it at recess, but looked at each other gravely, and then went into one of our tumultuous games.

But after recess, and all that afternoon, the spirit of indiscipline was on us all. I don't know what I did that was so wrong. Probably I threw spitballs, or blew them, as can be done, through a rolled-up sheet of paper. I scuffled my feet. I tried to trip up fellow pupils as they came or went between their seats and the front desks where we recited. Maybe I was no worse than any of the other boys. Maybe I was clumsier. Maybe I looked guiltier—I used to find it hard not to look guilty when any crime was committed, even though I had nothing to do with it.

At any rate, Miss Fillmore descended on me, and seized me by the collar. I don't think she had the slightest intention of doing me any harm. She had just had all she could stand from me, or any other boy, on that day—a day that had humiliated and perhaps frightened her. I wasn't the worst boy in school; I claim no such distinction. I was, I imagine, merely the nearest boy when her emotions overcame her. At this distance, I sympathize with Miss Fillmore's impulse. If I had been Miss Fillmore, which I find it difficult to conceive, I would have wished to grab some boy and twist his collar.

Miss Fillmore should have sent me out to cut a switch. This really did happen sometimes—once, indeed, to me. But she wasn't in a thoughtful mood. She merely twisted my collar until I had a passing difficulty in breathing. Later on, trying to justify myself in the eyes of my parents and others, I insisted that everything went black. I said Miss Fillmore had tried to choke me.

She didn't. Miss Fillmore, wherever you now are, I apologize to you, I am very sorry. You were a terrified and despairing woman, I was a scared boy, and we had much in common. I wish I had understood this then, as I do now.

Miss Fillmore sat me down, and then let me go back to my seat, but she kept me after school. It was my brother who had to go home with the melancholy news. He was a fair-minded boy who always told the truth; but the truth was enough to stir up my father, who was by that time home from his work at the granite sheds.

I think Miss Fillmore came to me after the others had gone home, and tried to explain the situation. Then she sat at her desk, facing the empty schoolroom, and I sat at mine, facing her; but it seems to me now we tried not to look at each other.

Finally she said, almost gently, "You may go home now, Robbie."

I walked sheepishly past her, mumbling some kind of good night, for I felt sorry now, and wicked, and disgraced. I didn't want to go home, and for a time I hid from public observation on the ice under the Pool Bridge. But it was cold there, and I was hungry, and I came up in the early darkness and started for home.

My father was coming toward me, anger in his bearing. I shrank back, for I had reason to believe he could be angry at me. But he wasn't; he was on his way to the schoolroom to have it out with Miss Fillmore if she was still keeping me after school. He was a stern-spoken Scot, who knew his rights; he would have kept within the limits of politeness to a woman, but I am glad for her sake and everybody's sake who was concerned, that he did not have to rescue me.

We went the short distance home together. He was kind with me, and I felt more like a sinner than ever.

The next day the news was all over town that Miss Fillmore had lost not only her pants, but her temper, and had nearly choked the younger Duffus boy. The day after that the news was all over town, and this was much more exciting, that Miss Fillmore had received at her boarding house a carefully wrapped package tied in blue ribbon, containing a new pair of women's drawers. This had come from the boys at the livery stable. Everybody would have known that, anyhow, but they bragged about it.

Miss Fillmore finished out the term, which was near its end. I don't know how she did it. I think we even had the customary last-day-of-school exercises, to which parents and other relatives came; and I spoke a piece about ten little Indians, and forgot the lines in the middle, and Miss Fillmore made me go to my desk and get the printed copy and read the rest. Dr. Freud would probably have known why I forgot.

Then Miss Fillmore went back to wherever she came from, and did not return for the spring term. I wonder if the livery stable boys would have sent that pair of drawers if word hadn't got around that she had been rough with the younger Duffus boy. I'm sorry, Miss Fillmore, I didn't mean to.

The snowstorm had been followed by an absolute clearing. Every snow particle glistened in the morning sun, against the blackness of trunks of trees, against the whiteness of birch, against the black and gray of rocks. I went up, alone, on the left of the falls, where tumbled masses of ice retained the effect of flowing water. I seemed to have to get over the edge of the hill and not see the familiar warm outlines of the place where I lived, any more, nor the village with its roofs and steeples. I wanted to be desolate in a white wilderness, in the untraveled Arctic, perhaps.

I came over the ridge to a place beside the brook which was well-known and friendly to me. Now it was strange, but not unfriendly. Now in this year so long after, I shut my eyes and I see a long slope and above it, because of the wind that still blows, and no doubt will blow forever, long after the time of man— and the time of ten-year-old boys—a drift curled over toward the brook, ready to fall. Because a boy is destructive and experimental, I climb up a few feet and send this beautiful wavering blade of snow down the slope.

Something inside me says, I suppose, nature will know I have been here now, she will have to rebuild that crest of snow and do that beauty all over again.

It is lovely here, and too lonely, perhaps, and I am a little frightened. Perhaps I ought not to have interfered. Perhaps I was not meant to be here today, perhaps I was not invited.

I retrace my steps. It is not far. I see again the spires of the churches and the houses in the village, and then the house where I belong, with its chimney smoking and dinner cooking.

CHAPTER TWO

---•◦•◦◦---

The Stingiest Man

I CANNOT speak for the other two Duffus children, my older brother and my younger sister; but I myself could not be called devout and I don't recall that the others were, either. We liked church suppers, whether they provided baked beans, oyster stews, or maple sugar on snow, with pickles and doughnuts; we liked anything good to eat; we also liked sociability within certain limits.

For this reason I think we, all of us, at one time or another, went to the Wednesday evening prayer meeting with my mother. Once we even had a religious cat, which followed my mother to church and up the stairs to the Sunday School room, where the prayer meeting was held, and sat on her lap, purring loudly, throughout the service. This must have been during the Reverend Blake's time, because the Reverend Jasper Pell, the old war horse who followed Mr. Blake, would have regarded the presence of a cat as sacrilegious.

But Mr. Blake, as I am sure it was, stopped and petted the cat as he came down the aisle after saying the benediction. "That's a good Congregational mouser," he said.

My mother was reassured. "Of course," she protested, "I didn't know he was following me."

"He wouldn't make noise in the snow," chuckled the Reverend Blake, for this was, indeed, a snowy evening, and we could see cat tracks all the way home in the almost untraveled road.

This was a pleasant incident, but things were always happening at prayer meeting. Once in a while somebody would start to, as we said, get religion; but neither Mr. Blake nor Mr. Pell, unalike though they otherwise were, cared much for emotionalism. We were expected to take our religion soberly and seriously, and not to shout about it in public.

The best way to stop anybody from getting religion too loudly at a prayer meeting in the Congregational Church in Williamstown was to call for a hymn. If Mr. Ainsworth was present, and he usually was, there was noise enough then.

Still, a prayer meeting was different from the regular Sunday morning service. It was more informal. In theory, anyhow, anybody present could offer a prayer or a personal statement, which he couldn't do, of course, Sunday mornings. The minister became a sort of moderator. I found this interesting, the way a play was, or an adventure book, because you never knew what would happen next.

So I would remember, even if there were not other reasons, the night Deacon Slater got up and said he had been doing a lot of praying lately. He was, he said, a naturally stingy man, maybe the stingiest man in town. He had been praying to the Lord to help him overcome this weakness, and he thought he was making some progress.

There was quite a silence when Deacon Slater sat down, because the truth seemed to most persons about as he had stated it. He really was a stingy man, perhaps the stingiest man in town.

Mr. Blake promptly called for a hymn.

I asked my mother on the way home what Deacon Slater meant and if he really was as stingy as he said.

She debated with herself for a while. Finally she shook her head. "If he was," she concluded, "he wouldn't say so."

2

I didn't then know much about Deacon Slater's story. A boy of ten doesn't—or didn't—know much about any adult's story. It seemed to a boy of ten that an adult had always been an adult. I knew my father and mother couldn't have been born at their present ages, as of 1898, but I couldn't believe with my heart and emotions that my parents had ever been ten years old.

(41)

So I thought of Deacon Slater as having always been Deacon Slater, even with the title of deacon tacked to him like a set of whiskers. But people said Albert Slater had once been a hired man, and I did know a hired man or two.

I knew a humorously self-pitying hired man named Blaine Stillson, who worked for Ed Gorham on the Gulf Road. The Gorham farm was pretty good land, and Ed did well by his wife and daughter. Mrs. Gorham chose to dress her daughter in styles of about ten years back, but that was not Ed's fault—he couldn't tell one style from another.

Ed's attitude and Mrs. Gorham's attitude toward the hired man seemed to be different. The hired man said he got eleven dollars a month for working between twenty-two and thirty-two hours a day. He was a serious young man, and I didn't dare question his figures. He also said he reminded himself of a hired man he knew who worked for a family where the lady of the house cut the bread so thin you could read the Bible through a dozen slices of it. The hired man watched me carefully as he said this, and I didn't express any doubt.

This hired man didn't look undernourished, and I thought maybe he got more to eat than he would admit. The customary complaint made by hired men, and sometimes by school teachers who taught in district schools and boarded around up in the hills, was not that there wasn't enough to eat, but that it wasn't good. I hesitate to tell about one teacher and what he found in the milk gravy with which the lady of the house surrounded the fried salt pork; I hesitate to do this, and I will not, though when I heard about it at the age of ten, I was glad I boarded at home.

But what I am trying to make clear is, that if this hired man with whom I was speaking had succeeded in saving enough money out of his wages to make a payment on a farm, and had then married a hired girl with a little less money than he himself had, and then acquired four or five children, he would have had to be stingy if he were to stay alive and keep his family alive. A generous man simply couldn't have existed under those circumstances. I suspect that the poor house and the cemetery had a large surplus of generous men.

So, although I could not think of Deacon Slater and Blaine Stillson as being alike, and they were not alike, I may have connected them in my mind without ever realizing it. I can do so now, at any rate.

The only men who got their land easy in Williamstown were those who inherited it. There were a few of these, the substantial old families. I suppose Mr. Ainsworth's land, which he did not farm except as he sold his hay on the stalk once or twice a year, was an inheritance. But even those who inherited farms couldn't sit around and let nature pour bounty in their laps. They had to work. Even if they had hired men to help them, they had to work.

Some farmers cut down their maple trees—their sugar bush, as we called them—for timber, and then sat around in late winter when they should have been sugaring. We didn't respect such men.

But there were also young men on their way up; and now I see that Deacon Slater must have been one of these when he was in his prime. To understand Deacon Slater one has to understand that this was no affair of buying for a certain sum and selling for a larger sum. What the young man who was to become Deacon Slater had for his earthly possession was what he produced out of the land with his own labor. Some of this he and his family ate, and some he sold; but it was his sweat and ache that gave it value.

That was what a dollar or a dime was to Deacon Slater: aching and sweating, doing more than he wanted to do, stumbling late into the kitchen after the chores were done, eating enough to make him sleepy and soggy but not eating for fun, the way we boys did, the way village folks who didn't work too hard seemed to do.

I could understand this situation at the age of ten. We village boys were really the only leisure class Williamstown had. We alone ate without sweat on our brows, we alone reaped where we had not sowed.

It was different for the farm boys who did their chores before coming to school and after getting home from school, and who all winter long got up by lamp-light. They knew what hard work was, they knew what a dollar or dime meant in terms of hard work, just as Deacon Slater did. My brother and I learned this, too, but not so thoroughly—not at that time.

I suppose this was how Deacon Slater lived when he was a boy. Still, I couldn't get it clear in my mind that Deacon Slater had once been ten years old, then had gone through all the ages up to twenty or so, then had got married and become what he was now. Deacon Slater was Deacon Slater, that was all there was to it, just as Stevens Branch was Stevens Branch, always had been, and always would be.

My maternal grandmother, marrying a second time after Josiah Graves' death, took for her husband a man who had started life as a bound boy—or apprentice. At the age of twenty-one, I think it was, he had been given a new suit of clothes and a hundred dollars. That was what he had in the world.

He was successful, according to his opportunities and the standards of his time. He was so successful that when the time came for me to be born my mother went home to her mother on a prosperous farm in Waterbury, on the Winooski River below the village, and made this my birthplace. Thus I could always say that I was born on a farm, though it was not until I was earning my way through college that I learned to milk a cow.

As Luther Davis (my step-grandfather) got ahead in life, he left the farm and moved into Waterbury village to a house where I later lived with my grandmother and my aunt, my mother's sister, during my high school days. My brother and sister also fondly remember this house.

Such was the achievement of a man who started with nothing but a suit of clothes and a hundred dollars. I think he valued money, as well he might have done; but he had a kindly disposition, and whenever he and my grandmother and my aunt came to visit us in Williamstown, which they did once or twice, I always wept at the parting and wanted to go back with them.

I remember my grandfather in his coffin, the first such sight I had ever seen. I remember, too, my grandmother saying that during his final delirium, in the crisis of the pneumonia that killed him, he thought he was driving his horses in the woods and was talking to them. He died working, so it now seems, leaving my grandmother with a modest competency. All this life of hard work had not, however, made him a stingy man; he merely knew what it was that gave value to a dollar.

Stingy and *mean* were words you used when you didn't like a man. If you liked him, or respected him, or owed him money, or expected to inherit from him, you said he knew the value of a dollar.

My grandfather Davis knew the value of a dollar, but people didn't use harsh adjectives about him, not that I ever heard of. The question was, however, whether Deacon Slater was or was not a stingy man, and maybe the stingiest man in town. When the Deacon had mentioned this matter in prayer meeting he had no doubt done it on the spur of the moment, and with a desire to humble himself and please the Lord. He hadn't meant to make an issue of it.

But he did. Not much was happening just then. There weren't any scandals worth talking about. The outside world didn't matter too much, even though some persons in New York and Washington were even then planning a war.

Maybe Deacon Slater wished he had kept his mouth shut before the Lord. But he couldn't unsay what he had said. He couldn't unpray what he said he had prayed.

3

One not too cold dreamy afternoon about this time, some of us were woods-roaming on an off Saturday, or maybe during one of those frequent vacations that come in a twenty-eight-week school year. There was a thaw, and snow melting, and a drip of water. I suppose Ralph Stevens and Jim Nutting were along, and perhaps my brother, and maybe one or both of the Linton boys. We weren't roaming for any definite purpose, although I believe the theory among us was that we were Indians, or pioneers looking for Indians. The theory didn't matter too much. It was wonderful just to be alive and out of doors. I shall never forget the utter freedom of those days; there is no such freedom now, anywhere. We weren't even hampered by a sense of guilt, for we didn't intend to steal apples, butternuts, or even turnips; and anyhow, the sense of guilt hadn't yet been invented.

We came unexpectedly out of the woods into a level pasture clearing, then into a meadow with some hummocks and bunch grass at the lower end and a cow or two grazing on withered grass from which the snow had melted; next we came to the hay barn and the cow barn, beside which was a neat brick house. At one side were the corn cribs, with open, out-slanting slats to let the corn dry, and nearby was the hen yard, with its white-washed coops and sharp but not unpleasant smell.

As we came up, a rooster crowed, a hen announced that she had just laid an egg, and there was an aimless, happy clucking from other hens that were doing nothing in particular except enjoy life. We boys understood that—we weren't doing anything in particular, either.

I had a sensation of utter peace, such as I rarely had even then, and have never had as an adult—except, perhaps, on an occasional camping trip.

I stood still for a long moment. I think we all did. I can still see, hear, and smell everything that came to my senses in that interval of time. Years later I went back to see if all I imagined was true: it was. Some of the magic had gone, but a red fox loped silently across the pasture and under a rail fence.

"He's a good farmer, anyhow," said one of the boys, Jim Nutting, maybe.

"Who is?" I asked, for I hadn't paid much attention to where we were going and didn't recognize the farm. Indeed, perhaps I wouldn't have recognized it in any case, for the dream lay hazy on it, and it was not a real farm at all, but a farm out of a story book.

"Deacon Slater," retorted Jim Nutting, giving the words a scornful intonation.

And in fact there was the Deacon himself, coming out of the cow barn with a pitchfork in his hand. He was not a smiling man, but he looked pleasant enough and greeted us in friendly fashion.

Is he really the stingiest man in Williamstown, I wondered. There wasn't anything stingy about the farm and its buildings, unless he had discovered that neatness and thrift go together.

We hung around for a while. On some farms the farmer would have called out to his wife, who would be working in the kitchen, to give us some doughnuts or cookies, or at least a drink of buttermilk. I didn't like buttermilk, but I preferred it to nothing at all. We eyed Deacon Slater somewhat hungrily, I imagine. But he didn't call Mrs. Slater. After a while he waved goodbye to us, with the remark that we'd better be getting home if we expected to be there for dinner, and went back into the cow barn.

Maybe that was stingy, I thought. But did it make him the stingiest man in Williamstown? After all, he hadn't been talking about giving doughnuts, cookies, or buttermilk to boys that evening at the prayer meeting; he had been talking about foreign missions and other good works to which he thought he ought to contribute.

Suppose he saved money by not giving us anything to eat, and then gave the money to foreign missions? Would that be stingy?

The other boys didn't debate this subject, at least not out loud. If they couldn't get anything to eat at the Slater farm, they intended to go where they could.

What I got out of that sunny winter day was a conflict of impressions: first, the deep sense of peace that brooded over Deacon Slater's land and buildings; second, the care he took of everything in them and on them. Whether or not he felt any peace was another question. I couldn't imagine him stopping his work long enough to look up at the sky and wonder about it.

Next day, when I went up to the Linton store to see what was going on, I heard that the boys at the livery stable had been putting up bets about Deacon Slater's remark at the prayer meeting. The only trouble was, they couldn't decide just how to prove who was the meanest and stingiest man if Deacon Slater wasn't.

My father asked my mother just what Deacon Slater said to stir up all this commotion, and she told him.

"He wanted to impress people," said my father. "He knows very well there are stingier people in town than he is." He gestured toward Mr. Ainsworth's side of the house. "Do you remember the time he gave what he called a party and served small green apples for refreshment?"

My mother did. "That was all he had, maybe," she commented. "He was taking his meals at the Monument House."

"He could have bought a bag of candy," my father said. This made him recall a man he had known when he was a young granite cutter in New Brunswick for a while. This man would have a fit of generosity and buy a large box of candy on a Saturday night to share with my father and perhaps one or two others. Then he would sit nibbling at it, after passing it around once or twice, and eat practically all of it himself.

"He probably had a craving for sugar," my mother remarked. I asked what made people stingy.

My father said they were born that way. There were just as many stingy people in Scotland as there were in Vermont— more, because Scotland was bigger.

My mother kept still for a while, and then suggested that people were stingy because they hadn't had enough when they were children and were afraid they wouldn't have enough when they were grown-up.

My father replied that this couldn't be true of Jim Beckett, who squeezed every penny he could out of everybody he had dealings with, and never let go of a single cent if he could help it. Jim might have been poor when he was a boy, but so was his brother George, in that case, and George Beckett would give the shirt off his back if anybody really needed it.

My mother thought you could be saving without being stingy. There was Mrs. Gorham's mother, for instance, Mrs. Caldwell, a lovely old lady who spent a lot of time rolling pieces of old newspapers into spills that could be lighted at the stove and thus save matches. There hadn't been enough matches when Mrs. Caldwell was young, and they had cost too much.

There were elderly people in our town who saved string, old nails, old newspapers—George Ainsworth practically cut his living space in half by the old newspapers he didn't read and wouldn't throw away—odd pieces of lumber, and clothes that nobody would ever wear again. This was what attics were for; they weren't good for anything else, except for the chimneys to run through and perhaps to keep the lower floors from getting too cold in winter or too hot in summer.

My father said it was a good thing for young people, especially boys, to learn the value of money by hard work. My brother and I did learn this lesson, in moderation. My brother once worked all day in a farmer's hayfield and received twenty-five cents in exchange. I suppose my father would have said about this that my brother learned the value of money, but that the farmer didn't have to—he knew it already.

All this set me to thinking of the time my brother and I contracted to deliver wild raspberries for canning to a shrewd neighbor of ours, at ten cents a quart. The berries were dead ripe and as we picked in the hot sun, they softened and sank a little in the pails. The result was that each quart we delivered came to maybe a quart and a quarter.

But this wasn't the way Mrs. Mims saw it. She said the berries were second-rate, and paid us eight cents a quart. We were too young to argue this matter with her, for in our world adults were generally held to be right. But I still think Mrs. Mims was a stingy woman, although she never got up in prayer meeting and said so.

The Slater farm wasn't far from the village, except, of course if you were a boy and found a lot to look at on the way. You cut across an end of Mr. Ainsworth's meadow, stopping in certain seasons of the year to eat black raspberries from a bush near the hay barn and get your teeth full of seeds, but they weren't too bad when they were full ripe; or maybe you found a gooseberry bush and if you had the patience to get the spines off the gooseberries, if they were of that sort, you could stand it to eat some; then you crawled under the fence and went up the hill to the left of the falls, and you might find some spruce gum if you looked carefully, and you could chew it if you hadn't any loose teeth at the time; slippery elm bark was also good to chew, though it was thought best not to swallow it; and if you didn't intend to drink any milk right away you could eat a chokecherry or two if there were any such; and at the right time there could be beechnuts, which tasted all right but required a lot of work to get at a tiny morsel of meat; and the brook came down and was worth looking into in case there might be a frog or two in sight, or a small trout hustling under a stone; or sometimes a small green or brown snake, though I didn't care for even harmless snakes myself.

The Slater farm wasn't far, but a boy might be delayed getting there. Yet I did go past there quite frequently, sometimes with other boys, as on the occasion I have already mentioned, and sometimes on a scouting expedition of my own.

Once Mrs. Slater came to the door, I think with a pail of kitchen scraps for the pigs. She looked neat and gray, thin and very tired, but friendly enough. It seemed to me that both the Slaters were friendly, but didn't have much time to work at it.

She said, "Hello, Robbie," though I was surprised that she knew my name.

I said hello, and stood still and fidgeted, wondering what to say or do next.

"Are you all alone today?" she asked.

I said I was. She seemed to think hard for a moment, then made up her mind. "You come into the kitchen and I'll give you a doughnut," she said. "And some buttermilk."

My spirits rose, then sank, but there wasn't anything to do but follow her into the kitchen. She laid out the doughnut on a clean table, with oilcloth shining on the top. Then she got the buttermilk.

"I always said," she remarked, "that if buttermilk was good for pigs, which it is, it ought to be good for growing boys." She drew a long breath. The Slater boy had grown to be a young man and had drifted off, nobody seemed to know just where.

"Yes, mam," I said, and gulped the milk down as fast as I could.

"Do you always shut your eyes when you drink?" asked Mrs. Slater with a faint smile.

I said I didn't know. I wasn't sure that the milk wouldn't be right back up again.

"Could I take the doughnut with me?" I said.

"If you want to. I'll have to be getting the washing in."

I thanked her and went out, carrying the doughnut like a big ring over the forefinger of my right hand. I wondered why she suddenly laughed, the first time I had heard her do that, as I left.

The buttermilk finally made up its mind to stay inside me, and in a few minutes I reached the hill above the village and sat down to eat the doughnut, pretending it was a strip of jerked venison.

Maybe she was trying not to be stingy, I thought. Or maybe it was just the Deacon who was stingy. I wondered if he was still praying to get over this fault and if his prayers were having any results. My own prayers usually didn't, but maybe, I reflected, that was because I prayed for solid things, such as a horse to ride, and not just to be a better boy.

I wanted to be a better boy, that was certain. What I was afraid of was that if I got too good I wouldn't have much fun. A really good boy wouldn't steal apples. Yet this might mean that a slightly bad boy would get more apples than a really good boy. What was the sense of it?

Yet I did get an apple not long afterward, without being a bad boy. I got an apple, free, from Deacon Slater. I had again drifted up to the Slater farm on a solitary ramble, without really intending to go there, and perhaps balancing the disadvantages of having to drink a big glass of buttermilk against the advantages of getting a doughnut or maybe some cookies. I suppose I was still worrying about Deacon Slater, and what kind of man he really was.

It was again about the middle of the morning and the Slater farm seemed as peaceful as ever, with the hens talking softly to themselves about what they had done or meant to do, and a rooster bragging at the top of his lungs, but not as though he really thought he would get any votes out of it.

Deacon Slater was sitting in the sun on a pile of sawed chunks of wood. This surprised me, and I stopped short. I had believed that when Deacon Slater was at home and not eating or sleeping, he was working. But he wasn't working. He looked puzzled and thoughtful.

I waited for him to speak. "I'm taking it easy today," he said, as if he were apologizing. "Something is wrong with my insides. I've got a pain. I couldn't eat my breakfast." He stopped. "I guess you ate yours. What did you have for breakfast?"

I had had twelve griddle cakes, with maple syrup. "Griddle cakes," I said.

Deacon Slater clasped his stomach and groaned a little. "I'd give a million dollars, if I had a million dollars, if I could eat something that tasted as good to me as those griddle cakes tasted to you."

"A million dollars?" The words jumped out of me. A man as mean as Deacon Slater said he was couldn't be talking in sums like that.

The Deacon corrected himself. "Well, make it a thousand dollars. I could raise that much on this farm. I've done a lot to this farm. It's worth a good deal more than that."

He got up painfully and began to walk me around as though he were a guide showing people the sights. "I painted the house," he said. "It hadn't been painted for years. That was after Gil went away, but I thought he might come back. I built that barn from the bottom up. Before that there was just one barn, with the cows down below and the hay up above, but it didn't hold all the hay we could cut and we had to buy some."

"I see," said I. I was interested but embarrassed.

He turned sharply. "No, you don't," he cried. "Nobody sees." He was talking to me as though I were a grownup. "Some people think I'm made of money, and don't have to work for it. When I say it's hard for me to give money away, they laugh."

We went on talking, he lumbering ahead, myself following with shorter and quicker steps. "There!" he indicated the stubby pasture land. "I cut the trees off that with my own hands—beech and birch and pine and an elm or two. I didn't cut my sugar bush, the way some men around here do. And I didn't have a hired man, and she didn't have a hired girl, except once, a long time back, when Gil was born. I owed that much to her; but she agreed she wouldn't want money we could save for Gil being spent for a hired man, or a hired girl, either. We've both worked hard, but she's never complained about it."

"I see," said I. I didn't know what I saw, but those were the only words I could think of.

"When a man is stingy," Deacon Slater went on, "he is stingy on account of something. He isn't just stingy. You remember that when you grow up, Robbie."

We walked on a little further, going up the slow rise of the pasture until we could look back at the house and the barns. A thin wisp of smoke was rising from the kitchen chimney.

I made the only original remark I had made that day—or for several days. "It's kind of quiet, isn't it?" I ventured.

He nodded. "Yes, it is. It's real quiet. I like it that way. Real quiet." He was still for a few moments. "Would you like to be a farmer when you grow up, Robbie?"

"No," I replied promptly. "I want to be an engineer."

"A what?" demanded Deacon Slater.

I was sure my answer hadn't pleased him. "An engineer," I repeated. "Like Mr. Webb."

Deacon Slater snorted in an un-Christian fashion. Then he sighed. "Gil must have felt that way," he said. "I don't know that he wanted to be an engineer and sit around all day pulling a throttle and blowing a whistle. Gil had some sense. But he didn't want to be a farmer." He paused, looking over his land and buildings with a sad sort of proudness. "Maybe he was right. When Ma and I are gone this farm as likely as not'll go back to woods again. I can raise good apples, but not as cheap as those from New York State, and they say they're bringing them in now all the way across from the State of Oregon. We can raise our own eating vegetables. I can sell some milk to the creamery, or I can peddle it at five cents a quart; but that's a hard way to get cash money." He shook his head. "Maybe Gil was right. And maybe it's no use trying to save a little for him, the way Ma and I have been doing for about five years. It gets to be a habit, saving." He turned abruptly. "Were you at prayer meeting when I said that?"

I nodded.

"Drinking liquor is a bad habit," said Deacon Slater, "and smoking is a bad habit, and women—but you wouldn't know about that—they're all bad habits and they're all sins against the Almighty, but maybe saving is a bad habit, too. That was what I meant."

"I see," I said.

"You're a good boy," the Deacon resumed. "You make me think a little of Gil at your age. I'm going—" he drew a long, resolute breath—"I'm going to give you an apple for yourself and one each for your brother and sister. Big Red Astrachans. Would you like that?"

"Oh, yes," I said.

I walked home slowly, eating one of the big red apples, with their thin skins and the white pulp, full of juice, underneath.

A few days later Mr. Ainsworth told my mother that Deacon Slater had been pretty sick and had had to have Dr. Watson come to see him. He got well, but I don't know how well. His voice in prayer meeting never boomed as much as it had once done, and Mrs. Slater, when she came with him, looked more tired than ever.

I don't know whether or not they ever heard from their son Gil. When I last saw the Slater farm, and that was years later, when the red fox seemed to feel at home on it, the house and barns were in disrepair and the land had long been out of cultivation.

4

When the livery stable boys had what they thought was a good joke, they treated it like a dog with a bone. They buried it and dug it right up again. They pretended to forget it, and then came back to it with a pounce. This habit of theirs can be understood, for they had little but their own slim wits to amuse them. Anyhow, this was what they did with the joke about the meanest and stingiest man in Williamstown—the one Deacon Slater unintentionally started.

One of their bright ideas about this time was to elect a stingiest man at the next town meeting, just as, in those days, many towns elected timber reeves, hog reeves, and other honorary but unnecessary officials.

Sheridan Dabney, who was a sort of spokesman for the livery stable hangers-on, took the idea around town. "Do you get it?" he would ask. "We elect him. Maybe the Deacon would win and maybe somebody else would."

Dab, as he was called, would then laugh uproariously, and as he hadn't any chin to speak of, and a big mouth, this was something to look at as well as listen to. He didn't seem to mind that most of the laughing that was done at his jokes was done by himself.

In another day or two he changed his mind. Maybe some-one had told him he shouldn't make fun of town meeting and its elected officials.

"What we've decided to do," he declared, "is to offer a prize. Maybe J. K. will let us set up a box with a slot in the top in his store and then anybody who wants to vote can pay one cent and do it. The man who gets the most votes gets the prize." He added, as he had done before, "Maybe the Deacon wouldn't win, maybe somebody else would. We've got a lot of mean men around this town. There'd be some competition if they all really went after that prize."

"What are you fixing for the prize to be?" somebody asked.

Dab guffawed again. Of course there was only one sort of prize he could think of; that was the sort of mind he had, as I perceived. "Hand-painted," he explained, "with roses on it, and a lid."

"Too bad you don't stand a chance for it yourself," said the man who had spoken before. "It seems to please you so much. But a man can't be mean without having something to be mean over, and that lets you out."

Dab didn't like that remark, but he didn't say much. He had never exercised enough to get up enough muscle to be any good in a fight. Besides, he was too lazy.

I didn't like Dab's kind of conversation, but it fascinated me. It reminded me of what I could find under a flat stone in a pasture if I turned it over, white worms and beetles and other unattractive forms of life. But I kept turning over stones in pastures, and I kept listening to Dab's kind of conversation whenever I heard him trying it out on a group of men in the store or around the stable. I couldn't always keep away from the stable, because I did like horses and kept dreaming of having one of my own.

But I didn't want Dab and his friends to send Deacon Slater, if he was the man they decided on, a thunder jug with hand-painted roses on it, and a lid. If he was a mean man, which I doubted, he was still a better man than Sheridan Dabney. I kept thinking of what it was like to stand beside Deacon Slater's barnyard and hear the hens clucking and the roosters crowing, and how Mrs. Slater had given me a doughnut, which I liked, in addition to a mug of buttermilk, which I didn't like, and how the Deacon had given me those Red Astrachans, and how the Deacon had talked about his absent son Gil.

I didn't want Dab, or anybody at all, to do anything to hurt the feelings of Deacon and Mrs. Slater.

And in the final outcome he didn't.

One day Philander Milton, as I shall call him, came down, in one of his rare visits to Williamstown Village, from his rocky farm around the far corners of the East Hill. Philander was the sort of man who wouldn't let his wife come to church more than once a month because the horses needed rest on Sunday, and ate too many oats if they were overworked. Mrs. Milton was a ghost of a woman, with unkempt graying hair and a lost and mournful look. How she got her husband to accept her mother as a boarder, nobody ever knew. Maybe Mrs. Milton had the strength that the meek often do have.

Philander grumbled about the arrangement but it continued until his wife's mother died. The funeral was as simple and cheap as it could be. The next time Philander came to the store somebody said, with an undertone of sarcasm, that it was generous of him to take the dying old woman in.

Philander coughed apologetically. "Well, I'll tell you," he said. "She never did eat much, all the time she was with us."

A slow smile spread over his face. "And the last two weeks she didn't eat nothing at all."

He looked around. Nobody spoke, though the story would be all around town by next morning and would be a tradition in Williamstown as long as any of the old timers lived there.

I thought of Deacon Slater and Mrs. Slater, and now they had a shining quality. I don't remember that after that anybody ever called the Deacon stingy—not even the Deacon himself, though, when he was well enough, he kept coming to prayer meeting.

Death reached for me early on a February afternoon, then changed his mind for a while. Do I remember this afternoon a little better because of what did not happen? Or is it the sum of many winter afternoons?

A thaw had come. The farmers knew it would not last. I heard them talking about it in J. K. Linton's store. Mr. Ainsworth said the climate was changing. It had never been this warm in February when he was young.

I went out aimlessly, drawing my sled. Slinging the rope around the rear crossbar of a heavy sledge loaded with logs for the mill, I rode part way to Mill Village. The snow was sliding off roofs, leaving wet black patches; and there were drippings at the eaves that would be icicles in the morning. The houses on the opposite side of town, visible as the road rose, seemed bleak; the sunken drifts of snow were gray and discouraged. There was no spring, or promise of spring, under this leaden sky; the south wind was ready to shift westward and northward and catch the unwary unawares.

The logs were like dead people, I thought—so straight and stiff. I let my sled rope slip loose and hooked on to a farmer's sleigh bound back toward the village. I wanted warmth, something that was not gray and drab, some lift and song, and there was none.

I don't know whether or not the farmer knew he had a free

rider attached to his sleigh. He went at a fair clip across the railway tracks, along past the depot, and then turned right; toward J. K. Linton's store. At this point he surprised me by swinging sharply left back of the store and coming in past a woodpile where a man with an axe was reducing chunks to stove-wood size.

The woodcutter waited, as I subsequently realized, to let the horse and sleigh pass by. He waited with his axe over his shoulder, ready to bring it down. He started to strike, then saw me, uttered a fervent prayer in which he Goddamned me to hell for almost getting my head split open, and waited again.

If he had killed me it would not have been his fault. Sleighs were not understood to have boys behind them. I lived. And, suddenly, how good life was!

CHAPTER THREE

The Italian Woman

*T*HE FIRST time I saw the Italian woman, though I had heard her spoken of by my elders, was when I went down into the basement of the Town Hall one day. She was in the cage down there, and crying. She was crying so loud and so hard that I wanted to cry, too.

Hers wasn't what some women in our town referred to as a good cry; it was a bad cry, with some terror in it, some rage, and a Mediterranean quality (which I felt, even then, but couldn't have found a legitimate name for) that didn't resemble the kind of crying that went on in respectable, self-contained, old-fashioned Vermont households.

Upstairs, the Town Hall was all that a town hall in New England should be. I suppose it had some of the town offices in it, though I can't recall what they looked like. The town clerk wasn't there at all, he was across the street in his harness office.

Upstairs was where the town meetings were held, for two or even three days in March when there was little else for the farmers to do and they could come down to the village, usually through snow or mud, but they got there. Upstairs was New England at its best, as I have since been told.

Downstairs was New England trying to decide what to do with crime and those who committed it. That was where the cage came in—a real cage with iron bars. It seems to me that it stood in the middle of a quite large basement room, but I may be mistaken. I seldom got down there, and I couldn't make myself look at it closely, it seemed so frightening. I have an inborn horror of being locked up. One Sunday, when I was about eight years old, I managed to lock myself into a bedroom in the house we were then living in, not the Ainsworth house. When I tried to unlock myself, the key stuck. I yelled with all my lung power and then twisted the key so hard that when my annoyed father finally got it out it was all out of shape.

My father removed me, after a while, through a window, and I broke the window. It was so good to be outside again and free that I hardly minded my father's remarks. But any locked place, any cage, gave me a shiver.

I don't even know, now, how the cage in the basement of the Town Hall was furnished. It must have had some facilities for the inmate's personal needs. It must have had a chair and a bed.

All I am sure of is that the Italian woman was sitting on something, no doubt the bed, and crying as though her heart were broken. It may be that Constable Nichols came along at this point and chased us out—for there must have been more than one of me. I didn't do risky things like that all alone; I tried as a rule to get some other boy to go first and see what happened.

I have never forgotten that weeping woman. I think I have dreamt of her more than once. This was not because I associated myself with her. I don't know what she looked like, except that she had black hair and it was all down around her face. She was no goddess to me, as Anna Marie Sylvester was to be. I did not want her to notice me. I am not even sure I wanted to help her. I just wanted her to stop crying. I wanted somebody to come and let her out. I wanted to be somewhere else.

She was not, of course, in quite as bad trouble as I supposed. She wasn't even a bad woman, in the technical sense of that word. Her sin was that she had sold alcoholic liquor, contrary to the law of the State of Vermont—and also, as we children were taught in school and church, and as many adults earnestly believed, contrary to the law and will of God. Our elders had some trouble explaining to us why it was a good thing for the Founder of Christianity to change water into wine at the marriage feast in Cana and a bad thing for this Italian woman, and other persons

of both sexes, to provide wine for modern marriage feasts and
on other occasions. But they tried, our elders did.

They tried by putting the evils of alcohol into our school
curriculum. Indeed, they poured them in. The teachers were
required to illustrate what might happen to us if we drank. They
did this by bringing some pure alcohol into class and dropping
an egg into it; believe it or not, the alcohol solidified the white
of the egg.

We children all knew that this was what happened if you
dropped an egg into hot water. We were supposed to infer, I
believe, that alcohol in the human stomach was as bad as boiling
water. In later life I never found this to be so.

The teacher also told us of certain diseases that came from
excessive use of alcohol in any form. We had an elementary text-
book in physiology that had pictures to prove this point.

In addition, the State of Vermont encouraged school children
to learn a song entitled *Touch Not the Cup,* the music and some
of the words of which still linger with me. The song stated in
so many words that liquor was "death to the soul." I have not
found it so. Or I have found it so and failed to notice my condition.

At any rate, Vermont in 1898 was existing under state-wide
prohibition—the second state, after Maine, to adopt this measure.

We all knew that some of our citizens didn't believe in prohibition and didn't practice it. The drugstores could get around
the law easily enough. Some people had liquor sent in from other
states by express, and no questions asked. Once on one of my
fruitless fishing excursions with another boy we noticed something unusual about the way the earth lay under a tree beside
the bank. It looked, indeed, as though something had been
buried there. Since we had just come upon an excessively dead
dog in the middle of the stream, we were thinking of death and
were full of morbid curiosity.

When we investigated, however, we found not another dead
dog, a dead human being, or anything that we considered
buried treasure. We found twelve bottles of beer.

I recall that we debated what to do next. Should we tell

Constable Nichols or somebody else in authority? Or would it be wiser to leave the beer bottles where we had found them and go on with our fishing? This last was what we did; we thought we knew whose hired man owned the beer, and we judged it sensible to keep on good terms with him. After all, he had seen us come up the brook and the stream was what we called "posted" against unlawful intruders.

On one occasion Constable Nichols and possibly some state enforcement agents raided the Rattlesnake Tavern, confiscated a large number of bottles of lager beer and disposed of their plunder in a handy and more or less legal way by throwing all, or most, of it off the little bridge where the brook slid down to Mr. Sibley's meadow, near the Ainsworth house.

Not all the bottles broke, though they were thrown off the wagon on to the stones of the stream bed. I wandered over— I will not incriminate my brother William—picked up a bottle or two, and took them around behind the barn. They were opened by springing the catch that held the cap down. Bravely I raised a bottle to my lips, intending to be thoroughly bad for once and learn what all this nonsense about alcohol really meant. I believed that beer must be like soda pop, only infinitely better.

This was a mistake. It took me years after that before I tasted beer again, and more years before I really liked it. I didn't get drunk—I just didn't like the stuff.

Such an experience might have embittered me for life. But what this one did was to convince me that perhaps my school-teachers, Sunday school teachers, and adult advisers were right. It made me wonder what some people could see in beer, wine, and liquor. All I was sure of was that they tasted bad, and in some cases made people sick to their stomachs.

There used to be a hotel or roadhouse in Williamstown Gulf, four or five miles below our town, and I suspect that at some time and under some managements alcohol was sold there. I recall two young men, obviously from Barre or Montpelier, driving through Williamstown one Sunday afternoon with a horse and buggy. One of the young men was making the horse go by lashing the poor animal with the whip. The other young man was leaning over the side of the vehicle and throwing up whatever he had been eating.

This did not make drinking seem a happy adventure. Still, my imagination played around it a little. There was drinking in some of the books I read—Dumas', for example—and it seemed to do the characters good.

Another kind of drinking took place among the farmers and others who had access to hard cider and, in season, to sap beer. Somehow the godly individuals in our town did not feel as reproachful and alarmed when a farmer drank hard cider as they did when he drank whiskey. Sap beer they were uncertain about, because though the beer part of the phrase might be questionable, the sap part was accepted by anybody who had ever tasted maple sugar.

In later days farmers drank a liquid that could be drawn off from the bottom of a silo, but this was a little after my time; at any rate, I knew nothing about it when I was ten years old.

But what the Italian woman had done was to sell wine at the Rattlesnake Tavern. And people in our town who winked at hard cider felt that it was wicked for the Italians to drink wine.

2

The Italians had probably learned to cut stone in the days when they were called Romans, and have never quite forgotten how. At any rate, they showed up in Vermont when the granite industry began to flourish there. I suppose they worked in marble, too, but we didn't have commercial marble in or near Williamstown. You had to go to Rutland or Proctor for that.

When the Italians came to Vermont, they brought Italy with them. Italy included a kind of bowling game played with one small ball and some big ones—a game I later saw being played in Sicily. Even Italian boarding houses, including the Rattlesnake Tavern, had an outdoor bowling alley.

The Italian granite cutters sometimes lived in the Tavern or a boarding house because they were young and unmarried. It seems to me, as I think of it, that few of them were married. I don't recall many Italian women, not to mention many Italian girls. Maybe some of them intended to go back to Italy when they had enough to live on in some small Italian village. Maybe they were younger than most skilled working men because so many of them died or had to give up stone cutting when they reached middle age. Stone cutting wasn't an old man's occupation—and men grew old in it early.

So the Italian granite workers brought to Williamstown their game of bowls, their quest for the women they hadn't yet found, and their habit of drinking wine. They would drink beer or whiskey if they couldn't get wine; but it was wine they preferred.

Some people said the Italians drank wine at every meal, including breakfast; they said that the Italians would pour wine into their coffee, stir it with their index fingers and drink it down; they implied that this was an extremely wicked way of drinking. Nobody said the Italians were permanently drunk. They couldn't be, and still do the delicate work required of them. We liked them, that is, our elders did; and we boys liked practically everybody. Their fault was that they weren't quite like the people of old Vermont stock.

I am sure Mr. Ainsworth and some of the other worthy citizens who did come from the old stock would have liked to turn the Italians into old-fashioned Vermonters—preferably of the Congregational or some other Protestant faith. I am also sure they realized they couldn't do this. The Italians would go right on being Italians—and being as a rule lovable, except when they were in love.

They would also go on being Catholics, as did the Irish and the French Canadians. This was inconvenient, for there was no Catholic church nearer than Barre; but it was probably not so inconvenient as it would have been for them to conform to our kind of religion. I believe even Mr. Ainsworth would have realized that. A hundred assorted Italians, plus some Irish and French Canadians, marching in a body into the Congregational Church on a Sunday morning and announcing that they had been converted to Protestantism of the Congregational type would have flabbergasted Mr. Ainsworth and everybody else.

Inwardly, I imagine all the townspeople preferred things about the way they were. I believe the townspeople of the medium good sort, not the extra professionally good, also preferred to let the Italians go on drinking wine if they liked to do so.

The law, however, had to make certain motions. If it was illegal to sell wine or other alcoholic drinks, including lager beer, the law felt obliged from time to time to make arrests and talk about penalties. I think this obligation rested heavily on Constable Nichols, who was a man not fond of trouble. Maybe he was prodded by state enforcement officers. Maybe people hinted that if he didn't make an arrest now and then, it was for corrupt reasons.

This was nonsense, for in our town nobody was corrupt. I really mean this. Williamstown wasn't large enough to make corruption worth while. There wouldn't have been enough money in it, for one thing; and for another thing, it couldn't have been hushed up, because everybody knew everybody else's business. A man couldn't even have an illicit sexual relationship in our town without everybody, including ten-year-old boys, knowing about it. An innocent ten-year-old boy, such as I was, not living on a farm, might be uncertain about the details; but he would hear from older boys, who in turn heard from still older ones, and so on into the adult range, that something wrong and exciting had been going on between Mr. X and Miss (or sometimes Mrs.) Y.

Nothing of this sort, so far as I ever heard, happened at the Rattlesnake Tavern. But though all the Italian boarding houses sold wine, the Rattlesnake Tavern was, for some reason, more dramatic than the others.

Its name may have had something to do with this situation. Vermont in my day had next to no rattlesnakes. I never saw one and never heard of any one else who had seen one. I don't know whether the Tavern was so named because somebody in the town's early history had seen a rattlesnake near by, or because it was supposed that some of the boarders drank enough to see one.

For some reason the Tavern was sinister, name or no name.

It stood under the edge of a hill on the edge of a swamp, so that it gave an impression of darkness. I remember passing by and hearing loud Italian singing from within. You wouldn't hear singing from houses inhabited by people of the old stock, not unless somebody was holding a family prayer meeting or a choir rehearsal or something like that. We didn't sing for the fun of it, just to express our joy in life, if we had any. We had to have a reason, and the Italians didn't.

Not that this singing that I heard going by the Rattlesnake Tavern was always gay. Sometimes it was sad, as though somebody had just died and the singer wished he—or sometimes she, for it could be in either voice—were dead, too.

I think I had once heard the woman who sold the wine singing, the woman who subsequently cried so hard in the cage in the Town Hall basement. Perhaps this was why her crying voice moved me so much, and why I have remembered it so long. What I remember of the singing voice she had is that it was not like something out of Italian opera, but like something out of Grieg; and at that time I didn't know any Italian opera or any Grieg. But now the woman, and the crying, and the singing voice, are all tied together in the things I remember. I must have been listening, and noticing, and seeing with some sort of special interest.

I suppose the woman's husband or somebody else from the Rattlesnake Tavern, or maybe one of the regular customers, for I am not certain she had a husband, came down as soon as he heard of her trouble and bailed her out. The town wouldn't have wanted to keep her in jail at its own expense, no matter what she had done, short of murder. Nor would it have wanted to send her to Barre to be locked up there. There was always the danger, which the selectmen avoided whenever possible, of having to spend a little money.

So I think the Italian woman didn't have to cry very long before Constable Nichols came down and let her out. I wouldn't have liked to be Constable Nichols, even then, for it was said later that she gave him a tongue-lashing that would have made any wife envious. It was, so people said, partly in English and partly in Italian, and she switched back and forth between the two, hunting for new words.

It was Constable Nichols, so it appeared, who had done wrong, not the Italian woman. She had been doing what she would have done in Italy, and no criticism from anybody. If any crime had been committed it had been committed by the man who had taken her from her home at her busiest time and shut her up behind iron bars in the basement of the Town Hall.

The Italians in general agreed with her. They felt that when she was arrested, in her own house, while attending to her own affairs, it was not she alone who was being persecuted, it was Italy and the whole Italian race that were being put upon. The Italians couldn't see why Mrs. Bianchi should be locked up in the cage in the basement of the Town Hall for selling or possessing wine when Mrs. White, up on the East Hill, could make or even sell all the coffee she wanted without being bothered by Constable Nichols or some stranger from Barre with a star on his coat.

Wine made you feel good, the Italians argued. Sure it did— they admitted it. Coffee also made you feel good. What was wrong with feeling good, in this world where so many people felt so bad so much of the time?

I heard these arguments being batted back and forth, and though I remained convinced that drinking wine was sinful, I found it hard to believe that our laughing, singing, quick-tempered, kind-hearted Italian neighbors were also sinful. They didn't look wicked. The woman in the cage didn't look wicked.

I knew well enough that in the big cities—maybe even in Barre—men got drunk and rolled around in the gutter. We didn't have any gutter in Williamstown, but I was certain that if we did have one it wouldn't be a nice place to roll around in. I knew, too, that drink caused poverty and sometimes even made men throw bottles at their little girls—I had seen a play called *Ten Nights in a Bar Room*. Drinking made the plaster come off the walls, so you could see the laths right through.

But the sight of the woman in the cage kept on bothering me. The case was talked about around town quite a lot. I heard one man in J. K. Linton's store speak up and say that he didn't see the use of bothering the Italians, even if they did drink a little red ink now and then, so long as they didn't make nuisances of themselves. Somebody else replied that a law was a law, and somebody down the counter a piece put in that it was easy to say that about a law you weren't tempted to break. Mr. Ainsworth came in about this time for a small purchase, and was pleasant to everybody, but the discussion ended there. Everybody knew what Mr. Ainsworth would say.

3

Everybody knew what Mr. Ainsworth would say. I repeat this observation because it was important. Mr. Ainsworth had a definite set of opinions about religious and moral questions— and the use of wine was both a religious and a moral question, the way he looked at it—and these opinions could not be changed by additional evidence.

Mr. Ainsworth was not a fanatic. He was not an unhappy or disappointed man, as I remember him. He was kindly in his conversation. If he indulged in gossip it was not out of malice but because of his real interest in the lives of other persons. This trait, indeed, assisted him in one of his occupational sidelines, that of being Williamstown correspondent for a Barre newspaper. Sometimes he wrote little essays and signed them "Gainsborough." I do not now recall what any of them was about, but it seems to me he had a smooth, rather wordy, old-fashioned style. People said some of Mr. Ainsworth's things were good enough to go in a book, and I don't doubt they were.

Mr. Ainsworth wasn't in the least like the drab creatures who were subsequently caricatured as prohibitionists, or other would-be reformers. He merely thought that liquor was bad for people and in a spirit of good will did what he could to keep them from drinking it. In the same way, I am sure, he was against sexual relations outside of marriage, and for the same reason, that they were not good for people.

He didn't want to hurt or humiliate the Italian woman. What

he was after was to keep her from doing harm to others—I mean harm in his own interpretation of the word.

The case of the Italian woman must have increased in importance after she had been bailed out of the cage in the basement of the Town Hall and had gone back to cooking and to serving wine to her boarders at the Rattlesnake Tavern.

There was more and more talk about it, some of which I overheard in J. K. Linton's store. It was even mentioned at home in the presence of us children. My mother said the poor woman might not have known she was breaking a law. On general principles my mother didn't believe in shutting anybody up in a cage unless the prisoner had committed murder or was getting ready to do so. She thought, as did also quite a few other citizens of both sexes, that it was especially wrong to shut a woman up.

The prevailing theory about women, in fact—and even many of the women shared it—was that they were delicate flowers and required protection and consideration.

My father was not sentimental about this or anything else. He said that Constable Nichols hadn't the sense he was born with. If he had had a small atom of sense somewhere inside his thick head, said my father, he would have known better than to arrest a woman. If he had to arrest somebody he would have waited for the husband or some other accomplice to show up, and then arrested him. He would have avoided what turned out to be a scandal.

Constable Nichols during this period went around town explaining himself and justifying himself. There wasn't any use in having laws, he said, if some people had to obey them and others didn't. He glared around him at the group in the store. What would they have done? That was what he wanted to know.

"If I'd been in your place, Henry," said somebody—a young farmer I believe it was—"I'd have known what to do. And it wouldn't have been what you actually did, either."

I didn't know quite what he meant, but I snickered, too, with the rest of them.

Constable Nichols looked around severely. "You ought at least to keep your dirty thoughts to yourself," he said, "when there's children around."

He then made his stately way to the front door, without looking back. I could have thrown an apple at him, for I didn't like to be described as a child. I knew I wasn't an adult; I was even glad not to be an adult and have to work at some dull occupation, other than railroading, for a living. But the word child suggested a small animal that couldn't be safely allowed out of its mother's sight. My young companions and myself were certainly beyond this silly stage. We were wood rangers, baseball players, mighty swimmers, and, in short, well able to take care of ourselves, except at mealtime and bedtime.

But I didn't talk back to Constable Nichols, partly because I was a polite and extremely shy boy, and partly because I believed he could arrest me and lock me up if I annoyed him. And I could see that Constable Nichols had arguments in his favor—not when he spoke of me as a child, but when he tried to keep his oath to enforce the law. He was worried, but not puzzled; he thought that if he could present his case to the whole town, one man at a time, he would be understood and appreciated.

With Mr. Ainsworth it was different. He had to say what everybody expected him to say. Then, somehow, he had to keep on saying it, as though to reassure himself. I didn't see this then, of course. I just thought it was nice of Mr. Ainsworth to talk to me about the Italian woman, as once or twice he did, as though I were an adult. He didn't precisely ask my opinion, but he seemed to wait at times for me to say uh-huh, which I obligingly did.

I suppose it was this trait of Mr. Ainsworth's—being democratic with small boys—that makes it hard for me to be severe with him. It wasn't that he was familiar or playful. Boys didn't like that sort of thing in adults any better than they liked snootiness. Mr. Ainsworth just seemed to forget how old he was and how young I was.

So I listened carefully while Mr. Ainsworth explained what he thought about wine and other sorts of alcoholic beverages, and what we had to do to stop people from drinking them except for medicinal purposes, and how it was sometimes necessary to be—well, severe—with those who broke the law, even if they were women.

Mr. Ainsworth said he thought the time was coming when no alcohol would be sold anywhere in the United States except on doctor's orders. "That will be a great day, Robbie," he went on enthusiastically, "and you'll live to see it, even though I don't. You see, we have to save some people from themselves. No matter what they think of us, we're really their friends."

I said, "Uh-huh, I see." To a certain extent I did see, for what Mr. Ainsworth and others told me about alcohol had sunk in. During my first year in high school, some two or three years after the date of which I am writing, I wrote what I thought was a good essay in which I compared liquor with the older forms of chattel slavery. If I had won a prize for this effort, I might have continued a prohibitionist the rest of my life. Five dollars might have done it. But all I got was honorary publication in the Waterbury Record.

So it has to be admitted that though Mr. Ainsworth expected me to remain a good boy and grow up to be a good man, I didn't quite make it. I am, however, glad I knew Mr. Ainsworth, because he made it impossible for me to dislike prohibitionists as much as I might have done when they became a power of the land. I could see their point. I wouldn't have dared say this between 1919 and 1933, the years when prohibition, so to speak, ruled our country. Now, perhaps, I can plead the statute of limitations.

4

The cage in the basement of the Town Hall was empty again, because I went down there to see. The arrest of the Italian woman was not followed by other arrests. Constable Nichols had done his duty that one time, but nobody expected him to go on doing it every day. For one thing, he wasn't paid enough. And, anyhow, he couldn't arrest the entire Italian population, the drinkers as well as the sellers of drinks. That would have been bad for business, so I heard people say.

There was a continued flurry of talk about the goings-on at the Rattlesnake Tavern. People said that the Saturday nights down there, after a pay day, were something to remember. They said that the neighbors for a half a mile around were kept awake as late as ten o'clock at night.

The Congregational minister made some reference to this in a sermon, but the reference hurt the feelings of some of his parishioners; his text was, "Judge not that ye be not judged." The Reverend Silas Blake was against liquor, all right; but he didn't have enough hell and damnation in his soul to please everybody.

Around the store I heard men discussing the relative results that could be had with whiskey, Dago red, hard cider, hair tonic, horse liniment, and rubbing alcohol. I wondered about this a little, because these were men I knew, and usually considered good citizens, and yet it seemed as though they had been experimenting with bad and unlawful drinks.

Adults puzzled me then. In fact, they still do.

Ralph Stevens and I finally decided to scout the Rattlesnake Tavern and see for ourselves if it were really as exciting as people seemed to believe. We could do this as Indians or, if we liked, as United States cavalrymen creeping up on a camp of Sioux.

So Ralph and I, taking care not to be seen by the Confederate pickets—for at the last moment we had enlisted in the Union Army—slid up the half-dry waterfall back of the Ainsworth house, turned left, and worked our way among the beeches, birches, maples, and small stuff back of the village.

It was pretty nice to be up there, for this was an early spring, and for a while we lay on our backs at the edge of the woods, gnawed at some apples we had brought along, and almost forgot the serious business of the afternoon. The village, with the churches, stores, and houses, looked sunny and friendly; but as soon as we had gone a little further along the ridge we would come past the stonesheds, which suggested men at work, and then into the shadowy stretches above the Tavern.

"They might not like to have us spying on them," I weakly suggested.

Ralph said I was a sissy. I said that wasn't true, but then I had to prove it wasn't.

"All right," I said. "I'll show you whether I'm scared or not." The truth was, of course, that I was more scared of Ralph's opinion of me than I was of anything that could happen if we slipped down into the back yard of the Tavern, and maybe looked into a window.

This, anyhow, was what we did. I think I realized then, without needing words for it, that Williamstown was not just one town, or one world, it was a whole series of them. It was my town, and Mr. Ainsworth's town, it was the Scottish granite cutters' town, it was the farmers' town, it was a good people's town and a bad people's town, a drinking town and a town that knew it would go straight to everlasting hell if it drank anything stronger than yesterday's cider.

And it was a town that had room in it for the Rattlesnake Tavern, just as it did for J. K. Linton's store and the Congregational Church and the Williamstown graded school.

But still the Rattlesnake Tavern and the Italian woman seemed to me mysterious and strange, overcast by some kind of shadow, in some way, I couldn't say what way, dangerous.

"I wonder what they'd do to us if they caught us," whispered Ralph.

"They wouldn't do anything," I answered. "Who's the sissy now?"

We came down through some shrubbery, keeping out of sight as well as we could, proceeding cautiously, each determined not to show the other how worried he was. There was nothing unusual about the house itself. Indeed, it somewhat resembled the Ainsworth house in being spaciously designed, with a broad front and an ell. It needed paint, but so did many other houses in our town. I may have been mistaken, but I thought it smelled differently from other houses: it seemed at once a little mustier, as though the sink water had been thrown out into the garden, and a little more pungent, as though the red wine that troubled Mr. Ainsworth so much had been spilled.

We were standing on tiptoes to look into what seemed to be a bedroom when I heard her singing; I had heard her sing on some earlier and more innocent passing, but today she seemed gladder than she had been before. Maybe, I thought, she was cheerful because she wasn't in the cage any more. Or maybe just because this was a sunny day, after a bleak cold spell, and the sunshine was falling for a brief period in this house that was for most of the day in shadow.

It was a sweet singing, in no tune I had ever heard, and perhaps no tune at all, as though the Italian woman were a song bird making up its notes as it went along. If there were words, as, once in a while but not all the time, there seemed to be, I couldn't understand them, and I concluded they must be Italian.

I wished I knew Italian, for suddenly I wanted to understand what she was singing about and why.

Then the singing stopped and we took another look into the room. It seemed like any bedroom, except that the bed wasn't neatly made and there were some clothes lying about on the bed and on chairs—women's clothes and men's too.

A door opened nearby, and the woman's voice said: "Why, little boys, what are you doing here? Do you want to see what it is like inside?"

It was too late to run, even if we had wanted to. I didn't want to, for there was no anger in her voice. I merely felt embarrassed as I turned to face her. I couldn't look into her eyes, but let my gaze drop. I don't think Ralph was any braver.

"Uh-huh," I said. "I guess so."

She laughed. "You want to see if I am a bad woman, that is what you want to see. You want to see if I keep my house clean, the way these Yankee women do. I think you must come in."

She held the door open, and we had to think so, too.

She led us through an entry hall that was like others we knew, with stairs on one side, doors opening on the other side and another door opening into the kitchen at the end of the passage.

She stopped at the entrance to the bedroom we had been looking into. "Tell your mamas," she said, "that when I am very busy maybe I do not make up the bed until afternoon, but I do make it up. I am just as clean and what you call tidy as they

(74)

are. But not the same way they are. Oh, no!" She laughed again, not so gaily this time.

There was a picture of a beautiful lady, kind of sad-looking, I thought, above the bed. The Italian woman caught my gaze fixed on it, and made a swift gesture with one hand, down and across. "You like her?" she asked. "You should. That is Our Blessed Lady."

I didn't say anything, nor did Ralph. We knew we shouldn't.

She laughed again. "You are so funny, you little boys, and all your papas and mamas, too. Now I am going to give you some cookies and—yes—something else."

The kitchen was like one of our own kitchens, only different. Like the rest of the house, it had a different smell—more spicy, or spicy in another way. It seemed to have more and larger and shinier pots and pans. There were a few bottles on a shelf.

The Italian woman saw us gazing at the bottles. "Those are what your constable says is so wicked," she cried. She picked up one and held it against the light. Part of it was covered with a kind of wickerwork, but I could see the lovely red shining through. "Pretty, isn't it?" she asked.

"Uh-huh," I agreed.

"Yes, mam," said Ralph, nodding amiably.

She hesitated. "It would be a good thing if I gave you some. Then you would know it is not wicked. But I am not going to do that. You are not little Italian boys, and you would not like it. Your constable would lock us all up in his cage, too. I shall give you some milk."

She poured out the milk, which was slightly sour but not too bad, and we all sat there drinking milk and eating cookies, for she ate and drank with us.

Finally we knew it was time to go.

She gazed at us in a suddenly motherly fashion. Then, as though we really were her children, she kissed each of us gently. I didn't see this coming in time to back away, and after it had happened it was, like the milk, not too bad.

"Now," she said, "I must get supper for a lot of grown-up little boys. You shall run along now."

We both said thank you, remembering our manners at the last. "And you will please tell your papas and mamas I am not a very bad woman," she called after us.

But we never did.

The promise of spring came before spring itself. The promise of spring was one morning when the crows proceeded, all together, all talking and proclaiming the glory of God, from the East Hill to the West Hill. I did not know, I do not know, what our crows did in winter; I know only that in the deep of winter they were not within sight or hearing.

The crows came over toward the end of March, making such a noise that we all ran out to listen. I think my heart could never lift to the song of the lark as it did to this multitudinous cawing of crows. A chill of sheer joy ran down my spine. I vibrated with an indefinable emotion, an inexpressible hope. All the world and all life opened before me. The crows were openly jubilant (and, as they should not have been in a Puritan community such as ours, openly sensual); and so, with no words to say for it and nothing to do about it, was I.

About this same time there was another sign of spring: the snow withdrew from the base of the hemlock tree in our front yard. Finally there was a morning when a boy woke up to hear the roar of flood water in the falls above the General E. Bass House, where the brook was coming down, in a great seasonal hurry, to join the bigger streams and get into the Winooski and Lake Champlain and the North Atlantic. When I ran out to look, the ice was gone and the yellow muddy water was tumbling madly where it had been.

Then I knew it was spring; then I knew the world was, and always would be, full of joy and beauty.

CHAPTER FOUR

Barre Quarries

*M*Y FATHER said, one day when I was eight and we
were living in Mill Village, that some day he'd hire a
horse and rig from J. K. Linton and take us all to see
the Barre Quarries. Two years later, when I was ten and we
were living in the General E. Bass house, we still hadn't gone to
see the quarries, but I kept hoping we would.

The quarries, in the hills above Barre and maybe four miles
from Williamstown, were the source of the granite industry in
that part of Vermont: they built a good deal of Barre and Montpelier, they gave Williamstown its brief flurry around the turn
of the century.

In my eyes they were among the marvels of the world, even
unseen. Of course we saw in many ways the traces and effects of
this primeval rock. From Graniteville a branch railroad wound
down to Barre; but there was also a steep dirt road descending
into Williamstown. Down this road, in some of my earliest memories, came the great stone-laden wagons, brakes making sparks
at the last steep pitch into our valley, horses holding hard back,
the drivers sometimes standing, reins tight in hand, and swearing blue blazes, and loving the admiration they drew from us
boys.

I don't know how many horses. Maybe four, sometimes,
maybe. Black horses, in my memory, with great, spreading hooves
and foam in their mouths and their ears laid back. And the
granite blocks they drew, or held against the rush of gravity, were
in a boy's sight half as big as a house, each one with a row of

chisel marks at juncture points where the quarrymen had drilled and blasted to get it out.

The quarrymen—the grown ones—I never saw in Williamstown, not to my knowledge. But I thought of them as giants with bulging muscles and their heads in the skies, bigger than ordinary stone cutters such as my father, who was only two or three inches over six feet, bigger than farmers, big and tough and full of wild words that even the teamsters didn't know.

Every quarryman's boy was tougher, it seemed to me, than the sons of granite cutters and farmers in and around Williamstown. They were as likely to be Scottish, or sometimes Welsh, as we were, but somehow of a more primitive breed.

Sometimes they would come down from Graniteville to play baseball with a Williamstown team. I wasn't playing competitive baseball at that time, because I was growing fast and was thought to be too delicate to indulge in much more vigorous exercise than was involved in running from the depot to the General E. Bass house, or tearing through the woods, or climbing trees—gentle things like that. But I could watch and listen.

I remember one youngster from Graniteville who seemed to be the captain of the visiting team, and who might have stepped right out of Aberdeen, Scotland, the way he talked and the scorn he had for native Vermonters of whatever race.

He was laying down the law, pounding the earth at home plate with the end of a bat. "Now you lads—" he began. I forget the rest of the words, but his eyes flashed fire and I thought he would as soon as not have taken on the whole Williamstown team in mortal combat. When he had finished, without being challenged by anybody present, of either team, he produced a cigarette—a real cigarette, stinking plainly of tobacco—and lighted it as calmly as one of us would have eaten a chocolate.

He wasn't a big boy, but he was wiry; he proved to be a good base-runner and a first-class yeller when the umpire made what seemed to him a wrong decision. He reinforced the impression I had of a race of giants, in strength if not in stature, living up in the granite hills to the east.

He made the Barre Quarries seem a long way off, as though

they were part of the big outer world to which Williamstown did not belong. He was wise in the way of that outer world, that was clear.

From that day on, maybe before, I thought of Barre Quarries as a distant journey, though they were, in fact, no further away than places to which we often went on our bicycles. Not as far away, really, as Barre itself. But I wouldn't have dreamed of going there alone, and somehow it never occurred to a group of us to bicycle up there.

This may have been partly because even then the quarries were two hundred feet down and our parents feared their boys might go too near the edge and fall in, or be too near when a blast went off and get blown back home in small pieces, or be mashed under a few tons of granite. I didn't ask to be allowed to go up with the other boys, and they didn't ask their parents, either, so far as I can recall. I waited for my father to find the time and money to take the whole Duffus family to see the quarries.

I daydreamed of how fine this would be. My father would drive; but maybe on level, slow stretches he would let each of us youngsters, my brother, myself, even my very small sister, as she was then, take the reins. We'd go up through the cool woods and come to the top where, I thought, there would be finer pastures than any I'd ever seen, with red and white cows feeding in them. And then there would be the miracle: the astounding, frightening hole in the ground and a great noise of machinery and much shouting and steam rising and the boom of explosions. I thought maybe I'd see blocks of granite rising dustily into air.

I kept this picture, and waited for the daydream to come true. I don't believe I've ever since been so interested in any prospective traveling.

2

So Barre Quarries represented to me, at the time I was ten years old, the dream of travel and adventure. When I say this I do not mean to imply that Williamstown, with only dirt roads leading to and from it and with only one rickety branch railroad line, was shut away like an enchanted village in a fairy story.

Even the Duffus family thought little of traveling twenty-four miles to Waterbury to visit my maternal grandmother and aunt. My father once in a great while went to Brooklyn, New York, to stay with his brother, the iron-founder. If my father talked of taking us all to the quarries, he also talked of taking us to his home in Scotland. I recall his discussion of such a journey one night, and his opinion that strong, healthy children such as we then were (but not always, for we had our setbacks) wouldn't be seasick. And he talked with a touch of sadness of Peterhead on the North Sea, and the fishing boats lying in the harbor at night, with their riding lights flickering like lightnin' bugs in the meadows in July.

Williamstown people traveled, all right. One Williamstown boy had become a well-known war correspondent and gone all over the world and been shot at; we boys envied him, though we never saw him. A Williamstown man, who had accumulated some modest means—perhaps by selling timberland to people from outside the state who didn't know too much about local timber and terrain—made an extensive trip one year. As Mr. Ainsworth put it in his column in the Barre newspaper, this adventurer "visited Europe, Asia, and Africa and expressed himself as very much pleased with what he saw." My father read this and remarked that Europe, Asia, and Africa would certainly be delighted when they heard of it.

Williamstown people with less money could go on excursions to Boston or Montreal for about ten dollars for the round trip. I think J. K. Linton did this sort of thing once in a while, buying things for the store.

If you felt very much like traveling you could also take one of the all-day excursions that left Williamstown in the early morning and got back late at night, picking up passengers at stations along the way and dropping them off again on the way back. In this fashion you could go all the way to Burlington, change to a Lake Champlain steamer, and go clear across to the New York side and see Ausable Chasm. This didn't cost too much, either; a dollar or two, I suppose. I never had the dollar or two at that time, but our family thought that some day we would have enough for all of us to go.

But my father never did promise to take us to Ausable Chasm. What he promised to do, as soon as we could afford it, was to take us to the Barre Quarries with a horse and surrey.

The trouble was that circumstances kept preventing this expedition. Sometimes work in the granite trade was slack and the stonesheds shut down. Once or twice there were strikes. On one of these occasions my father went to, I think, Manchester, New Hampshire, where he had heard of a non-union stoneshed that needed help. While he was gone we all got to thinking of how strange and exciting it would be to live in a big city like Manchester; and, besides, we'd see the world as we came and went. If we went that far we might some day go a little further and see the ocean, at Portsmouth.

But my father came back. He was an individualistic Scot and didn't think labor unions were perfect; but when he came right down to it he couldn't work in a non-union shop. The strike ended not long after, but there were bills to pay for rent and provisions, and we still didn't go up to Barre Quarries.

I think my mother, brother, and sister, and myself went as usual that year to spend a holiday in Waterbury, which was a happy thing to do even if it weren't so exciting and new as going up to the quarries would have been. The Central Vermont Railway of that day did all it possibly could to make a passenger realize he was traveling. It shot soot in through the open windows, it rolled and rocked going around curves, it backed and switched in Barre and Montpelier, it came down to the main line at Montpelier Junction and let everybody stand half an hour or so on a windy platform waiting for the train to come roaring down from Northfield and points south; in fact, there wasn't anything that railroad wouldn't do to make a small boy contented.

I don't believe my mother liked it all quite so well, for she had to look after her three offspring and see to it that none of them fell out of a car window or leaned too far over the track when the connecting train came into Montpelier Junction.

We were, in a fashion, seasoned travelers. No member of the Duffus, Graves, or Cooley families had ever been known to miss a train. In Williamstown we got somebody to take our baggage to the station on a wheelbarrow—or my father did this himself if he weren't working. We arrived an hour before the train was due to leave: in Williamstown and in Waterbury that was the rule, and we did it.

In Waterbury I remember looking wistfully down the track that led westward and northward to Burlington and the outer world; sometimes we would walk down this track a mile or two, crossing the Winooski River on the iron railway bridge at some peril to our lives, and coming into the town of Duxbury. I wanted to go further. It must, I thought, be pretty wonderful when you got around the curve and found yourself in Bolton, where the dam later was, and you could maybe see Camels Hump, and, as the scenery unfolded, all the wonders of nature and of man. But I did not go that way, not at the time of which I am writing.

And as yet we didn't go to Barre Quarries, though once in a while my father spoke of it again, and we all grew excited and began to plan. We decided to put up a picnic lunch and get out beside the road somewhere and eat it.

I talked all I could with people who had been to far-away places, but there weren't many such around Williamstown, and I was too shy to start conversations with strangers. I didn't talk with the teamsters who brought the blocks of granite down from the quarries. And I never figured out why some granite came this way, down the road, whereas other granite came up from Barre on flat cars.

In time, the prospect of traveling to the quarries or to New York, Washington, San Francisco, Paris, London, or other mysterious and alluring places came to seem to me much the same thing. All these places represented a kind of escape from a situation and spot I didn't really want to escape from. I wanted to go and I didn't want to go. I liked the familiarity of the house in which I lived, the bed in which I slept, the kitchen in which I ate, the stove, the table, the chairs, everything that was part of my daily life.

I wanted, I suppose, to make everything stand still, in the geographical place where it was, at the point in time that was just being ticked off.

I didn't know what a soap bubble it was on which we were all riding, how fragile it was, and how it wasn't necessary to do much planning to produce change.

3

As I said, I didn't readily start conversations with strangers; but I used to hear the commercial travelers called drummers talking in J. K. Linton's store and at the Monument House. They had grand airs, as men naturally would who had been around so much. They knew the world, and nothing could fool them— nosiree, as they used to say. They weren't the sort who would blow out the gas when they put up at a fashionable city hotel, and as for tall buildings they had seen them all—even, in some cases, the Madison Square Garden in New York City—and thought nothing of it.

A drummer was a good example of the sort of man I wanted to be when I grew up, assuming that I couldn't get into the army or be a cowboy. I could distinguish between dreams and possibilities, and I knew my parents would make trouble if I chose any life that seemed to them ridiculously dangerous.

A drummer would lean against the counter in a store and smoke cigars and tell stories—dirty stories if he thought no small boy was listening, but usually a small boy or two would be— and you could see that the drummer wouldn't be abashed by anything. He'd say hello to President McKinley the way one of us would pass the time of day with Jim Beckett—respectful, of course, but not scared.

Yet I was sure that even the most self-satisfied drummer had once been a small boy and had got where he had gotten by traveling around. It was the travel that did it, and this made me want more than ever to travel—even if I only went to the Barre Quarries with my family, which was not as good as going to California but better than not going anywhere.

And there were other sorts of travelers, stranger ones than

the drummers, who, after all, just traveled up and down the State of Vermont selling groceries or patent medicines or things like that to storekeepers.

There were the pack-peddlers, for example. I still remember one of these—or is this memory a combination of several peddlers? Anyhow, he had come to our door and my mother had let him in, and he had opened his pack, well-wrapped in oilcloth, on the kitchen table. I think there were fabrics of some sort, for I have an impression of soft colors and my mother fingering the stuff with the evident thought of making a dress or apron, perhaps for my shiny-eyed younger sister who was standing by.

But what sticks in my memory is something else: the bright packages of needles, thimbles, and knives of various shapes and sizes—jack-knives among them, I think. Indeed, maybe this was the peddler who sold my mother the pocket knife I treasured so long, which made the scar I still carry on the upper part of the little finger of my right hand. I look at this scar now and the intervening years are gone: the peddler, a dark little man with longish black hair, is holding something up for my mother to look at; he is honestly proud of his goods.

My mother hesitates, buys some trifle, perhaps the pocket knife. The peddler rolls up his pack again, snug in the black oilcloth, bows and smiles in a way not common in Williamstown, and backs out the door.

I watch him go, and envy him. I envied so many persons in those days.

On another day—and this, I think, was early spring—it was not a peddler who came. This stranger did not walk into the house but only into the yard. He approached from the south, along the dirt road that led to Williamstown Gulf and ultimately to such places as Randolph and Chelsea. I supposed he had probably walked all the distance from his own country, except as he had come to the ocean and had to take a ship. What he carried was not a peddler's sack, or a blanket roll, or any visible provision of the necessities of life. What he carried was a set of bagpipes, and as he walked he played upon them.

He was in full Highland costume, with a short jacket, ruffles, a kilt and sporran, and a rakishly-cocked Highland bonnet.

We all stared at him, because he was something out of a story book and not what you would expect in Williamstown. My Uncle Willie, my father's brother, had had his picture taken in Highland costume as a member of the Caledonia Society, I believe it was; but Uncle Willie wouldn't have come strolling down the road from the Gulf in kilts and playing the pipes.

My mother gave us each a penny, which added up to three cents and didn't seem, even to us, a vast sum, and we gave these bashfully to the piper. He looked at us from under shaggy brows and pulled his bonnet jocosely a little further over one eye.

Then he smiled and winked at us and saluted my mother, who had come to the front door, went through the motions of biting the three pennies, and remarked: "It's the mickles that make the muckle," and said some other words that sounded strange and wild which I presumed were Scottish. He was good-natured, and I thought he liked us all and wasn't too badly satisfied with the weather, the time and place, and the world and everything.

Why shouldn't he be satisfied? He didn't even have to carry a pack, the way peddlers did. All he had to carry was his pipes and the music he made up or remembered as he went along, which didn't weigh anything at all.

"Did you come from Scotland?" I managed to ask, overcoming my diffidence.

"That I did, Laddie," he promptly replied. "From nowhere else. And I'll play you a tune or two for asking." He hesitated. "Are you Scots now, yourselves?"

"Our father is," I said proudly.

"Well, he found a nice lady," observed the piper, and my mother couldn't help looking pleased. "That makes you children half-Scot, and that's far better than not being Scottish at all, like most of the unfortunate people in the world."

He began to play, looking reflectively around him and up into the sky. Some of his tunes I knew, like *The Blue Bells of Scotland;* some I didn't know, and some I wasn't sure about, because try as I would to enjoy this music the pipes did sometimes make the most unexplainable and inexcusable noises. My mother disappeared while this was going on, but I didn't know whether it was because she had something on the stove cooking, or because she didn't care for the pipes.

"It's bonny music," said the piper, when he had finished. He squinted at the sun and then looked at a big silver watch that he extracted from somewhere in his pockets—though I couldn't see where a pocket would be in a set of kilts. "It's bonny, isn't it?" repeated the piper.

I said it was. In a way, I was telling the truth. These unexplainable and inexcusable noises weren't the kind we were used to hearing around Williamstown. They startled me, and I almost wished the piper would stop making them; but still I knew, and this knowledge ran up and down my spine like a thrill and a chill combined, that they came from a long way off and a long time ago. There was a reason for them, even though I didn't know for sure what the reason was.

There was a moment or two when, listening, I wanted to dance; but of course, being a Vermonter and being myself, hemmed in by an impulse not to give way to impulses, I didn't dare dance.

The piper turned away at last. He had given us his three cents' worth and his passing friendship's worth, and that was that. We waved to him as he turned out our gate and proceeded toward the Pool Bridge. He kept on playing as he went—and this, I like now to think, was the mark of the true artist; for he could not possibly pick up even three cents between our house and the Pool Bridge.

My father was not sentimental about the piper when we told him about him. My father seemed to think the man was making a living of a sort out of being a Scot, and perhaps fooling people about a few things. He seemed to think the living the piper got was an easier one than the one the Scottish granite cutters earned in the stonesheds.

And my father tried to make us believe that now that he was an American citizen the songs and instruments of Scotland meant no more to him than those of Vermont. The trouble was, of course, that Vermont had few special songs and no special instruments. Vermont was a good state, and peculiar and different from all other states; but not even my father could make us believe that it was as peculiar and different as Scotland. The reason was, of course, that my father had been born in Scotland and hadn't found it too romantic to leave; but his wife and his children had merely read about it and been told about it, and to them it was a magic land.

"He will be going to the store tonight," said my father—he meant the J. K. Linton store—"and he will play on his pipes and pick up money." My father thought the whole situation over. "He will pick up more money than if he didn't wear kilties, which are not suitable for Vermont." There was a long silence. "He makes believe," said my father. "And after he has finished making believe here in Williamstown he will go up the hill to Graniteville, and down to Barre and Montpelier, and make believe some more there."

There was another silence, a longer one. "What did he play?" asked my father.

"The Blue Bells of Scotland," I said, anxious to please him. My mother and perhaps my brother and sister remembered one or two others.

"I would have liked to hear them well enough," said my father. "But at home they were not sung for money."

4

Sometimes it wasn't drummers, or a piper, or a teamster down from the Barre Quarries, or a man who had visited Europe, Asia, and Africa and liked them all; sometimes it was gypsies. The gypsies stirred a boy's wandering blood more even than the piper; a boy didn't precisely want to be a gypsy, he couldn't even imagine himself a gypsy; but he wondered and wondered and wondered about them and their way of life, and whether they liked it as much as they ought to have.

I don't suppose I ever even spoke a word with a gypsy. One reason was the usual one of shyness; another was the belief that they probably didn't speak English at all, but some outlandish language of their own. A further reason was that gypsies were

suspected of kidnapping children—carrying them off and bringing them up in their turn to be gypsies and kidnap other children.

Our parents warned us against taking risks, and we took none.
The gypsies fascinated us, but we didn't want to be kidnapped.

One lot of them camped one spring or summer night between
the General E. Bass house and the Pool Bridge. They had horses
and gaily painted wagons and carts; their women were in bright
colors, with much jewelry, and wearing handkerchiefs over their
heads; even their menfolk were picturesque with earrings and
sashes. No doubt their business was horse trading, and no doubt
they traded some. But for me they had the immense allure of
people who had no abiding homes, but who traveled wherever
they wanted to, all over the face of the earth.

Even if I didn't talk to them I could walk by them slowly and
look at them, and come back after a while and take another look.
Their camping arrangements were simple. They didn't have to
have hot and cold running water, the way they would now: nobody had hot and cold running water then, except President
McKinley, Queen Victoria, and J. P. Morgan, and I wasn't sure
even about them. And their other sanitary needs were easily
taken care of, in that free generation and place, when sanitation
wasn't even a word we knew.

So they unhitched their horses and let them graze beside the
road, which was anybody's property and didn't require permis-
sion if a horse wished to graze beside it. I am not sure what the
horses were like, but it seems to me they were black or brown,
with only once in a while a touch of white. The black, brown,
and sometimes white of the horses went well with the black, red,
and yellow, which is what I seem to remember, of the gypsies.

I loved colors, all colors, because we had so few of them, except in the fall, when the leaves turned.

I didn't want to be kidnapped by a gypsy, and I was not. But
I did keep thinking, as I saw this encampment, and especially
as I smelled what the gypsies were cooking in iron pots over
open fires, what it would be like to be kidnapped by gypsies,
and grow up and be, to all intents and purposes, a gypsy. Because, as a reasonably bright boy, and even without the vocabu-

lary that came and sat on my chest later, I knew that environ-
ment was an important influence. If I were kidnapped by gypsies,
I thought, maybe some morning I would wake up and find myself a little darker than usual, and maybe with gold earrings and
a black moustache—what wouldn't I have given to have a moustache, but I never had one, because when I could it was no
longer stylish—and I wouldn't have to go to school or be a
success in life.

I would have missed my family, though, my father, mother,
brother and sister. I knew that. I just wondered what it would
be like to be kidnapped by gypsies.

I wish it were possible, at this point, to bring in a gypsy, and
tell how he told me, a ten-year-old boy, the story of his life. Or a
female gypsy. But I can't do this. No gypsy ever told me the
story of a gypsy life. I didn't know any more about it until I
grew up and read George Borrow and some other authors.

But there they were, in Williamstown, Vermont, and how
could one tell, to look at them, whether they came from Egypt,
or from Rumania, or from Hungary, or where?

There they were, and with them was strangeness, and all the
glory and beating of drums and flags in the wind, all the color
and imagery, all the romance and the things that were so because they couldn't be so—all that side of life.

I did wish, so I thought at the end, as I turned home toward
my own house and bed and the good breakfast that would come
in the morning—I did wish I could be a gypsy and myself, too;
that I could be safe at home, with my mother looking after me,
and my father ready to make trouble if anybody killed me, and
my brother and sister usually in a kindly family mood; I did wish
I could also turn my face northward, or southward, or eastward,
or westward, and go with the gypsies, and be one of them, and
never go to school or church any more, ever, and eat the things
they were cooking, that smelled so good.

But next morning the gypsies were gone. I think they went
toward Barre, from which metropolis they could have gone to
Montpelier, Burlington, and the lesser cities of the world.

The next best thing to the gypsies that came to Williamstown, and that kept alive in me the spirit of travel and adventure, were the Uncle Tom shows and an occasional vaudeville show that played for a night in the Town Hall.

The Uncle Tom shows had a good deal besides Uncle Tom, Little Eva, Simon Legree, and one or more Lawyers Marks. They had a horse or two, sometimes an elephant, sometimes a man who walked a tight rope and did tricks on it, once in a while a trapeze performer, and a girl who did something or other and had spangles all over her. Everything that didn't have anything to do with Uncle Tom was called a Sacred Concert, and cost ten cents extra.

All the Uncle Tom shows and some of the vaudeville shows had parades, and often they enlisted local talent to make the parades look good. I recall the savage envy with which I saw a young acquaintance of mine named Lyle Burnham riding a horse in an Uncle Tom parade, down past the J. K. Linton store and as far as the school house and the Pool Bridge. Lyle looked as though he might fall off the horse at any moment, and I earnestly hoped he would, but he was wearing a bright red coat with gilt epaulettes and a soldier hat; and for this he was about to get a free ticket to the show.

I don't know how many Uncle Tom shows we saw in the course of our life in Williamstown. It could not have been more than three or four. But my father always said we certainly wouldn't want to see an Uncle Tom show again, because we had already seen it, and had read the book, and knew all about it, and he wouldn't have any boy of his carrying water to an elephant or a horse or even to Little Eva herself. Then, when we had given up hope, he would fish in his pocket and come up with whatever it cost to go. He did the same thing with firecrackers on the Fourth of July.

My mother didn't say anything. She looked at my father inquiringly, and when the dime or quarter appeared she just smiled.

So we did get to see the Uncle Tom shows, and maybe a one-ring circus or two—but I am puzzled about this, because my recollections are scrambled—in Williamstown; and I suppose one might say this was one manner of traveling. One didn't go all over the world, to Barre Quarries, and Burlington, and Quebec, and China, and such places; but the flavor and smell of the far-off rolled in upon us, under the big tents, and it was as if Williamstown had removed itself, for a night, to Burlington or Chicago or China, or one of those places.

A few traveling vaudeville shows came through, too, and did somewhat the same thing, only they were not quite so glamorous. Before I left Williamstown these shows usually carried a few reels of film and a motion picture projector. We thought this was wonderful and in many ways better than the magic lanterns we had at home.

What I chiefly recall of the vaudeville shows are the girls or women who kicked up their heels and danced and sang. There was one who had red ruffles under her dress, practically all the way down to her knees but no further, and I wondered if I ought to look at them.

The rest of the family, including my parents, my brother, and, I have no doubt, my sister, thought it foolish of me to waste ten hard-bitten cents on such an exhibition. My mother was willing enough to take me to an instrumental concert, or to a lecture which might be entitled "Hitch Your Wagon to a Star"; she wanted me to grow up to be a thoughtful and cultivated man; but she apparently didn't see how a girl kicking up her heels on the stage of the Town Hall could be of the least use to me.

But neither my mother nor my father told me not to go. This I gratefully remember. It was my ten cents, not theirs. If I spent it the way I wanted to, I couldn't spend it for candy or a baseball or a bat.

Afterward, and it was very late, almost ten, perhaps, I ran all the way home, pelting over the Pool Bridge with the suspicion that something might be lying in wait for me there to punish me for my small sin; but it wasn't.

"Did you have a good time?" my mother patiently asked.

"Yes, I did," I stoutly replied, but I hadn't, and she knew it.

Still my thoughts were with that vaudeville company. Where did they go next? What was it like to be completely outside of

Williamstown looking in at it, the way they did? Did that girl who kicked her heels up so high think we were funny?

Sometimes, most often at night when I was too tired to go to sleep right away, I would wonder about all the people in the world and what they were doing at that moment. If you could bore a hole right through the center of the earth, and China, as I supposed, was directly opposite Vermont, then if you went into that hole feet first, from the Vermont end, you would certainly come out feet first, and therefore upside down, at the Chinese end. It would follow that the people of China were all walking around upside down, even though they believed they were right side up. I wondered why they didn't fall off. I knew about the attraction of gravitation, to be sure, but I didn't really believe in it.

And what were the people of India doing, and the people of Australia, and the people of Africa, Asia, and Europe, and the Esquimos? They must be having a more interesting time than I was, for they lived in such interesting places. Why couldn't I have been born in an interesting place?

Then I would fall asleep and dream that I really was in an interesting place, which might be a happy combination of China and the Barre Quarries, and in it I would have the ability to sustain myself in the air by flapping my arms, and it wouldn't matter if I did fall into the quarries or was trying to walk upside down in China.

My father repeated that some day he would hire a rig from the livery stable and take the whole family to the Barre Quarries. He might as well have said that he would hire a rig and take us to San Francisco or Bombay.

He couldn't take us to the quarries because he never had quite enough money. This wasn't his fault, it was the fault of the granite industry. Today, if Williamstown still had granite-cutting sheds and he were still a granite cutter, he would have a motor vehicle of some sort, and all it would take to go to the Quarries would be a few minutes of time.

My father never took us to the Barre Quarries. His health

broke first, we children went away for our schooling after we had
passed through the Williamstown Grade School, and that was
the end of that.

I did not read, until a long time afterward, the story of the
man who never went to Carcassonne. But now I have been to
Carcassonne, and I have been to the Barre Quarries, and I am
sorry for those who wished to see them and did not.

5

Before I saw the Barre Quarries for the first time I had
crossed and recrossed the United States as far as San Francisco
and the Pacific; my father had gone to California, where he
died; my mother, too, was dead; the rest of the family was scattered geographically, though united by common affections, memories, and experiences.

Twenty-one years after the year in which these memories and
experiences at the moment tether me, I took my wife to Vermont.
That was 1919. The granite sheds were no longer operating in
Williamstown. Of the recollections of my childhood there sur-
vived the Williamstown Branch of the Central Vermont, soon
to be abandoned; the Monument House or its successor; the
J. K. Linton store, which had become a farmers' cooperative;
and the General E. Bass house.

The automobile had not then captured all the roads, especially
not the side roads. I said to my wife, "Let's hire a rig at the
livery stable and go up and look at the quarries." So we hired a
rig at the livery stable and went up and looked at the quarries.

My wife and I agreed that the quarries were too deep for a
boy to fall into safely, and that maybe it was just as well none
of us had been up there stumping each other, as we used to say,
to go as near the edge as possible.

I was glad enough I had waited for my father to take the
family there, some day when he had saved enough to hire a rig
from J. K. Linton.

But I was sorry, for him, to whom it made no difference any

more, that he had never been able to lay his hands on quite enough money.

———————

There came a time when the cowslips spread their broad leaves, and then bloomed yellow, in the marshes. We gathered them, my mother cooked them, and they were good. Later in the year we picked dandelion greens, and they, too, had a tang all their own; but they did not exult, as the cowslips did, at the coming of spring. At that period I had not heard of spinach, but I was just as happy.

I preferred cowslips to wildflowers, because you could eat cowslips. Wildflowers were of no use to anybody, except that they lured girls to go out into the woods to look for them, and girls going into the woods in 1898 needed male protection. I went along that year, I believe, with the nice little Sibley girl from across the road and some others.

I remember a flower called Johnny Jump-Up and another called Jack-in-the-Pulpit. I wouldn't be surprised if these flowers still grew, though I do wonder a little if boys and girls go out to look for them; boys and girls have so much to do these days, so much to worry about and be angry at.

The snow was all gone by the end of April, except for the very deep drifts in shaded places; but the woods were still wet, and there was a wind, fresh, damp, and cool, that ran among the trees and spoke of winter and of spring in the same gust.

But I thought of spring, and the other side of the world, and of the great happiness that would be coming to us all as the days warmed and lengthened.

CHAPTER FIVE

Williamstown Branch

I NEVER heard him called anything but Old Man Webb, though he must have had a first name, and maybe a middle name. I never heard anybody mention his relatives, though he must at one time have had a wife—if he hadn't had a wife somebody would have mentioned it, for elderly bachelors were always talked about, either because they ran around with women or because they didn't—and maybe he had had children.

If he had had a wife, she was certainly dead when I knew Mr. Webb. If he had children they may have been, as we often said, out west somewhere, but they certainly weren't around Williamstown.

Mr. Webb, when I knew him, if I can truly say that a boy of ten could then or at any other time really know a venerable engineer on the Central Vermont Railroad, lived in the Monument House. Hotel rates in small Vermont towns in 1898 must have been low enough to permit steadily employed workmen to board and room there. I wouldn't be surprised if Mr. Webb paid as much as six dollars a week or as little as four dollars a week.

Life in the Monument House was simple. When I revisited Williamstown twenty-one years later, the prices had gone up; but the guest still had to stroll down the hall to whatever it was he was looking for. I believe he no longer had a chamber pot in the so-called commode, but maybe he did. In Mr. Webb's day life in the hotel was simpler still, but simplicity did not bother Mr. Webb.

Mr. Webb's wife, if he had ever had one, must have brought him up carefully. Or maybe it was his mother who did this. Even in our informal town, people considered Mr. Webb informal. Mr. Webb didn't wait for the girl to clear the table after he was through eating. Other men might push their chairs back and go stamping out, chewing on cigars or full-bodied toothpicks as they went. But Mr. Webb picked up his plate, cup, and saucer, stacked them, and carried them out into the kitchen. He also tucked his napkin up under his chin and as far as it would go around the back of his neck, but this was not so unusual; a lot of men did that; it protected the vest. This might not have been necessary for a man who had whiskers, as Mr. Webb did, but it may have been a habit formed before he grew the whiskers.

But it wasn't Mr. Webb carrying his stacked-up dishes into the kitchen of the Monument House that impressed me most. What impressed me was what Mr. Webb did after breakfast and before supper. His lunch—his dinner, as we called it, and why shouldn't we?—he took with him when he left the Monument House in the morning, walked over to the railway station, and boarded his locomotive.

Mr. Webb's locomotive was a bell-stacked, wood-burning affair of the sort seen in pictures of the Civil War. For all I know, this very locomotive may have fought in the Civil War. Its fuel was chunks of wood taken from a wood pile under a big shed beside the tracks between the freight shed and the feed store.

Mr. Webb, I seem to recall, had a succession of firemen, each in turn attracted to railroading by the desire to travel and see the world, and each in turn repelled by the effect on the back muscles of spending the day heaving chunks of wood into Mr. Webb's engine.

But Mr. Webb, having passed this apprenticeship, seemed to know he had a good thing. When he got to his engine in the fairly early morning, the fireman would already have steam up. All Mr. Webb had to do was to climb into the cab, sink down into a luxuriously padded leather seat, and open the throttle. He would then back up to the baggage car and coach, or maybe half-coach and half-baggage car, that made up his train, wait for

Conductor Jim Kennealy to give him the signal, and go tooling away to Barre.

This would be about half-past seven in the morning, give or take a few minutes, of which there were plenty at that time.

Mr. Webb would descend the grade to Barre, back up into Barre station as his schedule required, unhitch his passenger coach and baggage equipment, and spend the day switching in the Barre yards. When his switching was over, he would re-attach his coach and baggage car, if any, and go home, up the grade, to Williamstown. He arrived there, I presume, around half-past six in the evening.

In the meantime another train would come up from Mont-pelier, this one with a coal-burning engine with a small stack, pick up passengers who desired to go out into the big world, and proceed with them, first to Barre, then to Montpelier Junction. At Montpelier Junction the passengers changed to the main line of the Central Vermont, over which they could go to Burling-ton, via Essex Junction, or, better yet, to Montreal and the West. With this afternoon train you could scoot clear out of Vermont. With Mr. Webb you were sure of getting home.

Sometimes I envied the engineer on the afternoon train; it was by that train, indeed, that we made connections at Mont-pelier Junction for Waterbury—which meant, at that time, a happy holiday with our grandmother and aunt, our mother's mother and sister.

But though I did want to be an engineer, pulling on a throttle and watching the world go by, I hardly expected to run an engine as far as Montpelier Junction, let alone Montreal. I was, in my way, a modest boy. I just wanted to be a Mr. Webb. It seemed to me there couldn't be any life a man could reasona-bly look for in this world that would be better than the one Mr. Webb led.

Yet I have seen Mr. Webb come out to the veranda of the Monument House after supper on a summer evening, put his feet on the railing, and sit there picking his teeth or chewing tobacco, or both, and spitting, and complain about how hard he worked and how tired he was.

The railroad and everything connected with it fascinated us boys endlessly. If we had been accustomed to seeing our parents step on the gas and go scooting off cross country on roads as smooth as J. K. Linton's new hardwood floor, we might have been less enchanted. But we didn't see many automobiles—and the few we did see were foolish and transitory models, whereas the Central Vermont Railroad operated with a good deal of certainty. Mr. Webb wasn't often very late getting his train up from Barre in the evening. He wanted his supper too much to be late, and I don't believe he was too particular about waiting in Barre for connections from the north.

Mr. Webb, in fact, gave the impression that although he co-operated with the Central Vermont Railroad the best he could, the Williamstown Branch was his own private enterprise. On a fine summer morning, he would lean out of the window of his cab, with his whiskers waving in whatever breeze there was, get the high sign from Jim Kennealy, and pull his throttle. The driving wheels would spin a little, the engine would get excited and begin to breathe hard, then it would whoosh a few times, and away it would go.

If I stood on the platform of the station and listened, which I was not always able to do at half-past seven in the morning, I would hear Mr. Webb's locomotive settle down into a steady puff-puff-puff-puff, in sets of four puffs with a slight pause in between; and at a distance I couldn't tell Mr. Webb's modest machine from the kind that went tearing northwest past my grandmother's house in Waterbury on its way to Montreal, in the lonesome midnights I well and happily remember.

Of course it wasn't always summer and not always bright and sunny when Mr. Webb left on his less adventurous journeys. I suppose Mr. Webb swore like a trooper some mornings and wished he had gone in for an easy life instead of railroading. But he had to get up and run his wood-burning antique down the grade to Barre. He couldn't just go out into a nice, warm barn and milk eight cows, the way a farmer could.

I wonder if he would have felt better if he had known how much some small boys admired him. I wonder what he thought about small boys. He must have had a lingering fondness for them, or a faint memory of how he had felt when he was a small boy himself. He was on occasion unexpectedly kind to us; and though he sometimes swore at us, he never told our parents when we did things we shouldn't have done.

I am thinking particularly of one episode that might have made Mr. Webb bite off a few of his own whiskers and swallow them. In spite of the fact that the statute of limitations has probably run its course several times over, I shall not mention the names of those involved. I shall not even suggest that my brother was present.

When a locomotive comes to the end of a branch line, it must do one of two things: it must find a way to turn around, or it must back up. In Williamstown, as at the terminals of other branch lines, this problem was solved by a simple device called a turntable.

This turntable worked by muscle power. Mr. Webb would drive his engine carefully upon it, taking pains not to keep on into the adjacent swamp. Then the fireman—never, I believe, Mr. Webb—would apply himself to a long lever and walk the engine round until its cowcatcher was where its rear end had been. Mr. Webb would make sure that the turntable track and the railroad track were locked in the correct positions, and then he would drive his engine off again.

This process was a miracle that happened twelve times a week, counting both trains into and out of Williamstown and not counting Sundays; but with myself and my young friends it never grew stale. We watched with bugged-out eyes whenever we had a chance, and we hoped that some day Mr. Webb would invite us into the cab while the miracle was being performed.

The next best thing was to wait till Mr. Webb and other employees of the Central Vermont Railroad were out of sight or busy at something else that kept them looking the other way, and then operate that turntable ourselves, though with no engine.

In addition to the rails provided for the locomotive, the turntable had its own rails to turn on. It was, one might say, a sort of circular railway. Mr. Webb's fireman, or somebody less important than Mr. Webb but more important than a whole gang of ten-year-old boys, would come out once in a while and grease the turntable. I wanted to do that—I still want to—but nobody ever let me, and now nobody ever will. There isn't any turntable on the Williamstown Branch any more, nor any timetable, either, nor any Williamstown Branch.

The rest of this particular incident follows almost as a matter of course. Any reader who lived in Williamstown, Vermont, in 1898 could figure it out for himself. If a boy can get his hands on a thing like a turntable, as we did, he is sooner or later going to run that turntable off its track. And this we did—myself and whoever was hanging around with me, loose and on the town, that day.

I don't know how we did it, for the turntable must have been built to stand wear and tear. At all events, it gave a shudder, a groan, and a hollow clatter and stuck tight about half-way around. We worked at it a while, growing uneasy because it was about time for Mr. Webb to pull in from Barre, and usually he turned his locomotive around before supper instead of after breakfast.

What was about to happen was as clear as day to all four of us—and again I refrain from mentioning names. Mr. Webb was going to be hungry. He was going to be annoyed with anything or anybody who delayed his arrival at the Monument House.

What did happen was a little worse than what we had expected to happen. As I have mentioned, Mr. Webb was in the habit of bringing his train in on time, regardless of what was taking place in other portions of the Central Vermont Railroad system. On this particular day he was three-quarters of an hour late because he had had to wait for a carload of guano that was coming in from Boston on the main line. Mr. Seaver, the feed-store proprietor, had been making a fuss about this guano, which stank to high heaven, but which did make things grow when properly applied.

Mr. Webb felt that fate had been unkind, first in this delay, and second, because he had to take time to set out the car of guano at Mr. Seaver's loading platform, where Mr. Seaver could get at it in the morning.

Mr. Webb therefore arrived in Williamstown hungrier than usual, madder than usual, and fully aware that the supper he was about to get at the Monument House wouldn't be as good or as cheerfully served as it would have been earlier.

I had come upstreet after supper, a criminal returning to the scene. Or almost to the scene, for I hung around J. K. Linton's store, waiting for the whistle. Seven o'clock came, and then quarter after seven, and I knew that my parents would be wondering where I was—or, assuming that my big brother was also upstreet, where we both were.

The wail of Mr. Webb's manfully struggling locomotive came at last from down the line a mile or so, near the Tud Holler one-room school building.

I wanted to go home, yet I was curious about what would happen. It seemed best not to wait. If I were the kind of boy who went home in the evening as his bedtime drew near I would be less likely to be suspected as a member of a gang that went around wrecking railroad turntables.

I listened as I ran, and after I had passed the Pool Bridge I looked across the meadow and the swamp to see if the engine had yet come down to the turntable. It hadn't. That worried me, too. At the age of ten, I was already a great worrier.

3

My mother asked me what I had been doing and I said I had been hanging around J. K. Linton's store. My father looked up from his newspaper and said there might be better things to do, and my mother said that if I never went to any worse place than J. K. Linton's store I'd be safe enough. My father said that when he was a boy of ten he was already working after school hours and tired enough at eight o'clock to be glad to have a chance to go to bed, and not hang around anybody's store. My mother said times had changed, and my father commented that they evidently had.

I lay awake for an hour or so, or maybe fifteen minutes, for lying awake was something I wasn't used to. Then I fell asleep and dreamed that the president of the Central Vermont Railroad had come to Williamstown, with a swarm of policemen all looking like Mr. Webb in his angrier moments, and that myself and three other Williamstown boys had been arrested and carried off to the reform school at Vergennes.

In this dream my mother cried and my father said he hoped this would teach me a lesson, and then tried to knock down one of the Mr. Webbs and rescue me.

In the morning, and because of the sense of uneasy leisure I had, I think this was during vacation, I ate my breakfast, still in a worried frame of mind and not sure—indeed, I am not yet sure—whether my brother or others of my young associates were also worried.

I thought it would be best to look into the situation, but in a cautious way that would not arouse suspicion. I therefore strolled, I hoped nonchalantly, toward the J. K. Linton store, then slid round the corner, and looked toward the station. The station was just across the track from a tall sandbank. It had always struck me as a happy coincidence that this sandbank, which was pierced near the loamy top with countless holes made by cliff swallows, was so situated that it left a flat place for the station and tracks. I have since decided that this result may have been foreseen by the men who laid out and built the Williamstown Branch.

The two cars that were to make up the early train to Barre that morning were still standing beside the station platform. This was unusual, for it was by now nearly nine o'clock, and Mr. Webb should have pulled out an hour and a half before.

Going a little further around the corner of the store and gazing past Fred Ainsworth's drugstore, I observed that Mr. Webb's locomotive was down by the turntable, a few hundred feet south of the station, and therefore to my right.

At the turntable itself there were quite a group of men, working and arguing; Mr. Webb, whose upper portion was leaning out of the engine cab, was almost visibly swearing. A man couldn't make the gestures Mr. Webb was making and still be talking in Sunday school language.

I then realized the dismaying truth. Mr. Webb hadn't turned his engine around the night before. He hadn't found out that anything was wrong with the turntable until his current fireman had tried to turn the thing around in the morning.

Then he had found himself stuck, and his plans for the day had immediately gone wrong. Some people said that Mr. Webb had a lady in Barre with whom he took midday dinner and carried on, but this was a joke and not real gossip. As I learned then, or later, Mr. Webb liked to take a nap during the noon period that was legitimately his, and which the Central Vermont Railroad wouldn't dare try to take away from him.

Now Mr. Webb was going to be so late into Barre that he wouldn't have time for a nap, and would be lucky if he had a few minutes in which to eat the slice of steak, the fried potatoes, the thick hunks of buttered bread, and the apple pie with which the Monument House had probably provided him—that or the equivalent. In the bottom of his dinner pail there would be coffee, which he could keep hot on the boiler, just as my father kept his own coffee warm on the boiler that ran the hoisting engine at the stoneshed.

Mr. Webb was annoyed. He was listening to loud advice from the men struggling with the turntable and was giving even louder advice in return. Nobody seemed to be getting anywhere.

As a normal boy, I longed to go over and watch the fun—and listen to it. As a criminal, interfering with the Central Vermont Railroad and possibly also with the United States mails, I judged I had better not do this.

I ducked over past the station on the north side, out of sight of any possibly suspicious eye among the men struggling with the turntable, scrambled up the sandbank and found myself with some of my fellow criminals in the grass at the top.

We watched the animated scene below. Indeed, this was a good vantage point from which to inspect the whole of Williamstown village: the three churches, the row of stores, the houses on Main Street and on Construction Hill, the stonesheds. I thought I might miss all this if I were dragged away to spend the rest of my boyhood in the Reform School at Vergennes. I did not feel bad enough to be willing to reform to that extent.

One of my companions suddenly drew a long breath. "He's going to back the train down to Barre," said this young man. "Judas Priest! Why didn't he think of that before?"

And this was indeed what that man of brawn and genius, Mr. Webb, actually did. He came away from the turntable with a whooshing of steam and spinning of wheels, picked up his abandoned tender, now well stocked with elm and maple chunks, hitched the front end of his engine to the train, blew his whistle as though he were letting out one last cuss word, and departed for Barre.

Mr. Webb did not enjoy this form of railroading. It was, to him, unorthodox. In addition, it gave him, as he told everybody who would listen that night and for some nights to come, a crick in the neck. But he did it because he wanted to get back home at some reasonable hour and not stick around Williamstown all day, letting the freight cars accumulate without his attention in the Barre yards.

In the afternoon a small wrecking train came up from Barre and straightened out the turntable between spits. The four or five men who operated this train were not mad at anybody, because that was what they were paid for, and it did not make them late for dinner to fix our turntable. In addition, they did not know one boy from another and did not care who had caused the damage.

So we boys went over and watched them while they worked, ducking out of sight only when the station agent seemed about to stroll over. The engineer of the wrecking train was younger than Mr. Webb, I thought, because he had no whiskers. He looked us over carefully, and then took a big chew of tobacco, and said he was surprised at how careless our fathers and mothers had been not to drown us when we were born; he said we were just the kind of boys who would grow up to be railroad men if we didn't look out, and it would serve us right.

Then he winked broadly, and I knew he was joking. At about

this time the work was done, and the wrecking train went away. The engineer didn't bother to test the turntable by turning his engine around on it. He backed away, blowing his whistle like mad, as though he was just as much at ease going backward as going forward.

We boys kept clear of Mr. Webb and everybody else connected with the Central Vermont Railroad for some days after this incident. I thought maybe Mr. Webb would tell our parents and make life difficult for us, but evidently he didn't.

My father looked at my brother and myself rather suspiciously one evening. "They had quite a lot of trouble with the turntable," he observed. "Somebody must have been fooling with it, they think." He paused. "If you were a little bigger I'd wonder if you boys weren't mixed up in it."

"They can't do all the wrong things that get done," said my mother gently.

"People missed connections all the way to Montreal," my father continued. He went on for a while with his dinner, and I could see, pretending all the while not to watch his expression, that his thoughts were drifting. He held his fork suspended for a moment. "Would you boys like to go to Montreal some day?" he asked.

I imagine we both gasped, as did my sister—his real favorite among us—who was not included in this suggestion.

"Montreal!" I said.

"Maybe," replied my father. "But keep away from that turntable after this. Understand?"

4

I seemed to know now that my father suspected the truth. I don't know how the other boys felt, but I had a wretched sense of guilt. To be estranged from the Central Vermont Railroad, and that was what it amounted to, was like quarreling with a loved one.

It was sad to have to keep away from the railroad station, sad not to dare venture near the turntable any more, sad to feel obliged to scuttle past the Monument House in the evening at the sight of Old Man Webb's feet grandly projected over the railing and Old Man Webb himself sitting so far down in his chair that his shoulder blades were where another portion of his anatomy should have been.

The fact is, I had lost my faith in the future. After what had happened I could never hope to realize the fondest of my ambitions. I might go West and become a cowboy. I might go to sea before the mast. I might enlist in the United States Army and get killed fighting Indians, the way General Custer had done; in that case I thought perhaps the Central Vermont Railroad might learn of what had occurred and feel sorry, but it would be too late.

We went exploring one lazy May day, down along the tracks toward Barre. There were bare wooden trestles at one or two places; if we wanted to be brave we would walk them, shuddering courageously at the depths below. I suppose people in authority thought the Williamstown Branch was to be a permanent institution, for once in a while they would send along a few gravel cars and fill in underneath some of these trestles. I wish I had the money they spent doing this; if any of them are still alive, they may wish so, too.

The afternoon train went by us twice, first on its way up, then on its way back. We didn't know this engineer, except by sight, because the way he operated he had to live in Barre or Montpelier. Still, he waved at us going and coming. We waved back half-heartedly, knowing that if he had all the details about us he would have been more likely to heave a few hunks of coal at us.

There were the usual job lot of passengers, visible through the half-open windows as the cars lumbered slowly by. I envied them, as I did everybody who was going anywhere on a train. I wished I could be among them, going somewhere to begin a new life among strangers who didn't know my past life. I thought I might be a well-behaved, upright boy under such circumstances.

Somehow the afternoon went by faster than we thought. It was a fine afternoon, with the sun sinking at last behind the

West Hill but leaving a good deal of light behind it for half an hour and more. We started home as it went down, walking slowly along the track and pretending we were railway trains. We could still do this, even though the Central Vermont Railroad no longer loved us.

We hadn't got more than half-way home, still following the track, when we heard a whistle behind us. It could be nothing less than Mr. Webb bringing up the evening train, tooting and puffing as he came up the grade, with the fireman ringing the bell and having fun at every cowpath that crossed the rails. Ah, what a life it was! I wonder if a transoceanic pilot has half the delight in his work that the old-style railroad men had—or should have had, for, as I have noted, Mr. Webb would never admit that he was anything but an overworked and underpaid slave of duty.

But I think he was trying to fool us—and maybe himself. I think this because of what happened.

We got off the track as Mr. Webb and his locomotive approached. There was plenty of time to do this, for Mr. Webb was not coming very fast. I suspect he was prolonging the sensation of being about to finish his day's work and get something to eat. And, anyhow, the ancient woodburner he was operating couldn't get up the grade at much more than seven miles an hour. If this strange machine had been an animal it might have been a subject of attention from the humane society. The snorting and puffing it made as it climbed the steeper parts of the branch line made me want to get behind and push.

But Mr. Webb wasn't worried. Mr. Webb, as we all suddenly realized, wasn't even mad. Mr. Webb had had a good day, whatever that meant to him. He was dead sober, I am sure. He was always dead sober while on duty. It was only when he had a few hours, or a whole day, off that he bought himself a bottle of Willerton's Stomach Remedy and got quietly and completely comfortable.

Mr. Webb saw us as the train approached. We were in a sandbank cut from which we could not readily escape, though we had plenty of room to let the train go safely by. Mr. Webb had his hand on the throttle; but as he did not have to steer he could take in the scenery, boys included, as he chugged along.

Mr. Webb leaned far out of his cab window and relieved himself of more tobacco spit than I would have thought any man outside of a circus would have been capable of. Then he gazed at us fixedly, and I wondered if a sheriff or some other species of policeman wasn't riding with him and getting ready to arrest us.

And then Mr. Webb winked. He winked a wink that began well up in his forehead and ended in a twitch along the left side of his nose.

We looked at each other, the three of us—or maybe that day it was four—and then let out a delighted and simultaneous whoop. Mr. Webb was our friend again, that was what that spitting and winking meant.

I felt as though I had been sentenced to jail and then pardoned. Maybe, I thought, as I pelted up the track in the wake of the slowly retreating train, maybe I could still hope, some day, if I were a good boy from then on, to sit in a cab with my hand on the throttle, and chew tobacco and spit out the window, and maybe wave at a group of admiring boys beside the right of way—maybe, maybe, maybe—the western sky was bright with maybes.

Just the same, when we came up to the station where the brakeman and station agent had just finished unloading the baggage and express, I was a little shy as I walked slowly past the locomotive. The other boys had disappeared altogether, and I was alone as I came up to where Mr. Webb was standing on the apron between the locomotive and the tender, and yawning and stretching himself as though he had just come out of a nap.

"Well, Robbie," he said, and I stopped as though I'd been seized by the collar. "I've missed you lately. You haven't been sick, have you?"

I said I hadn't, and he grinned.

"You must watch for the train when you're on the track," Mr. Webb continued. "It ain't a big engine but it would chew up a small boy if it hit him." He motioned. "We're going to turn her round, seeing there's time to do it tonight. Would you like to climb up and help?" He waited, as if I would have to think this one over.

"You're mighty spry," said Mr. Webb. I was—I was already in the cab.

"Uh-huh," I answered. I was breathing hard, not so much with the exertion of jumping into the cab beside Mr. Webb as with the excitement of being there at all.

"Well, now," Mr. Webb went on, taking his proper seat behind the throttle, but leaving room in front of him for me, "you set down and pretend you're the engineer. Take that throttle in your hand—it won't bite you. It only bites bad boys."

I took hold of the lever, feeling Mr. Webb's strong hand beside mine.

"All right," commanded Mr. Webb. "Pull back on it."

"But—" I stammered.

"Pull back, slow," said Mr. Webb.

I did this, aided and restrained, I suppose, by the engineer. The old locomotive breathed deeply, snorted and moved toward the turntable.

"Gosh!" I cried.

Mr. Webb laughed. "That's the way I felt, the first time," he said. "Easy there, easy now." I felt my hand go forward again as he closed the throttle, and the engine stopped. Mr. Webb gazed at me thoughtfully. "This turntable is what you might call a delicate apparatus," he observed. "It goes off the rails pretty easy. That's why we come up on it gentle, the way we're doing tonight. You take somebody playing with that turntable that don't know how it operates, and chances are they'll do damage to it."

He seemed to wait for me to speak. "Uh-huh," I said.

Mr. Webb was silent while he inched the locomotive upon the turntable, and the fireman, already in his proper post, turned it round.

"Runs like a sewing machine," remarked Mr. Webb, "since that wrecking crew come up the other day and oiled it."

"Uh-huh," I agreed.

We slid down toward the roundhouse where the ancient engine spent its nights.

"It's a tough life, being an engineer," said Mr. Webb as he climbed slowly down. "You boys wouldn't guess that, would you?"

"Nope," I said.

"I could have made a nice living cleaning out backhouses," mused Mr. Webb. "Maybe I'd have stunk worse than I do, but I'd 'a' been my own boss, you might say. How old are you, Robbie?"

I told him.

"In eight years you'll be old enough to be a fireman," Mr. Webb continued, inspecting me carefully. "You'll be a good chunk of a boy by that time. What do you want to be when you grow up, anyhow? How much of a damn fool are you?"

"An engineer," I replied breathlessly. "I mean—"

Mr. Webb laughed. "Just like I thought," he said, "solid maple from ear to ear. Well, I'll tell you, Robbie, if you want to be an engineer nobody can say you can't. If I'm still running eight years from now I'll take you on as fireman and teach you all I know. You'll be sorry, though."

"No, I won't, Mr. Webb." I found my voice at least. "I'm sorry about the turntable. We all are. I won't ever do it again. We all won't."

"Sure," said Mr. Webb encouragingly. "Sure you won't. And so far as I'm concerned you never did."

"If you'll take me," I went on bravely, "I'd like to be your fireman. I'll exercise and get real strong. I'm going to be an engineer, Mr. Webb—like you."

Mr. Webb came near purring. I'm glad I said this to him, for I suppose it made him feel like a success in the world. What more success can a man have than doing something that makes a boy want to come along in his footsteps?

But I never did become an engineer, though I repeatedly told my father, my mother, my aunt, and my grandmother that I wanted to be.

All I've done, aside from a little pick-and-shovel work, and

things like that, has been to play with words. I've never again
pulled the throttle of a locomotive.

---

*By the end of May and the beginning of June we were sure
at last that spring was not a time for going anywhere; spring
was a time for not going anywhere and not doing anything,
spring was a time for lying in the soft new grass, and maybe
even in the shade, and letting time go by.*

*Why did we let time go by? It would have been so much
better if we had not. But it did. It slipped through our fingers,
it ruffled our hair, it teased us with all sorts of promises, it made
itself seem valuable but nevertheless a value to be spent without
thought. In May, at the age of ten, we lay in the grass and let
time blow through us and change us. A few more springs—but
that was not then our problem; we did not believe that this
spring would vanish.*

*School would be out in May, because of the thrice-blessed
poverty of the Williamstown School Board. School would be
out, the agonies of speaking pieces done with, the long vacation
all ahead.*

*School would be out, and we ten-year-old boys lapsed easily
into the animal kingdom. First of all, after trying, usually in
vain, to catch trout or some other fish besides suckers and daice,
we wanted to go in swimming—"in swimming" was the phrase,
not a pursed-up "swimming." But in May the water in the brook
pools was often still too cold. We fell back on the fortitude of a
boy named Frankie Murphy, who was reputed to have gone in
swimming in March, and who had to live up to this reputation.
I remember Frankie, holding his heroic but reluctant nose, jumping into the West Branch and coming out fifteen seconds later
blue, shivering, and proud. The rest of us had to follow, or
Frankie would have been forever superior.*

*When the shivering stopped and the warmth of late May
and early June reasserted itself, we lay happily relaxed on the*

bank and listened to I don't know what birds and what wind whisperings among the trees.

Let us never go anywhere, let us never do anything in particular, let us never grow up, I thought, this is good and should last. But we did and it didn't.

CHAPTER SIX

Poor But Our Own

*W*ILFORD NILES was descended, as were his father, Ethan Niles, and his brother, Ira Niles, from one of the oldest families in Williamstown. This meant that in my generation the Niles family had been living around that vicinity for perhaps a century.

Besides being one of the oldest, the Nileses, as we spoke of them, were also one of the poorest families—poorest, that is to say, among our own people. The French Canadians, who came down to work at common labor in the granite sheds, the lumpers, were poorer still; but, good or bad, they weren't our own people. We weren't even sure they took Saturday night baths, the way we and all our people did.

But the Nileses were our own people, and they were poor. To add the finishing touch to their poorness, Wilford Niles was so feeble in his wits that he could never be more than a burden to his relatives. In his early teens, as I suppose he was in the year I am remembering, he had the intelligence of a small child.

Some persons said his mother had dropped him on his head when he was a baby. There had to be some explanation like this, for none of us, young or old, could understand that one of our own people could be stupid except accidentally. There was nothing wrong with Wilford's mother, Safira Niles (as she spelled her name); and Ethan Niles, his father, was a good, hardworking man, who would dig a ditch or clean out a backhouse when there was nothing better to do, and always paid cash for what he bought.

The Nileses were not only one of our oldest families, they lived in what was said to be the oldest house in town. This was not a beautiful house—oldest houses seldom are. It was the two-room outgrowth, as I learned much later, of what had been a log cabin. I would have envied the Niles family if I had known they were living in a log cabin—with memories, maybe, of the days when Indians lurked outside with the intention of scalping any Nileses who didn't have their rifles primed and ready.

There had never been any such days around Williamstown, but I could have invented some.

Mrs. Niles took in washing, and I remember an occasion or two when my brother and I—aristocrats with our father's steady income, in good times, of eighteen dollars a week—took our soiled linen, if that was quite the word for it, to the Niles house. The Niles house didn't smell quite like our own house. I took this to mean it smelled worse, but now I am not sure. Perhaps it just smelled different. Perhaps the Nileses didn't eat precisely what we did. Perhaps they ate more cabbage. Perhaps the steam produced when Mrs. Niles did our washing and other families' washings left an odor—for in those days, when people changed their underwear about as often as they took a bath, and really did take a bath only once a week, a washing was a washing, robust and vigorous.

Once, when we took the washing or went for it, the Nileses were all around the table in the kitchen, which was also a sitting room, a living room, to some extent a bedroom, and as much of a parlor as the Nileses could offer.

I don't know what the Nileses were eating. Perhaps, out of delicacy or shyness, I didn't look. I was sure, however, that because they were so poor it couldn't be as good as what we had been eating, or would be eating, at our house.

Somebody, I don't remember who, told me that he had once gone into the Niles house, or cabin, at meal time, and found them all eating Indian meal mush out of the same big dish in the middle of the table.

That was the kind of thing that got said about people who were, as we thought, poor. We had to say such things in order to separate ourselves from the really poor. Being poor was a rare misfortune, the way we looked at it. Sometimes, to be sure, it was caused by drunkenness or shiftlessness. In my mother's home town of Waterbury there was a man who was reported to have been graduated from medical school with one of the most brilliant records of his time; he took to drink, for reasons not inquired into, and when I used to see him he lived in a disreputable shack up the river road, and never raised anything but a little garden truck, and once in a while—but how he did this I was not told—a good deal of hell.

Being poor could also come from a death in the family, or prolonged sickness. Some extra good people among us thought that if folks were careful and saved their money, they would not fall into need at such times; but the medium good, and sometimes a few sinners, were sorry and tried to help.

Word got round in the very year of which I am writing that one family up on the Quarry Road—or maybe it was Baptist Street—was living on Montpelier crackers and water. I didn't think that was too bad, for I was fond of those heavy round soda biscuits that we used to buy in packages of one hundred for a quarter. My mother sometimes cooked them up tastefully with hot water, sugar, and cinnamon, and maybe slices of apple. But the church people got together and helped that family.

At any rate, somebody had to be poor in order to make the rest of us feel comfortable and reasonably well-off. We didn't mind J. K. Linton and a few others being rich and able to afford one, or sometimes two, hired girls all the time, and once a year or so make a trip to Boston. We didn't envy them, nor did we respect them except for qualities they might have that had nothing to do with their money. We—that is, the grown-ups—listened to them at town meeting because it was believed that men who knew how to manage their own property could be trusted with the town's property. But we didn't take orders from them, ever.

So our town had the rich, at the top, who didn't bother us much, and the poor at the bottom, who were about as scarce as the rich. We didn't look down on the poor, really, unless they had faults that kept them poor. We merely thought there had to be a few poor among us, because the poor were mentioned in the Bible as well as in less sacred books.

But there wasn't any class system, as I now see, except that we comfortable people, on eighteen dollars or so a week, were either better or more lucky than the poor of our own breed; quite a lot better than the French Canadians, who didn't always even speak English correctly; and different from the Italians, if maybe not better. The trouble with classifying the Italians was that though they were foreigners they earned as much as other granite cutters, and sometimes more.

Some Williamstownians rated the Scotch granite cutters a little below the native-born Vermonters. We did not worry much about this in our own family.

But, however you figured it, the Niles family was quite a way down in the social and economic scale; and Wilford Niles, being about the least intelligent young man in town, did his part, witlessly, in keeping it down.

Wilford's brother Ira, so Mr. Ainsworth and others said, was bright as a dollar; but whether this statement indicated merely that he was at least normal, or whether he had a trace of genius in him, I don't know. I wish I knew what became of him. He had a hard start.

We had compulsory school attendance in Vermont, even then, up to some age or other, but I don't know whether or not Wilford Niles had put in the required time. If he had done so it had not taught him anything, for I doubt that he could read or write or figure.

But he was harmless. Some queer and backward youngsters, even in that innocent and bracing atmosphere, were not altogether so—and this I think we boys sensed by some intuition. I recall one youth, freckled, cross-eyed, and somehow sinister, who was reputed to have his heart on the wrong side of his chest, and who was also said to have made strange suggestions to some of his companions. I don't believe anything came of this. There was an inbred normality in our lives. We didn't like strangeness.

We avoided the freckled youth, though it was asserted that he would eat dirt right out of the road, if you paid him a cent to do so.

Wilford Niles wouldn't eat dirt, and he did nobody any harm that I ever heard of. He could lose his temper if he were teased too much, but the most he did to work off his rage was to make uncouth angry sounds.

I suppose he passed his life in a kind of dream; not a bad dream when he was by himself, sometimes a nightmare when he was with others and felt himself underrated or a subject of laughter. We weren't unkind to him, any more than we were to Stevens Branch or the East Hill. Like them, he was a part of the scenery, a part of the town. As such, he had his place, he belonged to us, and we were neither ashamed nor proud of him.

In our fashion we were fond of him—all of us, boy and man. He was no rival to anyone. He had no pretensions. He wanted, touchingly, to be accepted as one of us, a member of the town. A boy could feel this, if not understand it, better than a man could. A boy was a little that way, too; he wanted to belong, and not be despised or laughed at. The difference was, of course, that a boy would grow up, which Wilford never would.

I suppose nowadays Wilford would have been in a "home" of some sort, learning to do some simple work and being as useful as he could. He might have liked that, because in such a place he might have found a few mortals who knew less and could do less than even he; he might have found himself slightly superior to such persons.

But in Williamstown, as Williamstown was in those days, he had something better. Everybody in town was used to him. Nobody turned to stare when he shambled by.

We boys, if we were not busy, might say to each other, "Here comes Wilford." We might ask him what he had had for breakfast or where he was going, because he never knew, and this amused us. We might let him go fishing with us, hanging over the rail of the Pool Bridge and persuading that calm and unworried creature we called a sucker to inhale our hooks. I believe he sometimes went swimming with us, tagging along behind like a faithful puppy, and never really learning to swim. We were aware of him at times, and at other times we weren't. But he was never a sideshow. He was a familiar part of the town.

Strangers might look at Wilford differently, but in those days there weren't many strangers in a small Vermont town. The traveling salesmen came through pretty regularly, and we envied them for their chance to see the world. But they weren't strangers. Many of them, I suppose, made the same rounds year after year, and J. K. Linton, or any other merchant who bought from them to stock his store, knew them almost as well as he knew his resident customers.

The drummers didn't bother Wilford. They felt, no doubt, that they had better not. To make fun of Wilford was possibly as bad as to make fun of the town itself; and part of their living depended on not making fun of any town in which they did business.

I believe, now that I think of it, that I once did hear a grocery drummer in the J. K. Linton store remark that if we thought Wilford was slow in the head we should see one they had over in Waitsfield. But he knew soon enough that he had made a mistake. Nobody asked any questions about the one over in Waitsfield.

2

Another sort of stranger came up from Barre in a livery rig and put on a show in front of the Monument House in the glare of brightly flickering torches. After the show, which usually included a few card tricks and other sleight of hand, and possibly a song or two, the stranger would sell patent medicines. He might throw in an exhibition of hypnotism as a dividend, and indeed I imagine his whole program was an exercise in hypnotism.

One of these visitors picked Wilford out of the crowd one night and had him up in front in no time. Wilford may have felt that he was at last being recognized, for he came willingly, and when the patent medicine man told him he had a bad stomach ache but would get well right away if he took a teaspoonful of the famous Kickapoo Indian digestive remedy, he at once had the stomach ache and just as quickly got well again.

"How did that taste?" the patent medicine man demanded.

Wilford said it tasted fine. He added—and it was a rare thing for him to add anything—that he wanted more.

The patent medicine man, winking at the crowd, said that more would bring the stomach ache right back again. "The beauty of the famous Kickapoo Indian digestive remedy," he went on, "is that one teaspoonful—just one teaspoonful, ladies and gentlemen—taken after every meal will relieve the severest case of indigestion. Save your money. Don't drink it. Sip it." He winked again. Since his version of the famous remedy was known to be almost pure alcohol, his advice was not taken too seriously in that prohibition state where liquor was scarce and costly.

The crowd guffawed. But the patent medicine man then made a mistake. "This bright young man"—he waited for the laugh and didn't get it—"will understand it when he grows up."

I caught a glimpse of Ira Niles, who I suppose had come there with Wilford. Ira looked unhappy—and indignant. But he wasn't much older than the rest of us boys, and there wasn't much he could do. There wasn't any word for what he wanted to say. So he didn't do anything or say anything.

But somebody did speak up. I don't know who it was. "That's enough of that, Mister," the voice said.

The patent medicine man's eyes went over the group—it couldn't really have been a crowd, though it seemed that way to me. The torches blew this way and that way in the shifting breeze of the warm June night. They had a hot tin smell that I would recognize if it ever came again—but it won't, and I can't describe it.

The patent medicine man patted Wilford gently on the shoulder. "Time for you to get home to bed, young man," he said. I saw Wilford step back and melt into darkness as Ira Niles took his arm and started him away. "And now," the patent medicine man continued, "I am going to offer this dollar bottle of the famous Kickapoo Indian digestive remedy, made from the roots of medicinal herbs growing in the swamps of upper Oswego County, New York—and don't ask me just where, gentlemen, or those swamps would be invaded by thousands of health seekers who wouldn't know what to do with a swamp if they had one— I am going to offer this one-dollar bottle of this priceless remedy for the small sum of fifty cents, one-half of a dollar."

He paused to get his breath. Wilford and Ira were gone, and whoever it was who had said that was enough of that had either had his say, or had gone home, too.

Nobody spoke and the patent medicine man resumed. "Some folks claim," he said, "that if you have heartburn or indigestion or inflammation of the spleen the best way to cure it is to put a mustard plaster over the spot nearest to it. Now, I'm a broad-minded man. I have no prejudice against mustard. I like mustard where God intended it to be—on a juicy slice of corned beef."

I let my eyes wander across the street to the front and spire of the Congregational Church, and wondered if the patent medicine man wasn't taking liberties with God that might get him into trouble.

"You might as well say," the patent medicine man was con-cluding, "that if you was hungry you could satisfy yourself by tying a beefsteak onto your stomach."

The bystanders laughed at this. I laughed, too. It seemed to me the patent medicine man was clever to think up things like that, one after another.

Then a few people came up and bought a bottle of the diges-tive remedy at fifty cents each, and all at once, after handing out a few bottles at the last minute for a quarter apiece, the patent medicine man whirled around in his wagon, doused his lights, whipped up his horses, and was off.

I don't know what made him do this. Maybe he thought he saw Constable Nichols lumbering down past the store ready to ask for his liquor or drug license and ready to take him into custody if he didn't have one. Maybe he always left town that way. He could do it in those days, in the dark, for the horses would keep to the road and there wouldn't be any other traffic to bother him—not at that time of night, after half-past nine, when nearly everybody would be in bed.

His customers, at a dollar, half a dollar, or a quarter of a dollar a bottle, wouldn't complain; for if they took a few good swigs before going to bed they would feel fine until morning; and if they didn't feel fine then, as they wouldn't, they would be too shamefaced to complain.

In any case, they would feel better than some of them did when they bought a few bottles of horse liniment from Fred Ainsworth's drugstore and made a night of it. The patent medicine man was a kind of public benefactor after his fashion. I never heard of anybody dying from taking his Kickapoo Indian digestive remedy; whereas some of our young townsfolk who drank paint mixers, hair tonic, or rubbing alcohol, although they kept within the strict letter of the state prohibition law, either died or came near it.

I saw Wilford Niles next day and reminded him of his adventure with the patent medicine man. After some prodding he recalled almost everything.

He smacked his lips. "It tasted real good," he said. His eyes were wistful. "I wish I'd had something like that when I was goin' to school. But Ira, he made me go home."

I don't believe I had ever thought, before this, that Wilford minded being himself, and not quite bright, any more than I minded being myself and somewhat brighter than the ordinary. But I could see, as I looked at him, that he was wondering about that medicine and what it might have done for him.

He was just wondering, though. He knew he'd never have any more of the magic in the patent medicine man's bottle. Ira wouldn't let him. Ira knew what was best for Wilford, and Wilford knew that Ira knew.

So Ira and Wilford and the rest of us went on as before, and there wasn't another patent medicine man that year, so far as I can recall, not in Williamstown.

But something else happened, and though I don't like to think about it even after all these years, I might as well tell it. It didn't happen in Williamstown, it happened in Barre; but it involved Williamstown, and it involved me and my character. I never did get to be very brave, even in that year of war when I worshipped bravery so much. But I wished then, and I wish now, I had been a little braver.

3

I don't know what was going on in Barre that day. It hadn't anything to do with the war, of that much I am sure. It could have been a fair of some sort, but everything has gone except for three things: first, that we rode our bicycles the six miles from Williamstown to Barre and back; second, that it was on this day that I had my first hot dog, which cost five cents, mustard included and tasted about as good as anything I have ever had outside of my own home, before or since; and, third, the thing that happened to Wilford.

I don't suppose I can make anybody understand what it meant to a boy then to ride a bicycle from the town where he lived to another and larger town. This was a sort of magic that opened up for my brother and myself when our Uncle Willie in New York sent us two bicycles that his family no longer needed. I suppose that for Uncle Willie and other sophisticated New Yorkers the bicycle craze was over.

My bicycle was a girl's bicycle, without any horizontal bar connecting the front end with the hind end. At first I was embarrassed about it, and my friends made fun of me; but it was a good bicycle and ran like a sewing machine and I could do tricks on it that couldn't be done on a standard boy's model. I could pretty nearly sit down on the pedals, for one thing. I could pretend I was an Indian, slipping under my horse's belly so the white hunters wouldn't see me, only to come up and puncture them with well-aimed arrows.

At any rate, the bicycle opened up a whole new world, and I suppose it meant more to us boys than the automobile meant some years later.

We had been used to going to Barre on the train, and at rare intervals. Now we could go there in less than an hour, since it was downhill nearly all the way, and come back in two hours, depending on how lazy we felt.

We didn't do this too often. Barre, being a big city, with six or seven thousand people in it and street cars, scared us some. We went on special occasions, and never alone. It is true that my brother once rode all the way from Williamstown to our grandmother-and-aunt's house in Waterbury, which is twenty-four miles; but he was bigger than I was.

Going to Barre on a bicycle, you went past the stores and the churches, over the bridge by the blacksmith shop, which must not be confused with the Pool Bridge, up the hill past the cemetery, and then, taking the left fork instead of going right to Mill Village, down a hill past a pretty fair swimming hole. You could get out of your depth in that swimming hole; and even if you tied a couple of empty gallon maple sugar tins under your armpits, it took courage.

But on the day I am thinking of we didn't stop at the swimming hole, there was so much going on (whatever it was) in Barre. We slid on down the hill. There are still such dirt roads in Vermont, I know, but this one would not be considered good enough for automobiles. Perhaps people ride horses over it today, for a horse is comfortable in dust or not too much sand and will ease past one of those ledges that the old road makers left across the road and didn't bother to blast.

There was a point, and I can shut my eyes and see it yet, where the road dipped into a sort of pass and then came out in the clear, and I saw the hills to the north, west, and east open out. There was the big world out there; there it was, all the beauty, adventure and danger a boy might dream of.

It awed me a little. I didn't want to go home. I might even have been glad to continue to Waterbury if I had been as big a boy as my brother. Still, there was a sort of menace in this scene. I was glad I had Williamstown to come back to.

Williamstown, as I left it for a while behind me, became something precious, and everything and everybody connected with Williamstown was in some way a part of me.

(123)

This was my town, my own, my people. We faced the outer world together, all of us. If we held together, and were loyal to each other, it could not harm us. If Williamstown had been an Italian city state of the time of Cellini I would have defended it with all my heart and strength against invaders from Barre, Montpelier, Chelsea or Northfield.

But now I was riding my bicycle down to Barre, and glad that some friends were with me to keep my bravery up to the mark. If any of the Barre or South Barre boys came out and yelled insults at us, there were enough of us to yell some good insults back. If a fight occurred as a result of these hard words, I meant to be a rear guard. I'd read enough about military operations during that military year to know that rear guards were necessary in any battle.

We advanced, therefore, into what might be hostile territory, passing the grimy South Barre station of the Williamstown branch of the Central Vermont Railroad, and coming into Barre itself.

When we turned right and swung across the river, the young Winooski wedded with our own Stevens Branch, we rode into Barre, big and terrifying city that it was, and came on a little stand-up restaurant.

There was a counter inside, and a man in a dirty white jacket saying next. I envied him his ease and self-confidence, which I supposed came naturally to men or boys living in big cities such as Barre. He seemed to be making change with one hand while with the other he hauled frankfurters off the grill, stuck them in a roll, smeared them with mustard as requested, and placed them in the customer's eager grasp. He needed about three hands for this, and I almost believed he had that many.

A young fellow in front of me hadn't been able to wait to begin, and was standing at the counter, the left side of his face bulged out with so big a bite of hot dog that he looked like a bad case of mumps. As I watched him he finished the other half of his roll, licked his fingers, and reordered.

"You rest up a while," said the man behind the counter unexpectedly, "and give somebody else a chance." He winked at the Williamstown delegation. "Jake here would kill himself with dogs if I gave him half a chance."

POOR BUT OUR OWN

He picked me out with his eye. "And now," he said, "how will you have yours, Judge—with or without?"

I felt embarrassed, the way I did when I had to speak a piece on the last day of school. "With," I answered. I hoped this meant with mustard, and it did.

We boys didn't want to be cramped in our style while eating a hot dog with plenty of mustard. We paid our nickels, which the man behind the counter tossed into a cigar box without even looking, and went out into the sunny street. It was a comfortable sort of day, not too hot, not too cool. We wolfed our hot dogs and began to feel at home in that strange big city.

Whatever was happening would be where the crowd was, and we didn't have to figure out where to go. Our bicycles we left around the corner by the hot dog stand, in a grass-grown vacant lot. Nobody would steal a boy's bicycle in Vermont— that much we took for granted. We locked them, though, just to be sure.

By this time we were beginning to feel as though we had lived in Barre all our lives and were as well acquainted with the city as though we had been born and grown up there. We swaggered a little, and looked around to see if any real Barre boys—or girls, for that matter—were paying any attention to us. None were, at least as far as we could tell at that moment.

Suddenly I found myself separated from the others. I had stopped to look at something in a store window, candy, maybe, or a bicycle, or a baseball bat and mitt (though I didn't play baseball much or well), or books and magazines, or fishing tackle (though no matter how much I fished the fish had little reason to worry about me)—something like that.

I felt lonesome and lost, even though I knew where my bicycle was and where Williamstown was and about where my friends would be. My confidence oozed out of me. I knew that nobody would mistake me for a Barre boy. I knew that every step and move I made told the truth—that I was a boy from a small town who didn't know city ways.

I felt apologetic, even though there wasn't anybody to apologize to, or anything to apologize for. Of course, this helps to explain what happened.

4

But how can the thing that happened be explained? How can a thing that ought to have happened and did not happen be explained?

As the truth comes to me now, Wilford Niles had become a symbol. He was Williamstown in one of its aspects, just as I was Williamstown in another aspect, and all the other boys, and J. K. Linton, and George Ainsworth and his brother, and George Beckett and his brother. He belonged among us. He had rights among us. We understood him, as other people and other towns and cities might not have done.

He was ours, that was the long and short of it. He belonged to us, and we belonged to him. Nobody in Williamstown would have said we were proud of Wilford, yet it wouldn't have been the same town without him. We had to have the wise and the unwise, the good and the bad, the weak and the strong; they were needed in order to make a complete town, all of them were needed.

I walked warily alone through the streets of Barre, a city infinitely greater and more terrifying in my eyes than New York, London, Paris, or Dublin could later be. I prowled like a beast in a strange jungle, a rabbit-like young beast on the watch for tigers and lions. I hoped that no other beast, big or small, would notice me. I intended to be brave if necessary, but I hoped the necessity would not arise.

I could not romanticize myself among these seemingly real dangers of a strange town where I knew nobody. I could hold back the Rebel charge at Gettysburg, I could stand resolutely on Bunker Hill, I could trail the Indians who had abducted the woman I loved, but this courage was possible only in situations that could not arise.

Barre was real. I walked with caution, looking around for my friends, who would give me back my confidence. I found them, but only after I had also found Wilford Niles.

I don't suppose Wilford had ridden a bicycle to Barre. Probably he didn't have a bicycle. The Nileses wouldn't have been able to buy him one, and wouldn't have trusted him with one. He had probably come to Barre on the morning train, which wouldn't have cost him anything. Jim Kennealy wouldn't have expected Wilford to have a ticket or money to pay for one. Jim would stand by Wilford in such a case, and let the Central Vermont Railroad take the loss. It wouldn't have been much of a loss, for no train in or out of Williamstown was ever more than a quarter filled with passengers.

At any rate, Wilford had reached Barre, led by the same attraction that had brought the rest of us. He, too, had got separated from his friends, just as I had. But whereas I could pass unnoticed, almost, Wilford couldn't.

Wilford stood out because he was different. We had our own word for his kind of difference. We said he wasn't bright. That meant his mind didn't work the way ours did. Were there some parts of his mind that worked better than ours? I ask that question now, a little too late.

The brave deed that was never done came too late, too. Wilford was in trouble and needed help. He didn't get any help.

Nobody was going to hurt Wilford, unless he first scared them by making them believe he was going to hurt them. If he had had a streak of violence in him he would have been in danger; but he didn't have.

What he needed, as I well knew when I came upon him, was somebody, some friend, to explain things to his tormenters, to make them understand that he was just Wilford Niles, from Williamstown, and all right, perfectly all right. This kindness to Wilford didn't require a man on a white horse riding home bronzed and weatherbeaten from the Civil War. It didn't ask for the kind of hero I liked in my daydreams to be. A boy ten years old would be enough. All the boy had to do was to recognize Wilford among these alien bees and hornets who were stinging him with their scorn, these dogs who were barking at him.

And Wilford, for once, at that instant, did seem like a bear or something of that size; and these Barre youngsters, city boys though they were, seemed mean and small.

But I was suddenly afraid. Not of any bodily harm that could be done me. Not of any mark that I would carry back home with me. I was afraid with a kind of strangeness, as though what was happening to Wilford might happen to me also if I were not careful.

What if they decided I was not quite bright, either, and turned from Wilford to me?

I don't know whether or not Wilford recognized me and spoke to me. I am not sure that he saw me and believed in his innocent way that I could rescue him from the trouble he was in. I hoped then, and I hope now, that this was not the case.

All I had to do was to say, hello, Wilford, just as I might have done if I had met him in front of the Monument House in Williamstown. How did you get here, I might have said, what are you up to so far from home?

There was an extremely funny saying, as we thought, in those days. Does your mama, we would ask, know you're out? I could have said this to Wilford, from the height of my ten-year-old superiority. I could make fun of Wilford, if I wanted to, without doing him any harm. These others couldn't.

But I didn't speak to Wilford. I pretended I didn't see Wilford. I pretended I didn't know him. I hurried by and left him to handle the situation, all by himself.

I betrayed Wilford. I also betrayed my home town, in the person of Wilford.

One of the other boys, whom I soon found, asked me what was the matter. Nothing, I replied, nothing at all. But I had little fun out of the rest of the day, and when we rode home I lagged gloomily and guiltily behind.

But the next time I met Wilford he was the same as ever with me. He even bragged a little about the fine time we had had in Barre. I didn't say much—I couldn't—but I went right into Fred Ainsworth's drugstore and bought Wilford a big two-cent stick of licorice, and he went away happy and grateful.

I think I was especially good to Wilford after that, trying to make it up to him. I did this even after it was plain he either hadn't noticed the harm I had done him, or didn't understand its meaning.

But I wish I had it to do over again: I'd walk up to that crowd of jeering youngsters and say, quietly but effectively, that's enough of that.

———

The little girl across the street had two cousins visiting her, another little girl—as I see her across the years, a pretty, brown-eyed, brown-haired child—and a boy whose name and appearance I have forgotten. They came from a long way off, a town near St. Paul, Minnesota, and this made the little girl the more romantic. She did not become one of my heart's desires—perhaps I had so many there was no more room—but I have remembered her.

I remember an evening, too, when we Duffus boys (I suppose our little sister was already tucked in bed) went across to play with our neighbor and her visitors. It was an evening in late June, perhaps the one the Scandinavians call Midsummer Eve. Daylight saving had not been invented, but it seemed as though the twilight would last forever and the red glow never die beyond the woods of the West Hill.

A sort of madness got into us. We ran and shouted tirelessly, without ever falling out of breath, while our elders sat decorously on the steps, the men with their coats on, I am sure, and the women with their long skirts gathered around them.

At first we were playing Hi Spy (and we never forgot to sound the h), and discovering each other around corners and behind shrubbery and shrieking to high heaven; and then we were chasing lightnin' bugs, which began to rise out of the grass on their nocturnal flight. Darkness was drifting down now, but these seemed almost to give enough light. The lawn, fields, and hills were soft with light and shadows, and maybe a moon was coming up, and maybe not.

(129)

The group on the steps rose with a flutter and a laugh and an honest yawn or two. It was time for us children, at least, to go to bed. But I would have saved that evening a little longer if I could have; I would like to be able to produce it now and show it to my friends and say, "Look, this is the way it was in Williamstown, in June, 1898." But though I have hunted for it, it is no longer there.

CHAPTER SEVEN

Blake vs. Ainsworth

*T*HE CASE of Blake vs. Ainsworth was never brought into any court, except the Court of Heaven, perhaps, where the Lord God and all His angels smiled at both sides and loved them both for their small sins and amusing ways as well as for their deep goodness.

I do, however, recall this battle between George Ainsworth and the Reverend Silas Blake. It may be that as I remember I impute to Silas Blake some of the qualities belonging to one or more other young ministers who briefly served the Williamstown Congregational Church. There was one young man, unmarried and very shy, who determinedly made a round of pastoral calls every so often and could usually think of nothing to say; my father didn't sit in on these calls, but my mother did, and her subsequent gentle laughter at the young man's awkward silences was mixed with a real and motherly affection for him. All the adults wondered that he was not picked up, married, and domesticated while he was in Williamstown; but I believe he got away untrapped and fell into the clutches of some designing woman —that was the way I heard his case spoken of by ladies who called on my mother—elsewhere.

The Reverend Silas Blake was of sterner material, and besides, he was already married when he came to Williamstown—married to a gentle and lovely woman, but not to one who would have let other ladies pay too much attention to the Reverend Blake, even if—which he didn't—he had wanted them to.

The Reverend Blake was a conscientious man. He was just

as conscientious as Mr. Ainsworth, which made the battle between them worse. If he had been suspected of any little moral laxities, such as smoking cigars, Mr. Ainsworth would have found it easier to deal with him.

But even Mr. Ainsworth had to admit that the Reverend Blake was a good young man, though a sadly mistaken one. For Silas Blake believed in the higher criticism, as it was then called, which I did not understand; and some of the things Mr. Ainsworth thought were wrong, Mr. Blake didn't think were wrong. Dancing, for instance, if performed under proper auspices. Play acting, for instance, if the actors and actresses were good, God-fearing persons. Mr. Blake didn't believe that playing sacred music on a violin in church was wicked; Mr. Ainsworth was certain it was. Mr. Blake argued that a piano was a stringed instrument. He also quoted the passage in the Bible which urged religiously inclined persons to make a joyful noise before the Lord. Mr. Ainsworth said that what we had in our church was, in fact, an organ, and it had no strings. Mr. Blake said he didn't want to believe in a God who would tolerate a toot from an organ but was offended by a twang from a string.

Mr. Ainsworth said Mr. Blake ought not to speak of God in this fashion. He said it was irreverent.

Mr. Ainsworth went all out against card playing. Mr. Blake didn't encourage card playing in church organizations or church circles; but he said he was sometimes puzzled when he was asked to explain why it was wrong for young folks to play with conventional playing cards, even if they did not gamble, but perfectly all right for them to play the game of authors—which also involved a pack of cards.

Mr. Ainsworth said he had prayed about this and the Lord had straightened him out on the subject. He implied that Mr. Blake ought to pray more. I can now see that Mr. Blake could have replied that he had prayed as much and as hard as Mr. Ainsworth, and that his understanding with the Lord had been different. But Mr. Blake didn't say that. I would have heard it, from conversations at home or from what later happened, if he had said it. And if I had heard it I would have remembered it, because I was always remembering—and still do—things of no particular use to me.

I should explain that a church crisis in Vermont at that time was a serious matter in more than the primary religious sense. What I say of our church—the right and correct church, the Congregational, as I then saw it—must also have been true of the Methodist Church. I don't know quite what the situation was among the Universalists, though they were respectable enough in their way. The Catholics, who had to go to Barre to confess or attend mass, really did take some trouble to be true to their faith; but since, on the whole, they didn't earn as much as the Congregationalists, we didn't worry about them. This is the truth of the matter, in spite of the high pay some of the Italian granite cutters—the very best, who could do you an angel or a wreath, in granite, that was almost as good as the original—in spite of what these men received. It was not so much the Italians who were deeply religious as it was the Irish, who performed their religious duties at some cost and much inconvenience by making the trip to Barre.

But the Congregationalists ran the town. This was not mainly because they were religious, although they were convinced they were, but because they included the old families, the ones with money. They also included old families without money, which my own family, on my mother's side, certainly was.

However, the church as a way of controlling things was not as important to most people, I am sure, as the church in its function of a club and social meeting place.

The horse sheds beside the Congregational Church told their story. These had not been built for the weekday delectation of boys, who could do tricks on the crossbeams or just sit around keeping out of the rain. They were to enable the farmer to bring his best buggy, with his best blankets, and his wife, to town, and keep the horse, buggy, and blankets under cover while he and his wife went to church.

I heard a good deal of talk about the loneliness of farmers' wives in Vermont. They didn't get to town as often as their husbands did. They stayed home most of the week, in spite of

Grange meetings and spelling bees and auctions and funerals.
J. K. Linton's store was a sort of club for the farmer; but it was
no club for the farmer's wife. She stayed home and attended to
her work; usually she did not go crazy, but sometimes she did.

The church stepped in and helped save her from this abyss
of loneliness, not only by its religious message, but also by pro-
viding a companionship that only the meanest and narrow-
mindedest husband could deny her. A man wouldn't ordinarily
dare refuse to take his wife to church on Sunday, and maybe,
if the weather were good and the mare hadn't gone lame, to
prayer meeting Wednesday or Thursday evening.

Church in my time didn't last morning and afternoon, as I
believe it did a century earlier. It lasted long enough, however,
for women to look at each other's dresses and bonnets, and for
them to indulge in a bit of decorous gossip afterwards. I saw
and heard this going on. I knew what it all meant to my mother,
though she was never physically isolated, the way the farm
women were.

Naturally, anything that interfered at all with the smooth
routine of church attendance and church services upset the whole
community. That was why the dispute, for such it came to be,
between the Reverend Blake and Mr. Ainsworth was more than
a matter of doctrine.

I could see—and things I heard my mother say to her friends
and even to my non-church-going father helped me to understand—that if you meddled with the church system in any way
you ran the risk of upsetting people's lives. Mr. Ainsworth must
have had quite a following, and I believe it was this sort of
worry that was behind most of it. The Congregationalist social
system was very good for those that were inside it; and nobody
could be quite sure that if you changed it, with the so-called
higher criticism, and card playing, and maybe dancing, it would
continue to be so comfortable and neighborly.

Mr. Ainsworth wasn't a fanatic. We didn't have any fanatics
in our church or in our town. He just felt safer with things the
way they were.

Mr. Blake didn't have the same need to feel safe, or so I

judge. He liked to use his mind, even on the religion he professed. And so there arose a quite considerable ruction in the Williamstown Congregational Church, part of which I understood.

2

Since Williamstown couldn't pay a preacher very much, it had to depend on preachers who were so old they didn't care to go anywhere else, or young preachers just out of divinity school who wanted to try out their wings. Mr. Blake was one of these; and he certainly did try out his wings.

I don't recall just how ministers were chosen in our church, but I do know that they were invited to come after a sample sermon or so, and that they were invited to go away again if they failed to suit the governing body of the church. In the case of Mr. Blake the trouble was that this governing body was split. Mr. Ainsworth, Deacon Slater, and several other extraordinarily respectable members of the congregation were on one side; and some of the younger married people, whose names I can't even think of now, were on the other side. I guess J. K. Linton was on the other side, though he had to be careful in community quarrels not to offend any customers.

Anyhow, Mr. Blake came and preached at the time there was a vacancy, and even Mr. Ainsworth liked the first sermon, for Mr. Blake, in spite of what seemed to be his youth and inexperience, was in favor of being good, just as Mr. Ainsworth was. The trouble later turned out to be that in that one sermon of about an hour in length Mr. Blake didn't have time to explain everything he meant by being good. The doctrinal part of Mr. Blake didn't come out and surprise Mr. Ainsworth until the deacons had voted, the bargain was completed, and the church had signed an agreement to pay Mr. Blake a salary for one year and provide him and his wife with a parsonage, rent free.

It was a beautiful parsonage, and still was when I last saw it: painted white, as most houses in Williamstown were except the brick ones and those whose owners didn't give a damn what people thought of them; it was on the west side of the main road

as you went toward Barre, and up a little rise, so that it over-
looked our village and valley. If a minister couldn't think noble
thoughts up there, he couldn't think them anywhere. He could
also walk to church in about six minutes, crossing the bridge by
Grover Caldwell's blacksmith shop and passing the Methodist
Church, but except in the rare instance of a union meeting, re-
sisting the temptation, if he felt any, to turn in.

Mr. and Mrs. Blake could have done much worse, assuming
that they were in a profession in which it wasn't considered fitting
to have much money. I imagine they had enough to eat; but I
now suspect they sometimes had trouble keeping themselves
looking as neat and stylish as they did. They didn't have any
children—not at that time. Maybe they were bride and groom
—I wouldn't be astonished if this were the case.

What did they talk to each other about, I now wonder, as
they sat at home on their little hill on their rare free evenings,
and looked down at the lights of Williamstown village—at the
lights of J. K. Linton's store, and maybe even at the Duffus and
Ainsworth lights, for it would have been hard to tell them apart,
glowing in the General E. Bass house beyond the brooks and
meadows. I wonder if Mr. Blake found it easier to think about
my father, who rarely came to church, than about Mr. Ainsworth, who came to all services and was an authority on what
the Lord God did want and didn't want.

But it must have been pleasant for Mr. and Mrs. Blake at the
start. Mr. Blake was the sort of young minister whom everybody liked, whether they wanted to or not; Mrs. Blake was
sweet and helpful and modest and firm. Nobody could find any
fault with Mrs. Blake, even, as the women of Williamstown
used to say, if a person went over her with a fine-toothed comb.

Mr. Blake was interesting and entertaining. He and his wife
kept thinking up plans to make life in the Williamstown Congregational Church more fun. Before he thought up the idea
that separated him from Williamstown and started him on a
more notable career, he thought up a number of other things.
He thought that a sermon needn't put the congregation to sleep.
He was in favor of all the virtues, just as his predecessors had

been; but he wasn't opposed to some rudimentary thinking, or even to touches of humor.

The higher criticism of which he was accused and which he may have practiced, I didn't understand. I listened to it as I sat in church waiting for Sunday School time to arrive, when Millicent Byrnes might smile at me or tease me or at least let on I was alive, but my thoughts were inclined to drift. I thought of all the things we boys did and might do, of swimming, fishing, butternutting, tramping through the woods, playing baseball, skating, having snowball fights; I thought of what fun it would be if I were a soldier in a real war, or a cowboy, or a sailor, or an explorer; but I never did get much idea as to what the higher criticism was about. I now believe that what Mr. Blake was suggesting was that there might have been mistakes in the King James translation of the English Bible.

Mr. Blake suspected, maybe, that it took the Lord God more than a week to create the universe. And this, as I learned, outraged Mr. Ainsworth.

I did some independent thinking about these matters. If the Lord God could create a universe at all, I reasoned, as He clearly had done, no other miracle was beyond him: he could do it in six days or six years or whatever time He had that wasn't needed for other jobs. So maybe Mr. Ainsworth was right.

On the other hand, the universe, and especially that part of it known as Williamstown, was pretty complicated. With my brother and other boys I had roamed the meadows, pastures, woods, and other natural features; I hadn't made careful note of the kinds of trees, flowers, grasses, and so on, or of the geological structures. My father said there was sand about six feet under Mr. Ainsworth's meadow and that there were seashells in the sand; but I wasn't sure whether or not my father was playing a joke on me when he said there may have been an ocean there at one time, or several times. I just didn't know, but it did seem to me that the Lord God must have been awfully smart to fix up all these details, and also to lay out China, Australia, India, and the North and South Poles, in which, I was sure, neither He nor we were as much interested, in the course of a single week.

Mr. Blake said the word "day" in the Bible might be a mis-translation. Or, he said, it might be a figure of speech for almost any period of time. After all, while the Lord God was laying out the world and putting the furniture around and planting the fruit, vegetable, and flower gardens, who was there to ask whether it was last Tuesday or next Tuesday? Because He came to the human race last of all. The House was there before Adam and Eve arrived, or before they needed one, or at least before they knew they needed one.

I am glad now to recall that my mother sympathized with the Reverend Blake rather than with those who were out to convict him of heresy and exile him to some other community. What she felt in the Reverend Blake, I think, was what I felt in him—a deep kindliness.

We young folks had proof of this kindliness because Mr. Blake, even when he was involved in difficult theological controversies, had a warm spot in his heart for boys and girls. I wished then he would see fit to mix the sexes in the classes he held at the parsonage, just as he did in the Sunday School classes where the lovely Millicent Byrnes sat and tickled the back of my neck.

However, he did what he could for all of us. I think he did have a class of girls, with which his lovely wife helped him. He also had a class of boys, of which I was one. We sang some hymns, I believe, but mostly we talked of boy problems—what we were going to do when we grew up, what it meant to keep on studying instead of going into the stonesheds, as many were tempted to do: the chance to amount to something and get ahead in the world, as we used to say.

It was a simple philosophy that the Reverend Blake had. Or perhaps it was not simple, either. He had seen strong men in early middle age succumb to the granite dust in which they worked; my father was to die of this less than a decade later, but of course Mr. Blake couldn't predict that tragedy. Mr. Blake couldn't attack the granite-cutting industry. He could, however, turn boys away from it without saying why. Even Mr. Ainsworth couldn't and didn't object to that, for Mr. Ainsworth didn't believe in tuberculosis or silicosis, and he did believe in getting ahead in the world.

So Mr Blake, like Mrs. Frankum in the graded school, put ideas into boys' heads. He even suggested that he might get up a class in Latin, to which we might come; he never did this, but he thought about it and honestly planned it. And Latin, in those days, might have seemed a way out of bondage. A boy who knew some Latin wouldn't spend his strong days pounding granite; he'd teach or be a lawyer or a doctor.

Mr. Blake had his following. My mother, for reasons I now clearly understand, was a part of it. And so was I.

And in the end, with neither man intending it, so I'd now say, Mr. Blake and Mr. Ainsworth faced each other, each with his following, like two armies with banners.

3

Mr. Blake's notions about the higher criticism might have precipitated the battle all by themselves. But a person who felt sleepy on a Sunday morning might doze off while Mr. Blake discussed the higher criticism, just as he might have done if Mr. Blake had picked out passages from the Sermon on the Mount and approved of them.

In the Williamstown Congregational Church it was not customary for the minister to hop around and yell as he did in some other respectable denominations, and as the so-called evangelists were expected to do. Mr. Blake had to keep his sermons on a calm and at least slightly intellectual plane. If he hadn't been willing to do this he wouldn't have become a Congregationalist in the first place. Excitable persons didn't become Congregationalists in Williamstown at that time, unless their parents made them.

Mr. Ainsworth wasn't excitable, either. He was merely firm. He knew what was right, and he intended, if he could, to make the right prevail.

What started the final set of fireworks was Mr. Blake's plan to stage a play for the benefit of the Ladies' Aid. There were only two plays on Mr. Ainsworth's approved list. One of these was *Ten Nights in a Bar Room*, which was a play, all right, but which, as Mr. Ainsworth thought, made people see the evils of drink. The other was *Uncle Tom's Cabin*, which showed how well-justified the position of Vermont during the Civil War had been.

But a play for the fun of it, even if it were intended to raise money for the Ladies' Aid, was something else. It was something worse. And what Mr. Blake proposed to do was to produce a play in which members of the Ladies' Aid would be the principal personages, and which had no moral in it at all that Mr. Ainsworth could discern. Even Mr. Ainsworth didn't argue that this play taught that sin was a good thing. On the other hand, the play didn't even hint that sin *wasn't* a good thing. It was, as Mr. Ainsworth seemed to think, altogether too neutral on this point. It didn't injure people's characters, but it didn't improve them, either.

My father and mother talked about this project from their two different points of view, neither of which resembled in any way Mr. Ainsworth's point of view.

My father's point of view was that it was foolish to make an issue out of a play; but that if the members of the Ladies' Aid wanted to make fools of themselves by acting in a play, he wouldn't argue against it. He thought that women of their ages might have more sense; but if God hadn't given them more sense it wasn't up to Mr. Ainsworth to interfere. Mr. Ainsworth's theology, said my father, was wrong in practically every respect; but in this instance there wasn't even any connection between play acting and theology.

On the whole, my father concluded, it would be a good thing for this play to be produced, and even for my mother to appear in it, because it would teach Mr. Ainsworth a lesson; it would show him he couldn't browbeat the other members of the Congregational Church. My father said he admired the Reverend Blake's courage. He said it was too bad a young man of that much character had to waste his talents by going into the ministry.

My mother shuddered a little and bridled a little as my father spoke, but she went on sewing. I don't suppose she ever stopped sewing when she wasn't doing some other kind of work. Except, of course, when she read, and she had to read carefully in order to be able to cite facts and figures to my father when he got off on the wrong side of an argument. Or when she played the parlor organ.

My mother said that in the first place a man who was a little older than she was wasn't in any position to make fun of her age or of the ages of the other members of the Ladies' Aid. She went on to say that the play wasn't being produced in order to make Mr. Ainsworth feel bad. She liked Mr. Ainsworth, as she liked practically everybody who hadn't committed a felony, and she hoped he would get over his present feelings and maybe even come to the play.

She then digressed from the main argument and said she wished my father would not say uncomplimentary things about the ministry in front of my brother and me. The ministry wasn't too good for even the most gifted young man, she said.

Not if he wanted to make money, said my father.

They both looked at us boys, and I was afraid one or the other of them might ask us whether or not we wanted to be ministers. They wouldn't ask my sister that question, in spite of the fact that the Universalist preacher was a woman.

I would have had to lie if I meant to please my mother; and I wasn't even sure I wanted to please my father and make money. What I wanted was an interesting, exciting, and heroic life—without too much danger, of course, but I always thought I could handle that problem when it came up. I didn't want to be rich, for that implied being stuffy and pompous, like Jim Beckett, or working and worrying all the time, like J. K. Linton; I just wanted to have all the money I needed when I needed it.

But I did not wish to be a minister, I simply did not. A minister had to speak pieces once or twice a week, and I didn't care for that; and all he got out of it, so far as I could see, was that he was sure of going to Heaven when he died, whereas the rest of us would wake up sweating in the middle of the night and wonder about it. Besides, I didn't want to die; I didn't want even to think about it.

So I didn't want to be a minister, not even the kind of minister Mr. Blake was, even though I had heard Millicent Byrnes and some of the other little girls say he was perfectly adorable.

Luckily, neither my mother nor my father asked me, nor did they ask my brother, either.

They were too much interested in the play, some of which I remember, though the essentials of the plot are a dozen layers down in my memory, like the first walls of Troy. I think, however, that what we had was a variation of the Faust legend.

To get this story down to the terms of a ten-year-old mind in Williamstown, Vermont, in the year 1898, there was this salesman who came to a small town—our own, for example—with a machine for making elderly persons young again.

As set up on the stage of the Town Hall, the machine seemed to consist of a sort of hopper, like a big coffee-grinder. The candidates entered at the top, after ascending a ladder. The ladder was placed at the back of the contrivance, of course, so that the audience could not see their ankles, let alone their legs, as they ascended. The youth salesman, as I may call him, then turned the crank, or pretended to, and the elderly ladies who had entered came out at the bottom through a little door, young and beautiful.

The plot didn't seem to require any elderly gentlemen being transformed into handsome young beaux. Perhaps that was why there was a plot; because it would stand to reason, the way we thought of things in those days in Williamstown, Vermont, that an old gentleman who had grown fond of an elderly wife after a long period of putting up with her whims and tolerating her virtues, would find a lovely young wife difficult. She'd want to go out when he wanted to stay home, for one thing—though where she would have gone in our town on the spur of the moment, I can't imagine.

There were quite a lot of ladies in the cast of characters, and perhaps only one man. I wish I could remember who this man was. He would have had to be a passable actor and a good stage manager, and at the same time an undeniably pious member of the Congregational Church; and this would have been difficult.

There were, I believe, weeks of rehearsals, in spite of the simple nature of the drama. I believe some members of the cast renewed their youth in this innocent way, possibly for the last time. Of course those of my mother's generation weren't really old, not by today's standards. My mother was in early middle age; and though she suffered from sensitive nerves was still healthy and, as I thought, pretty. I remember how pleased she was when I said to her, as an observation of fact but not consciously as a compliment, "Your hair isn't red, Ma—it's gold."

I suppose my father and mother as they were in 1898, she with her golden-red hair, he with black hair and sometimes a mustache—and a handsome man, too, in his prime—would seem young to me now.

"Did you get a lot of giggling done this afternoon?" my father asked one evening.

"I don't giggle," said my mother. "I never did. You know that."

"Isn't it in the play?" my father asked. "It ought to be."

But I could see that somehow, in his restrained Scottish fashion, he was proud of my mother being in the production; and little by little he made it evident that he intended to see the performance. Somebody had to be there to look after the children, he said. He didn't say that he would have gone in any case because he didn't propose to let George Ainsworth dictate to him.

As for George Ainsworth himself, he was in a sad fix. As a journalist and a man interested in all details of village life, he should go to the play at the Town Hall. As a conservative member of the Congregational Church, he couldn't go. And there was no provision possible that would have kept him present but not much in sight, as did his familiar rear-left-corner chair in the church. He had to go, or not go.

He didn't go. I felt sorry for him then. I still feel sorry for him, for I couldn't hate George Ainsworth. Nobody, man, boy, or beast, could hate George Ainsworth. My father cherished him, I am sure, for my father, being a Scot, liked to have somebody around to argue with.

I can now see, after many years of journalism, how George Ainsworth must have suffered in having to pick up the details of the play second hand, and not see them at first hand. He did insert an account of it in the Barre newspaper. In this account he said that the play had been produced, listed those who had parts in it, stated, as the truth required, that there had been a large attendance, and mentioned the sum taken in by the Ladies' Aid for its good purposes. I respect George Ainsworth as a journalist. When the truth had to be told, even though he did not approve of it, he told it.

4

So it happened. The Ladies' Aid of the Congregational Church of Williamstown, Vermont, produced a play called, perhaps—I don't remember—*The Youth Machine,* and this play caused a split in our church. Or it dramatized the fact that there was a split.

That is history. It happened. It may be more important than the Spanish-American War if you take it as a symbol and understand that what could happen in Williamstown could happen all over Vermont, and—after a decent interval during which the rest of mankind would catch up—elsewhere.

That was the way we felt about it, and the way we felt about it, even the way boys ten years old felt about it, is also history.

I forgot to mention that I myself had once been in a play staged in the Town Hall. It was a school play, which even Mr. Ainsworth couldn't associate with hell-fire and damnation. I believe it was about the Revolutionary War, which was the most respectable war there was, exceeding even the Civil War, in which people from Williamstown took part and got killed or wounded.

About all I remember about that play was that I carried a wooden gun and forgot my lines. I always forgot my lines under stress, and this is one of three-and-a-half-dozen reasons why I didn't choose the stage as a career. I didn't want to have lines. I wanted to be out front, enjoying myself. This I usually did, as at one local-talent minstrel show—yes, we had those, too, but Mr. Ainsworth didn't seem to mind, since in some way he associated them with Appomattox and the Emancipation Proclamation— when I discovered that if you tore a narrow strip from the program, held it tight between your thumbs, and blew on it, you got as good a whistle as you could extract from a strip of marsh grass, similarly held. I urge American youth to try this.

However, what I started to say was that having been on the Town Hall stage, I knew how it felt to be up there. In my opinion, it did not feel good. The audience might be friendly; but what friend would sit down there in a comfortable seat—anyhow, a seat—and watch somebody else squirm?

But the ladies who took part in the skit that may have been entitled *The Youth Machine* didn't seem in the least to mind being up there. They had an audience that included not only the Reverend Blake's portion of the membership of the Congregational Church, but also a number of Methodists, a few Unitarians, some Catholics, an atheist or two, and a recognizable scattering of citizens who would have preferred to be Baptists or some other denomination if a suitable church had been available.

Mr. Ainsworth had unintentionally done the enterprise a good turn. A trained press agent couldn't have accomplished more. Mr. Ainsworth had stirred up curiosity as to what this scandal in the Congregational Church was all about. The Town Hall auditorium was filled. I don't think that even the glass-blowers' show at which I won the glass deer surrounded by artificial snow, or the most daring of the vaudeville shows, with girls kicking up their heels and showing all their red petticoats—I don't think any of these ever drew a bigger crowd.

My father liked this, and he didn't. So I thought then, and so I think now. If any lady of the Ladies' Aid was to be prominent in that play, and be recognized as a little better than the others, he was willing that it should be my mother. It was the same as having my brother, my sister, or myself at the head of the class in school.

Still, he wasn't sure, or so I believe, that he liked to see my mother up there on the stage, being stared at by anybody who had twenty-five cents, or whatever it took to buy a ticket to the benefit.

But it went off wonderfully, the way I saw it. The members of the Ladies' Aid looked as old as the hills when they approached the miraculous machine. They had white hair and wrinkles, they were stooped and rheumatic, some of them had canes. Of course some of them, in real life, were not as young as my mother. But even my mother, as she was made up for this stage debut, startled me. Would she, some day, have white hair and wrinkles? Would she some day falter in her walk? Would her shoulders be bent by age, some day?

I couldn't believe it. I can hardly believe it now, after all the years.

But when she went into the machine in her turn, an old woman, and emerged at the bottom a woman who had recovered her youth, I wasn't sure even my father didn't catch his breath.

Who knows what his mother really looks like? Or the woman or women he later loves? All I was sure of was that this aged woman made young again by the magic of the machine was the prettiest of them all.

It was so long ago, and nobody who was young then is young any more, not even the babes in arms. But I like to think that for a few minutes youth returned to my mother and to the other members of the Ladies' Aid of Williamstown, Vermont. The machine was no silly contrivance, after all; it worked; it kept forever, like the images on the Grecian urn, a picture of our town as it was in that year and at that moment.

Dear town, dear moment! After all the years, it lives. After all the years our family walks home again together, my father poking his own kind of fun at the whole affair, my mother modestly proud, for she knew she had done well; myself, and perhaps my brother and sister, marveling that for once, for this one night, we knew a real actress.

My mother said, as though she had read our thoughts, she certainly wouldn't care to go through that again; but, after all— well, she could see what some people saw in it.

My father said there was no sense in the whole business, but he thought my mother had done a lot better than some of those other old hens.

My mother said they weren't old hens, they were God-fearing women trying to help their church, and he needn't make fun of them. But, in a way, I hardly knew why, she was pleased.

We were all pleased. After we got home my mother made cocoa for the family, and we children, even though we were beginning to get sleepy, were allowed to sit up long enough to have some, with caraway cookies on the side.

I wish I had some caraway cookies on the side now; I wish we all had that evening back. The only one who wouldn't want it back, if he were here and could express his opinion, would be Mr. Ainsworth. This wasn't one of Mr. Ainsworth's triumphant evenings.

There was a light on his side of the house as we came in. My father looked at it as he fumbled for the knob of our own front door—not the lock, for we didn't lock our doors then, or there, any more than the people in Longfellow's *Evangeline* did.

"No," said my mother warningly. "I don't think he'd care to talk about it tonight." She reflected. "I'd like to send one of the children in with some cocoa, but I think we'd better not."

"Well, we licked him," observed my father. "I hope this will be a lesson to him."

5

But of course we hadn't licked Mr. Ainsworth. Nobody licked Mr. Ainsworth. Mr. Blake might have done so, maybe, if Mr. Blake had been willing to stake his whole future on what happened in Williamstown, Vermont. But Mr. Blake wasn't hemmed in by the East and West Hills, he could get out. Mr. Ainsworth couldn't get out. He had to live and die in Williamstown.

So that was the way it was.

The play about the youth machine had been a financial success, and the Ladies' Aid had almost more money than it could spend. Mr. Ainsworth couldn't say this was wrong. He was full of ideas for spending the money, including putting a fresh coat of paint on the church. Some of the ladies believed it would be better to paint the parsonage, which was homelike inside, but was beginning to look dingy outside. Deacon Slater proposed to increase our contribution to foreign missions.

Mr. Blake thought it would be a good idea to fix up the church basement so that church suppers could be cooked right

there, and save a lot of running around. Mr. Ainsworth didn't
like this idea; he said the House of God wasn't intended for bak-
ing beans.

In this sort of argument the dispute over whether the play
should or should not have been given was almost forgotten. But
Mr. Blake went on talking about the higher criticism, and
though I still didn't understand what he was arguing about in
his Sunday morning sermons, I could see Mr. Ainsworth, in his
chair at the far left-hand corner, wriggling and getting pink. And
Mr. Ainsworth went home as soon as the service was over, not
waiting to shake the minister's hand at the door.

This sort of thing lasted for a few weeks, and then it began to
be taken for granted that Mr. Blake wouldn't be asked to stay
for another year.

I knew this almost without being told. I knew it even though
Mr. Blake went right on preaching and making calls, the way he
always did; and when he came to call on my mother she subsequently observed to my father that he hadn't said a single thing
about the church trouble or about going away.

"I wonder what he would have said if he had met George
Ainsworth," mused my father.

"He probably did," my mother replied. "If he did he probably
said good afternoon."

The Sunday came when Mr. Blake preached what we all knew
to be his farewell sermon. I haven't the slightest idea what it was
about, but I am inclined to believe that it had a good deal to do
with brotherly and neighborly love and not much to do with the
higher criticism.

After that we had Sunday school as usual, and when we came
downstairs Mr. Blake was still standing there and we all shook
hands with him. He had a firm warm clasp, and a friendly but
sad look in his eyes. This time his wife was standing beside him,
and she too shook hands with us.

"Be good children," she said—something like that.

When the Blakes actually left, which was during the following week, the deacons went to the depot to see them off, and so
did many of the congregation. Even Mr. Ainsworth was there,

and I thought this was odd. My mother, who had dragged me up in front of everybody to shake hands again, wasn't surprised; she seemed to take it for granted.

Mr. Ainsworth walked home with us. "A fine young man," he observed, after a while. "When he gets a little older and settles down he'll be a good minister." He was silent for a while. "A fine young man," he repeated.

"One of the very best," said my mother. Mr. Ainsworth looked at her sharply.

So this was the way the case of Blake v. Ainsworth turned out. The next minister we had was a rheumatic veteran from somewhere or other who believed in hell-fire and plenty of it. Mr. Ainsworth liked him.

On my birthday some of us went berry picking in a burned-over patch beside the railway tracks of the Williamstown Branch. I remember the date for the very reason that it was indeed my birthday, and this was a way of spending it. I may have returned home to presents of one sort and another, and a feast with cream cake in it—and oh, Dear Lord, may there be cream cake in heaven if ever I manage to get in there, and, may I pray the Court please, have that same appetite for it. But what has remained with me, the ultimate birthday present that has never worn out or been eaten or broken or outgrown, is a berry patch in the sun.

The wild raspberries came in July, my natal month, and the blackberries later. We wandered through the rich growth with our tin pails, never completely stripping one bush before we saw another and, as we thought, richer one, and moved on.

But there would always be raspberries in that place, so we believed, and every year the sun would shine as warmly as on that day, and we and the raspberries and the sun would all be there together. There were small green insects on some of the berries; they had a bitter taste and I did not approve of them;

(149)

but now I wonder, is that raspberry patch still there, and are there still small green bugs that taste bitter, and little boys, who will never grow up, to eat them by mistake?

The shadows slanted westward; for a while there weren't many shadows, and we stopped to eat our lunch; and then the shadows swung to the east, more and more, but there were still humming noises in the woods, peaceful twirrings, buzzings, and little, sleepy, contented snorings, and we went on putting some raspberries in the pails, and eating some.

This was my birthday, my tenth birthday. This was my birthday party. The berry patch, Williamstown, all of Vermont, the whole world, dozed happily around me; and I was utterly happy, too, but did not know it.

CHAPTER EIGHT

------◄•••►------

The Chicken Croquette

*T*HE DAY Mrs. Linton took her Sunday School class down to Williamstown Gulf brought me good luck and frustration. It also taught me a little more about little girls, in a negative sort of way, but this did me no good at the time, or for a long time after.

The good luck was that while we were racing up one of the paths at the sulphur spring reservation that made Williamstown Gulf smell the way it did, I found a dime. This was the first money I ever found lying around that way. I did not find any more in that way until some twenty years later, when I was hiking with a friend along an almost unused dirt road in the Sierra Morena, west of San José above the Santa Clara Valley in California, and came upon a bright silver dollar. The dollar in 1918 meant about as much as the dime in 1898, which I suppose is an evidence of inflation.

The bad luck was that I had an encounter with a chicken croquette, and the chicken croquette won. This must have been one of the times when the Gulf House was being managed by persons who respected the state prohibition law, or Mrs. Linton would not have taken us there. Still, I did have the feeling that this was a worldly and potentially wicked place, and no doubt this gave the chicken croquette an advantage it would not otherwise have had.

I shall have to fill in the background of this situation in order to make anybody believe what happened—or to make anybody believe that what happened mattered one way or the other. It did matter, partly because there were little girls around, looking on and giggling when little boys made mistakes, and partly because I felt that Mrs. Linton was introducing us all into a world above the one we were used to—or different, anyhow.

For one thing, few of us ever ate in a restaurant. There were no restaurants in Williamstown, unless you called the dining room of the Monument House a restaurant; and even Mr. Brown, George Brown's father, who was then running the Monument House, would hardly have done that. A hot dog stand wasn't a restaurant, and anyhow the nearest hot dog stand was in Barre, six miles away.

So eating at any restaurant—and especially one as stylish as the Gulf House—was wonderful but rather awful. Because what fork did you use, if there were more than one? Did you tuck your napkin under your chin, as you were likely to do at home, or what? What about corn on the cob? What about bones? Did you use fingers after all else had failed? Could you talk to the waitress—because usually it was a waitress—in case you could think of anything to say? I couldn't, but if I could, should I?

The presence of my young companions at the Gulf House helped a little, but there was a catch there. Two of them, the Linton boys, who, as I have explained, came of a well-to-do household, had traveled; they had been to Burlington, I am sure, and I believe they had been as far as Montreal and maybe Boston. They were sophisticated, they knew what to do.

Finally, there was the outstanding position of the Lintons in our community. And that takes some explaining, too.

2

There may have been a dozen citizens of Williamstown who could have sold out for more than J. K. Linton. We had an intellectual aristocracy in the persons of two or three professional men—say, two doctors and a lawyer. And the ministers, of course. Then there were Charlie Seaver, who ran the feed store, and Grierson, who owned the biggest granite shed.

But J. K. Linton, without putting on any airs, seemed to be our most important citizen. In 1898 he had, under one roof, a grocery store, a drygoods store, and the postoffice. Our post-office box was Number Ninety-nine. It hasn't done me the least bit of good to remember this all these years, but there it is—I do remember it.

The Linton family had quality, and this I won't try to define. At the time of which I am writing J. K. probably felt easy as to his status and his prospects. He indulged in certain luxuries. The hired girl was one of them. Another was an inside privy, which didn't flush—as far as I know, there wasn't a modern flush toilet in Williamstown at that date—but did have real toilet paper instead of old newspapers. And it wasn't illustrated, the way many old-fashioned outhouses were.

Mr. Ainsworth's, for example, was an education in itself. To this day I recall what the steamship *Great Eastern* looked like on her maiden voyage to New York in the late 'sixties of the past century; she was pasted on the wall as she came into harbor, flags flying and cheering throngs awaiting her. There were one or two religious motifs, for Mr. Ainsworth was a devout man. One of these showed Jacob in the House of Laban—that was its exact title. The older pictures came, I think, from *Harpers Weekly*. I don't know who was responsible for a more modern type: for instance, a drawing of a soubrette kicking up her heels so that you could see nearly to her knees and singing (so the caption said) a song entitled: "O, I am awfully shy, boys; I am, and I cannot tell why, boys."

A good, respectable outhouse decorated in this fashion was not in the least vulgar; on the contrary it was, in its modest field, as cultural as the Metropolitan Museum of Art. It was educational. It took one's mind off mundane matters.

But progress led away from it, just as progress led away from the horse and buggy and other comparatively quiet phases of life. And J. K. Linton was not showing off when he built his indoor, unillustrated privy; he was just keeping up with the procession as he saw it. He was a public-spirited man who played in the band—and we had a very good one—and did other things to make Williamstown a better town to live in. Finally, he was kind-hearted, with a twinkle in his eye for small boys. This kept us from standing in awe of him. Yet he and his equally kind-hearted wife and his two sons seemed to be a little set apart.

The boys made no parade of their father's affluence, even though they once had a pony all their own to ride, and either one of them could walk into the store and take a chocolate or two out of the candy counter without feeling guilty; and in the year of the Spanish War they had sailor suits and could pretend to be home on leave from the Battle of Santiago, whereas the rest of us had to remain civilians.

The Lintons had a summer cottage and camp at Mirror Lake (the old settlers called it Berlin Pond), a few miles from Williamstown. People in Vermont were just beginning to realize that it was a healthy thing to get away from home for a while in the summer, but not many of them had yet figured out how to do it; the Lintons had, however, and once they invited me over for a day or two. It was a marvelous experience: I slept in a tent for the first time in my life and was awakened in the morning by the singing of a bird, whose shadow I could see against the canvas near the cross pole; I got stepped on by the pony and had most of the skin taken off the top of my right big toe; I fell in love with a nineteen-year-old girl, as I was doing from time to time in those days—I wonder where she is now and whether I would still love her; finally, I went swimming, and a snapping turtle, as we supposed, nipped a sizable chunk out of the bottom of my left foot as I was wading ashore. Everybody was sorry for me, including the nineteen-year-old girl, and I felt almost as much of a hero as I would have done if I had gone to war and had a piece shot off the bottom of my foot.

I think I crippled myself before I got around to doing any fishing; but some of the others caught perch and I remember to this day how good these tasted fried in cornmeal. And I got to ride the pony who had stepped on me, and I didn't fall off.

I felt that this was the life I had been born for—to ride ponies, to be slightly injured now and then, but not too painfully or durably, to sleep in a tent, to be awakened by a bird, and not to have to work much or go to school, except in bad weather when there was nothing else to do. My father had told us that there was once a King Duffus in Scotland (as, indeed, there was, until his subjects caught him in a careless moment in the town of Forres), and I wondered if my taste for the finer things of life wasn't partly due to the royal blood coming out. I didn't mention this theory to my brother or sister, who should logically have felt the same way, but somehow didn't seem to.

Anyhow, this was what the Linton family stood for, in my dreams. J. K., modest man that he was, would have been amused.

3

Mrs. Linton was a good Sunday school teacher. Sunday school was held after church, upstairs in the room also used for prayer meetings and for meetings of the Junior Christian Endeavor. The point about Sunday school and also about the Christian Endeavor was only partly that they taught us religious truths. They also brought boys and girls together under what our elders evidently hoped were uplifting circumstances. I don't know just how uplifting it was when Millicent Byrnes, sitting behind me in Sunday school, tickled the back of my neck with her muff; I suppose I would have to ask a psychiatrist about that. The back of my neck felt as though it were turning red, and Millicent and two or three of the other little girls giggled so hard that I forgot my carefully-memorized Golden Text when Mrs. Linton asked me to repeat it.

Mrs. Linton was patient. She said she realized it was hard sometimes to keep our minds on Sunday school, but maybe we would be glad when we grew up if we could remember some verses out of the Bible. She added that we surely had enough time when we weren't in Sunday school or ordinary school, and could use that time for play.

I think it was that day, but it may have been another, the way the days kept melting into one another, that Mr. Ainsworth, acting as Sunday school superintendent, stuck his head in the door. As luck would have it, he picked me out to recite the Golden Text, and again I failed, and again I heard muffled girlish giggles.

I decided then and there to become a trapper in the Rocky Mountains after I got a little older, and never see a girl or woman from one year's end to the other. Millicent Byrnes could smother herself with her muff, for all I would care. But this mood did not last. I made new plans, many with females in them.

"You're so quiet today, Robbie," Mrs. Linton said kindly as we were filing out. "You're not unwell, are you?"

"Nope," I replied. I ran down the stairs two at a time, nearly upsetting the Reverend Silas Blake, who stood at the door to say goodbye to us. I saw Millicent Byrnes come down a few seconds later, a demure little figure with her hands in her muff, and a saintly expression on her face.

"Such a sweet child," I heard Mrs. Linton say to Mr. Blake. "But—" she nodded her head smilingly—"full of mischief."

"If they weren't at that age, I'd worry," agreed Mr. Blake, who often shocked his more conservative parishioners by his mildness. People said, sometimes approvingly, occasionally with a touch of doubt, that there was no hell-fire in Mr. Blake. He wasn't the least bit like the Reverend Jonathan Horner, a stern old character who had spent nearly half a century ministering to the needs of Williamstown's Congregationalists, and who had been known to say that religion without hell in it was like a meal without salt. Mr. Horner was gone before my time, and I was not directly exposed to his influence.

After Sunday school I went across with some of the other boys to the horse sheds near the church. There were crossbeams on which we could chin ourselves, but it didn't matter too much what we did. After being in church and then in Sunday school, it was necessary for us to relax. We could stand being comparatively good little boys just so long, and then it was time to be healthy little animals, yelling and showing off.

But this did not last long. Sunday noon dinner was the best meal of the week. In our house it might mean roast beef or boiled tongue—which I adored—and once in a great while it would mean chicken. My mother never had to scold any of her three children for being late to Sunday dinner.

I have mentioned the meetings of the Junior Christian Endeavor. The cast of characters here was about the same as in Sunday school, though Mrs. Linton didn't attend. A good deal went on at Christian Endeavor meetings that our elders did not know about. It was customary, for example, for one small boy or girl to be chosen to lead the meeting. This meant that he—or she—sat up in front, read a passage from the Bible, gave out the hymns, and asked somebody to lead in prayer.

Except for one of these privileges, nothing could have tormented me more than having to be the leader. But I did love to ask one of my helpless boy friends—somebody I had quarreled with, as a rule—to lead in prayer; I loved to watch the expressions of wrath and dismay chase themselves over his face; I loved to look between my spread fingers as he groped for words, usually beginning with O Lord and ending with a stammer. I don't suppose any deity ever enjoyed being prayed to half as much as I did making someone else do this praying in front of an audience always ready to snicker at his embarrassment.

Sometimes, when my opportunity came, I turned on one of the Linton boys in this way. I had to show them that in spite of their wealth they were no better than the rest of us. I might also take a whack at Jim Nutting or Ralph Stevens, not out of malice, but just to see them squirm.

The little girls I didn't bother. How could I have called on Millicent Byrnes without getting red all over and revealing my innermost secrets—one of them, at any rate?

But either one of the Linton boys would as soon as not call on the beautiful Millicent; and somehow Millicent liked to have this done. I didn't understand women, at that time.

I trust these remarks about religion among the young in Williamstown in the year 1898 have made the situation crystal clear. I am speaking, of course, as a Congregationalist. The Congregationalist Church, and I say this in all modesty, was socially on top. When Mrs. Linton took us on our annual Sunday school picnic, in what I remember as a sort of nine-seated surrey with a fringe on top borrowed from her husband's livery stable, we felt ourselves to be about the best that Williamstown had to offer. We did not look down on other religions, we were merely thankful that we didn't belong to any of them.

It is not easy for me to make a mental picture of that surrey. I am not even sure that it had two horses in front. I think Mrs. Linton borrowed one of the livery stable boys for the occasion— one of the more refined among them, of course. I seem to recall that he rolled up his sleeves after we had arrived at the Gulf House and played throw and catch with another young man; and I wondered if I would ever have biceps like that.

I am not sure, either, how many there were of us. Something like a dozen, maybe. If we didn't all get into one surrey there would be another, for when J. K. Linton did things like this, he did them in style.

When you went to Williamstown Gulf you went south. You climbed a little, leaving the watershed of the Winooski, which ultimately delivered into Lake Champlain and thence into the St. Lawrence and the chillier part of the Atlantic. You came into the watershed of the White River, which emptied (as it still does) into the Connecticut, and so helped keep up the level of Long Island Sound.

You went down past Cutter's Pond, which I believe has a fancier name now, where we boys swam and fished. Then you got down into a low-lying pass, with sides so steep that the word Gulf was appropriate enough.

This was the old stage road, and not much better in the days I write of than it had been in the stagecoach days. It had been a corduroy road once, and some of the cross-logs could still be seen, covered with a few inches of gravel, in the swampy parts. It was dark and damp down there even on a sunny day. It was a place to go to on a picnic, but not all alone, and not, at the age of ten, after dark.

But it was cheerful to be going down there. This was one of the happy days, except for the adventure of the chicken cro-quettes.

I think it was a happy day for Mrs. Linton. She seemed to me, as did my parents, quite old and staid; but I imagine they were all in or near their middle thirties. They differed, of course, from persons in their middle thirties today, because it was not then considered right for anybody much over thirty-five to relax in public, and have lighthearted fun.

But a woman of thirty-five, if that was Mrs. Linton's age, could easily remember when she had been twenty-five and even when she had been twenty or eighteen; and she might sigh at times for her lost youth.

Anyhow, we sang—I even sang a little myself when the others were making enough noise to drown out false notes—and Mrs. Linton sang with us. Then we played some sort of word game, the kind you can play on a fine day in a surrey. We did conundrums, I imagine. After half an hour of this we were all reasonably silly. Mrs. Linton smiled understandingly, the way adults did when children were in this mood.

Then she suddenly gave a little laugh, quite unlike her usual polite expression of amusement, pulled off Ralph Stevens' hat, and sent it sailing into the bushes. It was the kind of hat that would sail—wide-brimmed, low-crowned, and light in weight. You could buy one at J. K. Linton's store for fifty cents at the beginning of the season and about twenty-five cents in July.

Ralph started a yell of protest, thinking one of the girls had been guilty, then flushed and stammered when he realized who it was. Mrs. Linton flushed, too, as she turned to the driver.

"Now why did I do that?" she asked. "I didn't think I was still such a goose—at my age, too!"

I think I knew then why she did it, and now I am sure. She was reaching back toward her youth. She had tried to make believe, for a moment, that she was one of us, and not just a dignified, motherly, Sunday-school teacher.

Ralph jumped out and had his hat in a jiffy, not at all damaged —you could hardly damage that kind of hat with anything but an ax. But he didn't bring back Mrs. Linton's lost girlhood.

4

At some stage of any mixed gathering of young persons in Williamstown, somebody would suggest playing what we called kissing games. At the age of ten I didn't care much for this amusement. It seemed to me effeminate, though I didn't know that word. A cowboy or a trapper or a cavalryman wouldn't belittle himself to play a kissing game, I thought. The problem of a fond caress for the beautiful young woman he would occasionally rescue from Indians or some other fate worse than death would arise in due time, I realized; but it wouldn't have to be dealt with in the middle of a jeering ring of companions.

So on this occasion, when this proposal came up, to fill in the hour before dinner—and by this I mean the midday meal—I caught Ralph Stevens' eye. The two of us slid around the corner of the front porch of the Gulf House before anybody noticed what we were up to. As we scrambled up the steep trail we heard our young friends singing:

> You're married, you're married,
> You're married away;
> You don't know what to do or say;
> You're married, you're married,
> You're married away.

There was more, much more, but I imagine the words convey what the situation was.

"Who do you suppose they got?" asked Ralph, somewhat tremulously.

"One of the Linton boys, maybe. It's their party, kind of."

Ralph nodded. "And maybe Millicent Byrnes. She's kind of soft on Merrill Linton."

My heart sank. For a moment I wished I hadn't ducked the game. It wasn't that I wanted to be involved in an exchange of wet smacks with Millicent Byrnes in the middle of the circle. But if I weren't going to kiss her I didn't want Merrill Linton to do it.

"How do you know she's soft on him?" I demanded.

Ralph made a lordly gesture, in his best man of the world style. "They all are," he replied. "Besides, I can tell. Anybody with two eyes can tell."

"If he wants to play with girls he can," I said bitterly. "Personally, I don't intend to be a sissie."

"It's funny about girls," Ralph mused. "They're kind of silly. They're always getting hurt and yelling about it. And they think they're awful smart. A girl don't like to get dirty."

"They don't even like it when we get dirty," I added. "They're almost as bad as a set of mothers."

"Same time," Ralph continued, "I kind of like to look at them. Of course I'd rather be where there weren't any girls most of the time—I'm no—no sissie—but once in a while I don't mind so much. It would be queer if there weren't any girls, wouldn't it?"

I agreed. At the distance we had now reached, the voices sounded pleasant. I almost thought I could pick out the clear soprano of Millicent Byrnes—it had a sort of lilt in it.

"When I grow up," Ralph said, "I suppose I'll get married, like everybody else. There has to be somebody around to do the housework. But no girl is going to boss me around. I'm going to be the boss."

Our steps grew slower. We were feeling lonesome. I sat down on a flattened-off log beside one of the sulphur springs. Ralph did the same. The smell was villainous. The taste, when I filled a tin cup that was tied to a near-by stake and took a big swallow, was worse. "It must be awfully good for you," I observed.

"It is," said Ralph, making a wry face. "It cures pretty near everything, they say."

"So would a rotten egg," I commented. "Stands to reason it ought to. It tastes just the same."

There was a silence while we brooded over this and other mysteries.

"They're a little quieter now," said Ralph lonesomely. "Maybe they're not playing that marrying game any more. Of course there may be some sense to it. It's like drinking this sulphur water, maybe—tough at the time."

"Some of them like it," I ventured.

"The boys don't," Ralph stoutly insisted. "They only do it to get in with the girls. It's the girls that like it."

"But why do they—the boys, I mean—take all the trouble?" I could see why anybody would want to please Millicent Byrnes, but girls in general—no.

"Why do men get married?" retorted Ralph. "They don't have to."

"Sometimes they do—" I said. I was thinking of what happened when an unmarried girl was going to have a baby and the town authorities were able to find what was known in such instances as The Man.

"I didn't mean that," said Ralph indignantly.

We were silent again.

"Maybe they'll be having dinner," I remarked nervously. "We wouldn't want to be late for dinner, I guess."

We sniffed at the thin smoke that rose from the Gulf House chimneys. It seemed as though some cooking was going on in the kitchen. The smoke smelled good.

Ralph got to his feet. "We can argue all we want about other things," he said, "but there's no argument about dinner. I guess I like about everything there is that can be eaten."

We ran back down the trail and then strolled as nonchalantly as we could around to the front of the inn. Our friends were sitting in a row near the dining room door. One or two of the girls snickered when they saw us.

"Didn't want to play, didn't want to play," said some bit of femininity.

Millicent Byrnes looked at me disdainfully. "I think you're mean," she cried. "Both of you."

Not knowing what to say to this, I didn't say anything. I did not reason that if Millicent was angry with me she must be at least a little interested in me; I did not reason at all when it came to girls; it did not enter into my head that it was a good sign that Millicent had noticed I wasn't there when the kissing game started.

Merrill Linton caught my eye and grinned knowingly.

"We had fun, anyhow," Millicent resumed. "I'm sure we didn't miss you—either of you."

Mrs. Linton came down the porch, part hostess, part teacher, part mother. "Is everybody having a good time?" she asked. Then her eyes fell on Ralph and me. "Why, where have you two been?" she inquired. "We looked everywhere for you. And we've been having such fun. Haven't we, Merrill?" She waited for her son to help her out.

"We certainly have," Merrill agreed.

Everybody laughed. Millicent blushed. I was sure the worst had happened. I was sure Merrill had kissed Millicent Byrnes. Maybe I could have done this if I had been there. But I was not sure I would have wanted to. Why couldn't Millicent sit up on the edge of a cloud, or drift in and out of my dreams, and not pay any attention to any other boy—and not to me, either, when other persons were around?

"Are you all hungry?" asked Mrs. Linton. "I'm sure that even Robbie Duffus and Ralph Stevens are hungry."

We were. There was no doubt of that.

"Well, then," said Mrs. Linton, "we'll have dinner and see if that doesn't make us feel better."

I thought there might be one big table inside, but there wasn't —there were a number of little tables. I found myself at one of the small tables, with Mrs. Linton, Merrill Linton—and Millicent Byrnes. I felt my ears grow red. I hardly dared look at Millicent, she was so beautiful, with her glowing red hair and dark eyes; and as for talking to her or anybody else, all I could manage was a yes or no. Millicent smiled. The Queen of England couldn't have been more calm.

5

It was under these circumstances that I ordered the chicken croquette. It was the name and the shape that made this item a mystery and a menace. My mother made potato balls, which consisted of mashed potatoes pressed into a flat cake and fried in hot fat in a frying pan. My aunt, my mother's sister, made fish balls, which were spherical and about the size of a crab apple; these she fried swiftly in a kettle of deep fat until they turned brown and crisp, and at one time I could eat a dozen of them and still want more.

But nobody had ever told me what a croquette was.

I had already indicated, in a mild and embarrassed voice, that I would like milk, rolls, roast beef, mashed potatoes, mashed turnips, squash, apple pie, and ice cream. Then Merrill, studying the menu like a world-weary club man, said he would like all that and a chicken croquette, too.

Mrs. Linton then asked Millicent and me if we, also, would like to have a chicken croquette. Millicent said daintily that she did not. For some reason she was not being sweet to Merrill, even though he had kissed her in the marrying game. I said I would.

Presently the waitress appeared with all the other things we had ordered, and the croquettes for Merrill and me. The croquette was about the shape and size of a large carrot. It was nicely browned, and I could imagine myself eating it.

But how did you eat a croquette? You ate a fish ball or a potato ball with a fork, but this object was shaped differently. It was shaped so that you could pick it up with your fingers if you wanted to. But perhaps it was too soft to do this. In that case, did you eat it with a fork or did you use a spoon?

There was, of course, a simple solution. So I thought. I had only to wait until Merrill, who was undoubtedly familiar with this item on the menu, attacked his croquette. I would then eat mine in the same way.

But Merrill didn't touch his croquette. He ate his roast beef, his potatoes, his turnips, his squash, but he worked clear around his croquette. I waited, also, and fussed with other things. Then, as it seemed to me, a situation began to develop. It seemed to me that I caught a torturing smile on Merrill's face, as though he understood perfectly what was going on in my mind. It seemed to me that Millicent Byrnes was eyeing me with a cool disdain, as though I were a pretender who didn't belong in that place and in her company.

Of course I was wrong. Millicent was annoyed at me, I now think, because I had gone off into the woods at a time when there might have been a chance for me to kiss her. I am conceited enough now to imagine that she wanted me to do this; but what she really wanted, no doubt, was one more tribute of admiration from a boy of about my age—however unworthy of her affection.

On the other hand, I am not sure now that I was completely unworthy of her affection. I came of respectable parents, I was reasonably intelligent, and I did know a pretty girl when I saw one. I wish I knew where Millicent is now—I would ask her. But I don't know, and she might not remember.

The knowledge of my predicament seemed to me to spread through the entire dining room of the Gulf House. It took in the rest of Mrs. Linton's class at adjoining tables, and included a number of strangers who had hired rigs in Barre or Chelsea and driven to Williamstown Gulf to find out what effect the waters would have on them. Or just to see the scenery.

I felt as though practically the entire civilized world was waiting to see what I would do with my chicken croquette. Such is the egotism of the shy, the young, and the intimidated.

I was in love, at that instant, with Millicent Byrnes. I was in love with her because she was there, and being in love with her did not make me disloyal to two or three older girls who were not there, or to a number of completely imaginary girls.

Being in love with Millicent, I wished to appear to good advantage in her eyes. I wished to be brave, dashing, a man of the world, a potential cowboy, soldier, sailor, explorer. But because I wished such things I was never capable of being any one of them while Millicent was around.

So Millicent's lovely presence was the crowning ignominy of my pathetic adventure. I almost hated her.

Mrs. Linton, good, kind soul that she was, must have understood the situation, even though she may have eaten hundreds of chicken croquettes and could not realize that I had never eaten a single one, at least under that name.

Said Mrs. Linton, looking at her erring son: "Merrill, why don't you eat your croquette?"

He mumbled something I nearly didn't catch. After all, he was the lord of the manor, he didn't have to be polite to his own mother. He made no motion to eat his croquette. Mrs. Linton sighed.

"When I was a little girl," she observed, "we used to say that willful waste makes woeful want."

Merrill still didn't eat his croquette. I didn't eat mine, either, because by this time it would have choked me, no matter what tool I ate it with or how; and after a little while the waitress came and took it away. Then we had the apple pie and ice cream, which I ate with relish, in spite of my sorrow and humiliation. I knew now that Millicent would never love me. I knew also that there would always be apple pie and ice cream. Life was dark but not unendurable. I wasn't even sure that if I had to choose between never seeing Millicent again and never having any more ice cream, I wouldn't have selected the ice cream.

And now, as by an unspoken consent, the boys and girls of Mrs. Linton's sunday school class again separated. This was not for the obvious reason, after so long a lapse of time, though that was certainly a part of it. It was because boys and girls at the ages of ten to twelve couldn't stand more than a certain amount of each other's company, and didn't care to do precisely the same things.

The girls, I think, walked slowly to one of the nearest of the ill-smelling sulphur springs, and there, making disgusted feminine faces, tasted the water—and screamed. They would not have been little girls in 1898 if they had not. Their screams, not too desperate, filled the valley with a not unpleasant sound, like the singing of birds.

We boys went tearing into the woods, yelling and whooping —not screaming; and I suppose we sounded more like bird dogs than birds. A sort of release had come to us. We didn't have to be genteel and polite any more. We weren't in competition, spoken or unspoken, for any little girl's favor. The competition was to see who could run fastest, or climb a steep rock or a tree, or jump farthest.

"Beat you to the top, bee line, path or no path!" cried Merrill Linton.

I followed him, panting, up the steep slope, plunging through the underbrush, scratching myself and tearing my clothes on briars, until we came suddenly out of shadow into sunshine, where the ridge met the sky. We looked east to the trees on the other side of the Gulf, west over level forested land.

"I'd have beat you if you hadn't had a head start," I gasped. "I wonder what they're doing down there."

He grunted. "Playing dolls, probably." He mused. "Seems to me it can't be much fun being a girl. Maybe you and Ralph had some sense when you stayed away."

I stared. It was strange to hear this successful man about town saying this, the conqueror of womanhood admitting a trace of boredom.

But I thought of Millicent Byrnes. "I guess you had fun enough," I said sourly. Strange how little I wanted from Millicent, yet how hard it was for me to think of any other boy having anything from her.

"There's all sorts of fun," Merrill conceded.

We loafed around a while, looking westward into the unknown—for this stretch of woods above the Gulf was out of our territory. It might as well not have been discovered for all we knew about it.

"I wish—" I began.

"Me, too," Merrill agreed. "Only we might get lost."

"We could make a fire," said I eagerly, "by rubbing two sticks together. We could live on nuts and berries, the way Robinson Crusoe and Swiss Family Robinson did." This was quite farsighted of me, I must now admit, as I had not yet heard about Boy Scouts—there weren't any.

"We better go back," I said.

He nodded. "I guess we're supposed to get home before dark. That was what my mother said."

We drifted down the trail—though I think we called it a path, and reserved the name of trail for something west of the Mississippi—and for some reason I kept ahead of Merrill and the others.

So it was I who found the dime.

None of the boys in Mrs. Linton's Sunday School class could have lost it, nor any of the girls, for they wouldn't have been strong enough to climb that far. A stranger must have dropped it—maybe somebody from Barre or Chelsea, who would be almost as foreign to us as a person from China. It was strictly finders keepers, as we used to say.

But I knew what would happen if any of my boy friends saw

me pick it up. I would be compelled to invest it in lemon drops or licorice or some other cheap and bulky edible, and divide.

This was before reaction time had been invented; but I must have had one even then, for the moment I saw the glint in the path I knew it was money, and the moment I knew it was money I pretended to stumble, grabbed the dime, recovered myself, and resumed the race downhill to the Gulf House.

Ralph Stevens, who, like myself, was poor, may have suspected something. "Whatja pick up?" he demanded breathlessly.

"Nothing," I replied. "A whole handful of nothing. Want some?"

I had the dime in my right-hand pants pocket, where I used to keep the little polished oval stone I once found in the West Branch. I had lost the little stone, and felt bereaved; but now I had a dime, a shiny new dime.

My luck had gone, but now it had come back to me. Not luck for any particular thing, not luck that would make me loved by Millicent Byrnes or any other, possibly even prettier, girl, not luck that would bring me adventures and fame, which I wanted a little more than I wanted Millicent, because you could do something with adventures and fame, whereas not with Millicent; just luck, just plain luck.

Something sang in me, something selfish and a bit cruel. With a dime I could buy two bottles of ginger ale, or so many candied dates that I could be generous with my brother, or two bags of peanuts, or two copies of Old Sleuth, or a baseball that would last an hour instead of half an hour in a game.

But the real joy was not in what I could buy with the dime. I might even give it away. The real joy was that the boy who had felt abandoned and frustrated when the chicken croquette deceived him had received a special mark of favor from the gods.

Maybe some day Millicent would like me a little, I thought, as we rode home, some singing, some paired off, myself in a back-seat corner brooding. And if she never did, I had, at least, found a dime; I was the sort of boy who found things; the future was full of wonderment.

August was a month when time stood still, like a grandfather clock interrupting its pendulum at the end of a swing and hesitating before letting the weight slide back. There was such a clock in the front hall of the General E. Bass house, and often there seemed to be a long time between the tick and the tock. In the end, of course, there were ticks enough and tocks enough to carry us through August, and a great deal further.

But August did seem to linger. I forget how many times in a summer the Ainsworth meadow was mowed, but it was certainly mowed in August. There was the clackety-clack of the horse-drawn mower, the rattle of the horse-rake and tedder, the shouts of the men. As the windrows dried there would come the most enchanted and enchanting fragrance in all the world. Why perfumers do not stock it, why women do not use it to bring young men from the country swiftly to submission, I do not know.

Hot and muggy days, thunderstorms, clear days almost cool, with a faint hint of chilly weather to come and a suggestion of far northern places, a boy's foreboding of school days approaching, and his not too unhappy anticipation of them—that was August.

But we still went barefoot, we still swam in the meadow brook, the dust of the road after sunset was still pleasant to our toes as we ran shouting.

We wanted to hang on to August, which gave us much and asked little of us—and especially that August of 1898. But we also wanted fall and winter, we were homesick for change.

CHAPTER NINE

———◄••••►———

Mr. Ainsworth's Brother

*W*HEN I found the shiny new dime in the path above the Gulf House on the day of Mrs. Linton's picnic— when I found this dime and successfully concealed it from my predatory friends in Mrs. Linton's Sunday School class—I had to decide where to spend it.

I couldn't spend it in J. K. Linton's store, for in that case Merrill and Roswell Linton would have known what had happened and would have demanded some of the loot—this in spite of the fact that if they wanted candy all they had to do was to rifle the showcase when their father wasn't looking. Other boys, whose fathers didn't have stores or who didn't have fathers, Jim Nutting, for example, or Ralph Stevens, might have wanted to be cut in on the transaction.

My older brother was as generous and easygoing a boy as could have been hoped for, but this only made the matter of conscience worse: I ought to have told my brother that I had found the dime and asked him to share in the subsequent jubilee. But I didn't. I let him have some of the dates when I stole the lead pipe from George Ainsworth's cellar, but that was a crime and I needed an accomplice, however unwitting; whereas in this case I had honestly found a dime, not stolen it, and I didn't have to be big-hearted. I had a hankering for sweets. I was a growing boy, and, as I subsequently found out, sweets are good for growing boys.

Anyhow, I wanted more candy than was good for me, and for good reasons I went to Fred Ainsworth's drugstore—he was

George Ainsworth's brother—to get it. At the other drugstore, which had a soda fountain—a miracle which astounded me every time I went in there—I might have met a friend, a boy friend, not Millicent Byrnes, bless her dear heart, and he might have suggested that ten cents would buy two five-cent sodas, one for him and one for me; or ten chocolate effigies, any one of which might have one cent inside and so enable the fortunate purchaser to buy another.

So I went to Fred Ainsworth's store, which was on the right-hand side of the street as you went down from Main Street past Linton's store toward the depot.

We didn't often go to Fred Ainsworth's drugstore, I don't know why. Perhaps it was because it was so neat and clean, and we boys didn't especially care for neatness and cleanliness. Perhaps it was because Fred Ainsworth was a sort of stranger among us, that is, among us boys. We didn't quite know what to make of him.

This wasn't because he ever did anything or suggested anything that could scare a boy or make a boy uneasy. We knew that kind of threat, even though I don't recall that it ever crossed any of our paths in Williamstown—except in the case of the strange young man who had his heart on the wrong side, and ate dirt if you gave him a cent to do it. Fred Ainsworth wasn't that sort of man. He didn't appear to have any wife during the time I knew about him; but whatever trouble he had with himself, or nature, or sex, he kept to himself, so far as I know.

His fault, if it was one, as I suppose, was neatness. He had an almost alarming neatness. It didn't seem right for a man to be as neat as that. A druggist had to be neat, maybe; but the way it was in Fred Ainsworth's store, if you went in there when he was out in the back room and you moved a red flannel chest protector on top of the counter a half inch, Fred would notice it when he came back and put it back half an inch to where it belonged.

I heard a young woman say she'd like to be married to Fred Ainsworth, because then she wouldn't have to put up with men tramping mud into the kitchen and emptying pipe tobacco ashes all over the place and hanging up their overalls on the floor; but she didn't expect to be married to Fred Ainsworth, and no other young woman did. Young women had had a try at him before this, and it hadn't got anywhere.

He was too damn smart to get caught, the boys at the livery stable said. He knew a good thing when he had it and wouldn't clutter it up with women. Or maybe—because that was the way their minds ran—he had his women, one at a time and a dollar or two at a time, when he went to Burlington, or even to Boston, to stock up.

I don't believe this. I didn't believe it then. I felt then, without thinking it, and I think now, without feeling it much except as part of the general sadness of life, that he was drawing inside himself, that he was scared of something, he didn't know what, that he was afraid of being anything except clean and neat.

There was, certainly, a strangeness about him; but it wasn't a strangeness in anything he did. It was, rather, what he didn't do. It was remaining solitary in a world where men were expected to mate; it was not going to church, where I don't believe I ever saw him during my time in Williamstown; it was not belonging to anything, not being a lodge member of any kind, not playing in the band, not hanging around J. K. Linton's store when the crowd was there, not going to sociables or oyster suppers or singing school. It was in choosing to be alone; or at least in being alone, for maybe he didn't want to be alone.

At any rate, this was the way things were with Fred Ainsworth. He had a fence around himself, and you didn't know what was inside. The fence was always just the same. He never seemed bad-tempered and he never seemed gay. I wouldn't have thought him an unhappy man, but I wouldn't have thought him a happy man, either. I didn't really ask myself such questions, of course, but if anybody had asked me if I would like to be Fred Ainsworth, I would have said no. Yet this meant nothing. I wouldn't have wanted to be any adult at all—they had to get up so early and work so hard.

It may be, of course, that I sensed something a little desperate under Fred Ainsworth's outward serenity, and that I chose to forget it. Perhaps I let some of what I saw of him erase itself from my conscious memory: we didn't know anything about the unconscious in those days, but I must have had one.

2

I didn't want to have anything to do with unhappiness. I didn't want to believe that anybody, anywhere, was unhappy. If this weren't possible, I didn't want to believe that anybody in Williamstown, Orange County, Vermont, was unhappy. By this I mean deeply and permanently unhappy. I knew that people died and that their surviving relatives mourned them for a while. I was sometimes unhappy myself—I ate too much of the wrong thing at the wrong time, as, indeed, I planned to do when I took my dime into Fred Ainsworth's store, and I suffered from unrequited love and similar afflictions, but not too much.

But I knew that some persons were wrong and lonesome, and not fitted into the kind of life people were expected to lead in Williamstown. There were, indeed, other strangers; and stranger strangers than Fred Ainsworth.

One day, a Sunday afternoon, I imagine, Ralph Stevens and I went out for what we called a walk. A Sunday afternoon walk was not considered sinful in our branch of the Congregational Church, and my mother wouldn't have considered any gentle and natural act sinful if she had been asked about it. So Ralph and I went up to Mill Village, which may have been anywhere from five miles to a quarter of a mile from Williamstown Center, depending on how much hurry a boy felt when he wanted to go there. Mill Village consisted of houses, or it wouldn't have been a village, but also of a mill pond, a sawmill, and a gristmill. I loved Mill Village, and would go back there if it still existed.

Since the day was Sunday, Ralph and I could not watch the circular saw as it cut into the spruce, maple, elm, and oak logs that were brought to it. Nor could we stand in the lower level of the grist mill and watch the jiggle-jiggle of the canvas conveyor tube as it shook the cornmeal, or wheat flour, or buckwheat flour down into the waiting bags.

We did what we could do, of course. The sawmill had a little railway, with a little car on it, which could pick up small wood or sawdust, or small boys, and slide this cargo up or down past the saws. On days such as this one, when the mill wasn't running, we could push this little car up to the top of the incline, then get in it and ride down.

We could also look at the saw, which wasn't running, and we could wonder why it was, and how it was, that the man who fed the logs to the swiftly-turning jagged wheel didn't lose a hand or two every morning. Of course, he sometimes did, but not always, not every morning; that was what individualism, and no workmen's compensation, and the devil take the hindmost, meant at that time; and if we boys thought about it, we didn't think hard or long.

After we had looked at the quiet gristmill and the quiet sawmill, and coasted down the little railway a few times, Ralph and I went down to the edge of the pool and inspected the water wheel. If we had been able to start this apparatus we would probably have done so and these words would not be written; but we weren't.

We then went outside and rowed a small and leaky rowboat around the pool, with an imminent chance of falling in and drowning ourselves. Even though we both could swim, after a fashion, it is likely that if the boat had tipped over or filled through its many leaks and sunk, we would have gone down with it. A boy's life is—or was—full of such chances.

We put the boat away after a while and loitered aimlessly around the dam and up to the crest of a grassy slope that ran down to the stream. This was, of course, one of the branches of Stevens Branch. It was quiet on that hillside; and yet, I don't know why, not quite cheerful even before we both caught sight of the lonesome figure below at the edge of the water.

He did not see us, nor do I suppose he ever knew we were there, so deeply absorbed was he in something, I don't know what, some dark mood, some object he saw and others did not see. I don't remember his face, for I did not see him then clearly. What I remember is the lonesomeness.

Ralph Stevens, that wise young man, so much more experienced than I in the ways of the world, pointed and spoke in a hushed voice, as though his words could carry clearly across some hundreds of feet of space. "That's So-and-So," he said, and I couldn't even remember the name afterward. He paused. "He's a morphadite," he added. "Everybody knows that."

I didn't ask him what a morphadite was. After a fashion, I knew. A morphadite—and I give the word as we pronounced it—was a person who was part man and part woman. Only, I asked myself, which part? I didn't know much about feminine anatomy. And this was, in general, a man. Ralph used the masculine pronoun in referring to him.

Maybe he wasn't anything of the sort. Maybe Ralph was trying to horrify me, as he sometimes did. But a shiver went up my spine, and down again. I thought this person was suffering. I thought he was cut off from the rest of mankind.

"Let's get out of here," I said. "He might see us."

Ralph sneered. "Aw, what you afraid of?" he demanded. "He couldn't do us any harm. We got a right to take a walk, the same as he has."

But the man stirred a little, as though about to get up, and we slid quietly away. There wasn't any use in taking chances. And yet it wasn't so much anything that the poor fellow could have done that dismayed me; it was the thought that he existed and was so sad, so lonely. I wanted everybody to be good-natured and genial and at ease in the world. This man wasn't, whatever the matter with him may have been.

The queer thing about this experience that Sunday afternoon was that I do not recall seeing the man after that day, any more than I recall seeing him on any previous day. Perhaps Ralph Stevens made him up. Perhaps he wasn't there.

Still, I was left with the uneasy feeling that all was not always right with the world, and that there were some ailments that neither time nor anything Dr. Watson could bring in his black bag could cure.

3

Caesar Salvatori was another stranger, in that he differed somewhat from the general run of men. But Caesar differed in a way that didn't seem to make him unhappy, except for brief intervals, and that rendered him an object of admiration and even envy among his contemporaries.

Caesar's distinction was that he was almost exclusively interested in women and almost invariably successful with those he pursued. Boarding as he did at the Monument House, Caesar ate heartily. He also drank. He was a good stonecutter, one of those Italians who did the very finest work on tombstones—work so exquisite that some people said it was almost worth while to die to have a man such as Caesar Salvatori carve the winged angels, weeping willow trees, or floral wreaths that went on the stone.

But the situation was such that whenever an unmarried girl in town produced a baby the authorities inquired first if she had known Caesar Salvatori. If she did know Caesar, even though she didn't accuse him, the authorities would try to get Caesar to admit parentage. Or they would sit around patiently for the baby to get to an age where it would resemble somebody, in the hope that Caesar would concede that he was the man it resembled. But he never did.

For some reason, perhaps because Caesar's air of injured innocence on such occasions hid an active intellect, the town fathers were never able during my time in Williamstown to make Caesar get married, or even to extract a sum of money from him for the care of a child who otherwise had no known father.

If Caesar Salvatori was indeed what he was said and believed to be, he was doing wrong. This I knew to be the case then, for I knew it was wrong for any man to take advantage of a girl before she was married; and it never occurred to me in those days that a girl might sometimes take advantage of a man. I still think Caesar was in some instances wrong, but not so much because he and some woman had amatory impulses and indulged them, as because he refused to pay the resulting expenses afterward.

I should add that despite many careful explanations by Ralph Stevens and by boys older than either Ralph or myself, I was not quite sure, at the age of ten, just how Caesar took advantage of a woman. Caesar himself provided no answer. Of course I could not ask him what went on. I was just another wide-eyed little boy. Ralph Stevens' answer or Jim Nuttings' answer did not satisfy me. And I thought, at the age of ten, that I ought to know all the answers already, and not go around asking foolish questions.

It was, of course, the village boys who were innocent or ignorant, whichever the correct word is. The farm boys knew, because the mating of animals on a farm, though not romantic, did produce a fraction of an income.

I had watched a mare being inducted into sex and motherhood. The mare seemed puzzled, although the stallion did everything but yawn to express his relative indifference to the procedure, except at the critical moment. It seemed to me that this was not the right way to produce colts; but at my age then —and even at my present age—no better method had, or has, suggested itself. I am sure the colt was produced, and I suppose it was a Morgan horse—in Vermont the gasoline engine of the era that preceded the gasoline engine.

Caesar Salvatori was a sort of Morgan horse, and I have no doubt the human breed was improved by his activities during his creative years. It is to his credit, and I lay this wreath wherever his ashes are, that nobody ever said he was unkind to any woman, except in refusing to pay her bills; or that he ever misrepresented himself to any woman, except in suggesting that maybe now, with her, he felt like settling down. He must have been in his middle twenties during the years I knew of him, and there was time for him to settle down, or not settle down, according to the way he felt about it. Women, in our town and in that time, were more restricted; if they desired, as most of them naturally did, to get married and have children, they had to count the years.

On the whole, I must conclude that Caesar Salvatori was a very bad man. Yet the truth was that he did not depress me as did Fred Ainsworth, a very good man according to his lights; or as did the nameless wanderer Ralph Stevens and I saw that afternoon up by the mill pond. Not wishing to be depressed, I rather liked Caesar, though I do not suppose I ever spoke a word to him.

Caesar, to most of his fellows, was not only a hero, but a gay adventurer. Even the married men among them, even the contented ones with three or four children and a hard time paying the monthly bills at the store, seemed to look up to Caesar. I remember him sitting on the porch of the Monument House on a Saturday afternoon in summer, when work was over for the week, and everybody could rest and be easy, and maybe go over to J. K. Linton's and buy something, or around to the barber shop and get shaved, out of a private mug, or go home and argue with his wife, if he had a wife, and everything was young and hopeful and would always stay that way.

Caesar wasn't set apart on those occasions, as the man at the hill had been or as Fred Ainsworth seemed to me to be. He was one of the crowd, and everybody was interested in teasing him and then finding out what he had to say in reply. He had plenty to say, and a rich smile to go along with the words. I wouldn't have said then that he was ever worried about anything. I am not so sure now. But Caesar isn't here any more; or if he is here, he is past the follies of his youth.

The picture he presented was that of a popular man. I didn't ask then whether a popular man was always happy about being popular, or whether he didn't sometimes wish he could drop back into the crowd and be neither popular nor unpopular, but just one of the boys. Caesar couldn't ever be just one of the boys, not so long as he stayed in Williamstown. He couldn't be just a good stonecutter, whose winged angels were better than other men's. He had to be a specialist—a specialist in taking advantage of women, or winning women's affections, or getting into trouble with unexpected babies. The crowd on the front porch of the hotel, or in the Linton store, wouldn't have respected Caesar merely because he had a way with women: what they respected in him was his unfailing ability to produce babies, or so they thought.

Poor Caesar! He could not admit to the village fathers that he had ever caused a baby to be born. He could not deny to his friends of the Monument House that his smallest touch was enough to make a woman pregnant. He was caught between his pride as a man and his fear that somebody would lay claim to a part of his wages.

I lingered around the edges of the group a few times while Caesar's cronies were questioning him about his technique. "What is there about you, Caesar," somebody asked, "that makes a woman willing to put up with you?" And they went into more intimate details.

"It can't be his good looks," said somebody else, "because he ain't got none."

The truth was that though Caesar had curly black hair and black eyes and a moustache that he kept carefully trimmed, he was a little too fat for our Yankee style. Or the Scottish style, either.

But he had to grin at everything that was said. He had to keep on being popular in case some of these men, some day, had more than a passing interest in some woman he had been with. He needed friends at court.

"I'll tell you," he said at last. "You got to take an interest in them if you expect them to take an interest in you. You got to give a little time to it. That's all. Besides," he added hastily, "I ain't admitting anything, am I? I can't help people talking, can I?" He laughed, to show that he was not too serious. "I can't help it if women like me, can I?"

It didn't matter what he said, of course. He was the great lover in our town. He was the man young girls had to be warned against. He was the man young girls looked at over their shoulders, even when they were out walking with the young men they were determined to marry.

How much of all this did I understand at that time? At ten I was not myself a success with girls. I wondered hopelessly if when I grew up I would be like Caesar Salvatori.

I didn't want to be. Yet, in a way, I did want to be. I wanted to be Caesar Salvatori and not have the troubles he evidently had, and the worries, just as I wanted to be a hero in a war but not get shot in any unpleasant or unattractive way.

My father had no doubts in this matter. "I see Caesar Salvatori

is in trouble again," I heard him tell my mother. "I don't wonder. If there ever was a male tom cat—."

My mother held up a finger and nodded toward us children.
"There couldn't be any female tom cats," she said. "Besides—."

"Well," replied my father, "I stick by what I said." He looked
at my brother and myself as though he had intended to admonish
us not to be like Caesar Salvatori when we grew up. Then he
subsided into his newspaper.

But I went on thinking. I didn't want to be completely like
Caesar Salvatori. I was sure of that, because the other men,
even while they envied and admired him, were also laughing
at him; but I thought I might like to be a little more like him,
when I grew up, than I then was.

4

But I didn't want to be even a little like Fred Ainsworth. For
I perceived, without understanding why, that Fred Ainsworth
was afraid of life and that in his drugstore in Williamstown he
had found a sanctuary where he was less afraid. His very neatness, the spotlessness of his store, the clean smell it had, were
a sort of victory over an outer world that may have terrified him.

It seems to me that he slept in the back of the store. If he
didn't really do this he might as well have done so, for the store
was in his blood, it was a part of him, it was his refuge and his
strength. It was not his gift, as it was Caesar Salvatori's, to
be the father of problem children, or of any children. I don't
think he ever, in his youth, went buggy-riding, and pulled the
buggy off the road and tied the reins, and put his arms warmly
around the girl he was with.

I don't think he ever did this, or really wanted to. I think it
was one of the things he was afraid of. His trouble was, maybe,
that he was afraid of what he knew he ought to desire, of what
other men desired, and he felt sad and guilty, though he didn't
know the Freudian words for it.

Well, as I was saying, I took my dime to Fred Ainsworth's
drugstore to spend it. I didn't know what kind of candy I
wanted, except that I wanted a lot, the most a dime could buy.

Mr. Ainsworth must have heard the door open and shut, for he had one of those fascinating contrivances that rang a bell in the back when anybody came in at the front. This was as wonderful to me as the H-bomb now is, and much more comfortable to think about.

Still, there was a moment or two for me to be alone in the store, since there was no other customer, and look things over. I wish I could remember what was there; but unhappily all I now see clearly are the red flannel chest protector and a few hot water bottles. Fred Ainsworth had patent medicines, I am sure, including some that helped young men to endure the assumed absence of alcohol in their diet. They had to get this beverage, as I have elsewhere indicated, under other names. The hard cider season didn't last all year, and neither did the sap beer season.

But I don't believe Fred Ainsworth intended to help any young man get drunk and I am sure he stayed wholly within the letter of the law. His shelves, on both sides of the store as you entered, were shiny, clean, and well-arranged. You could find anything on those shelves that was admittedly good, in a medicinal way, for man or beast.

I thought Fred Ainsworth ought to be the healthiest man in the world, except doctors, for all he had to do if he had a pain or illness was to come out into the store and take something off a shelf—a few pills or some pink liquid—and pretty soon he would be well again. My mother once asked me if I wouldn't like to be a druggist. I said maybe I would, for half of me would have liked being safe and secure, like Fred Ainsworth in his store, even though the other half was selling his life dearly in a battle with the Indians and coming home, wounded, weary, and romantic, to marry Millicent Byrnes.

After a while Fred Ainsworth came out from the back of the store from behind a partition, and greeted me. I suppose he may have wished I were a well-to-do farmer from up on the hill, with a wife or son or daughter sick enough to need some medicine, if not sick enough to need Dr. Watson. Maybe he was disappointed when all he saw was me.

But he smiled pleasantly, clasping his hands as he recognized me. "Well, Robbie," he said, "what will it be today? Something for your rheumatism, maybe? At your age you have to be careful. You can't run around the way you did when you were—let me see—" he paused judiciously—"seven or eight years old instead of ten. You're getting on, Robbie, you're getting on."

I felt embarrassed, but I managed a laugh out of the left-hand corner of my face, as I usually did under such circumstances. He was making fun of me, but I didn't really mind it.

"I want some candy," I said.

"What kind of candy?" He moved behind the candy counter. "Would you like a whole lot of candy, or just a little very good candy?"

It was a test question.

"Well—" I began.

"I see." Fred Ainsworth nodded sagaciously. "You're like everybody else around here, Robbie. You're like everybody else in the world, because the world is just like Williamstown, no matter how far you go." I couldn't find words to answer this. "You want a whole lot of very good candy." His laugh died down and suddenly he looked sad and tired. "You can't have both," he concluded. "You just have to make up your mind."

"What's that?" I pointed. It looked good, and somehow there seemed to be a lot of it.

He smiled again. "That," he announced solemnly, "is called pig's delight. I can give you more than you ought to eat for—" he examined my dime—"ten cents."

"I guess I'll take it, then," I said. Then I thought of the implications of this remark. "I mean I'll take some, anyway," I concluded.

Fred Ainsworth laughed again, that surface laugh of his that never so much as shook the buttons on his vest. "You don't have to be ashamed of what I called that candy," he observed. "You have to be a pig or you wouldn't grow up. Growing boys need sugar."

The ten cents' worth he gave me was quite a bag-full. Indeed,

I almost wished I had let my brother or one of the other boys in on this adventure.

But I took the candy and went out, conscious that Fred Ainsworth's eyes were following me, and wondering what he really thought about boys and people in general, and why it was he seemed so sad. What was there to be sad about in Williamstown?

I went up on the hill above the depot and the sandbank and ate my candy slowly. The cliff swallows didn't like my being there at first, but after a while they got used to me, or pretended to, or forgot about me. They were busy and had a good deal to talk about. I pulled a small dry bit of root out of the edge of the bank, chewed it a little, and then tried to light it and smoke it. We called these roots rattan; they weren't rattan, but that was what we called them. We never could smoke them, though sometimes they would stay lighted for a while, and we could pretend. The thing to smoke was either cornsilk, well-dried and rolled in toilet paper if you could get any or in a bit of newspaper if that was all you had; or a manufactured cubeb cigarette.

Fred Ainsworth had cubeb cigarettes in his store; I had bought them there, and now I was sorry I hadn't got some instead of candy. They were thought to be good for colds in the head, but my parents were not enthusiastic about their sons smoking them—they believed, and rightly, that if we smoked cubebs in childhood we would be tempted to smoke tobacco when we grew up. My father smoked tobacco in a pipe; but he sometimes said he wished he didn't.

Anyhow, there I sat, pretending I was smoking a real cigarette, pretending I was an enemy spy during the Civil War studying the defenses of a rebel Virginia stronghold, but mostly daydreaming about nothing in particular.

I fell into what I suppose was an animal-like state of contentment, and in this state I ate candy almost mechanically until my stomach began to protest. Then I waited a while and ate some more. It wasn't good candy and it wasn't bad candy; it was just a whole lot of candy for ten cents. I could see why it amused Fred Ainsworth.

One didn't have to be very high up to see the whole village. I could watch, in a lazy way, what was going on. To my right were the stonesheds. I could hear the whoosh when they used the stationary steam-engine that hauled granite blocks back and forth by means of its overhead track and pulleys. I could even hear the clack-clack of hammers on stone—and I won't ever forget that sound, heard near or far, until the day I die. It was a deadly sound, because granite dust killed men if they breathed it long enough; and it was a cheerful sound because it meant employment and money to pay the rent and grocery bills. It was cheerful, too, for me, because I wasn't employed at anything but enjoying life.

I could see the three churches and the Town Hall, all in a row, west of Main Street and a little above it. They were cheerful, too, though the churches had their weekday look and nobody was going in or out of the Town Hall. I hoped nobody was in jail there, the way the Italian woman had been; it was so fine a day I didn't want anybody to be in jail anywhere—at least not anywhere that I had to know about.

The village would have seemed sleepy to an outsider, I suppose, but a good deal was going on, even outside the stonesheds. The station agent came out of the depot, looked up at me, and waved. A wagon was backed up in front of the feed store, by the track, loading what looked like bags of fertilizer. One or two men were piling cordwood, ready for the wood-burner the next time she came up from Barre. There was some movement, on foot and in horse-drawn rigs, along Main Street—people going in and out of J. K. Linton's store, the other drugstore and Seaver's general store, and a rig or two standing in front of the blacksmith shop by the bridge while the horses that belonged to them were being shod by Grover Caldwell inside. I could see the cemetery, with its blooming of white stones, not too sad on a sunny day. I could see the house, not far from the cemetery, where Jim Nutting lived with his uncle; I even saw Jim come out and look around; I could almost have made him hear if I had yelled at him, but I was lazy and didn't try.

On the other side, to the left, I could look across the meadows

and the winding brook, to the General E. Bass House. My mother
came to the kitchen door and looked around, just as Jim Nutting
had done. I took another bite of candy and wondered if I would
be hungry when I went home for what we called dinner—that
is, the middle-of-the-day meal.

I even saw George Ainsworth making his way uptown, coming
along the rickety plank sidewalk to the Pool Bridge, then dis-
appearing for a while among the trees.

During all this time nobody went into Fred Ainsworth's store
or came out. I speculated as to how much he made on the things
he sold and how much he had to make in order to keep his store
going and provide for the needs of life. I thought it might be at
least a dollar a day, and wondered if I could ever earn that
much.

About this time George Ainsworth came into sight again, well
up toward the Linton store. He moved fast enough when not
interrupted; but every now and then he was brought to a halt
by meeting somebody or by turning to speak to somebody in a
front yard. As Williamstown correspondent for the Barre newspaper he had to know what everybody was doing; besides that,
it was his native impulse to find out all he could, including things
he couldn't print.

Finally he came in front of the Linton store, where I couldn't
see him, and I began to daydream again. Looking at George
Ainsworth had made me think again of Fred Ainsworth. A
thought struck me that I couldn't then put into words: it was
this, that that neat man, Fred Ainsworth, and his neat store
didn't really belong in such a town as Williamstown, which was
so sprawling and comfortable, usually not worried, and never
really tidy. The meadows, pastures, and woods kept crowding
in on Williamstown; they were what made it what it was, much
more than the buildings men had put up; that was the way it
looked to a ten-year-old boy. Fred Ainsworth's store didn't belong in the same picture with the rugged East Hill, or Stevens
Branch winding every which way through the marsh. And Fred
Ainsworth didn't belong in the picture, either, not the way the
blacksmith did, or the stonecutters, or the farmers. He was like

somebody from Barre or even a big city like Burlington, which was said to have twenty thousand people. Maybe that was why he was so lonesome.

It seemed a long while, but there was lots of time, so far as I was concerned; and then George Ainsworth came out of the side or north door of J. K. Linton's emporium, and turned his steps toward his brother's drugstore.

This surprised me, because the two brothers, though reported to be on friendly enough terms, were not often seen together. I suppose that Fred Ainsworth, even though far from being the village atheist, differed with George Ainsworth about religion and many other things. Their temperaments were different, too. Fred seemed to turn in on himself and away from the world, whereas George exploded all over the place; and one couldn't imagine him sitting by himself and wondering if life were worth while.

At any rate, George Ainsworth walked briskly to his brother's front door and turned in, as though he were in the habit of doing this thing a dozen times a day.

I didn't wait for him to come out. I was tired of Fred Ainsworth, tired of being alone on the top of the hill above the sandbank, tired of eating candy—and the candy was now about gone. I finished it hurriedly. I felt unusually sad, partly because my insides hurt a little.

I slid down the sandy slope, ran swiftly kitty-corner-wise across the empty lots behind the Monument House, and scooted up the hill to Jim Nutting's house.

Jim was still there, standing meditatively in the front yard.

"Whatja been doing?" he asked.

"Nothing," I assured him. "Just loafing around."

"You better come in," said Jim. "My uncle's away and I found some doughnuts."

So we ate quite a few doughnuts each, and then cut through the cemetery to see if Mr. Slater's Red Astrachans were ripe, but they weren't; and then I went home and ate a good lunch of my mother's codfish chowder.

5

Maybe this day was a condensation of many widely separated days in which Fred Ainsworth incidentally figured. I don't know. I know that that was the way I afterward remembered him—that sort of day, a happy, lazy sort of day for everybody but Fred Ainsworth and one or two others; myself ten years old and never counting, really, on ever being any older; and George Ainsworth coming upstreet to call on his brother Fred, the way a brother should.

If I was looking into anything potentially tragic on that far-off morning I tried not to see the tragedy, and possibly tried not to remember what of it I did see.

My picture of Fred Ainsworth, filed along with the pictures of other Williamstown neighbors of that year, will always show him neat, composed, taking time for harmless banter with a ten-year-old boy, a man at home in his drugstore but not really at home anywhere else. Somehow this picture will not seem to belong with the other pictures in the collection, not even with that of his brother George.

It will be as though it belonged in some other town or city, and got into the Williamstown album by mistake.

I cannot tell the end of the story without stepping out of my framework of time, just as Fred Ainsworth stepped out of his when he stepped into Williamstown. But the end of the story did not surprise me too much when I heard of it ten years later. Something of what the young man of twenty learned in 1908 the boy of ten had unconsciously guessed, I believe, in 1898.

By 1908 the Duffus boys were undergraduates at Stanford University, California. One day my brother and I received a clipping from a Barre newspaper with the strange story of a Williamstown man who had come to a fantastic end. This man, living alone, had risen one night and put on the oldest clothes he could find. Seemingly he had even sewed rags to them to make himself look as much like a tramp as he could. Then he had taken a coil of rope and wandered out into the night.

A farmer, hearing a noise in his barn, had gone out with a lantern and a shotgun, found the supposed tramp, and fired, wounding him fatally.

The tramp was, of course, Fred Ainsworth, and this last insane act of his had evidently been a final revolt against all that he had cherished and endured in his long, lonesome life.

Dr. Watson did all he could for him, but he died. George Ainsworth took the trouble to write about it to my brother and myself. He wanted us to know that Fred Ainsworth was out of his mind when the shooting occurred, and that in a rational moment before the end he had murmured his belated acceptance of George Ainsworth's version of the Christian faith.

But I remember him, neat, calm, and smiling, scooping out perhaps twenty cents' worth of candy for a boy who had only a dime.

Now it was September, and in the faint shadow of a butternut tree too high and branchless to climb we built our ceremonial fire to the gods of the seasons. We were tired of summer, and more restless, even, than we had been in spring. We were tired of everything whatever that we had so far known; but we thought maybe if we waited something interesting would happen, something that would make our hearts leap.

We put potatoes in the ashes and let them cook till they were burned on the outside while still raw inside; then we ate them, pretending that nothing cooked inside a house, on a stove, by any boy's mother whatsoever, could be as good. Jim Nutting and Ralph Stevens didn't have to pretend, because they had no mothers—all they had were uncles.

We had no salt. Jim Nutting said this was all right; the Indians hadn't any salt as a usual thing, either; when they wanted salt they went to a salt lick and licked some salt. We could find a salt lick if we had to.

If we had enough potatoes, I said, and there were a few

blackberries and butternuts left, we could camp out all the time. I said houses were foolish. Ralph Stevens said, how would I like to camp out all the time when the snow was six or eight feet deep?

But there wasn't any snow then. It was the middle of a September day, and though there might be frost by morning, there was no frost then. I put another fragment of a fallen branch of the butternut on the fire. The flame was as yellow as the sun seen through the haze.

"I wish winter would hurry up," said Ralph Stevens.

A cool wind came down the little valley through which the brook ran on its way to the falls below. "I guess it will," said Jim Nutting. "I've had enough of summer."

CHAPTER TEN

◄••••►

Once More Unto the Breach

*M*Y MATERNAL grandmother, a wise and dearly beloved woman, used to say she never could abide telegrams.

They had so often brought bad news during the Civil War that bad news was all people thought about when one of those yellow slips arrived.

This is one of my close links with what is called history: it was not history for her, it was things, mainly unhappy things, happening to human beings. She had no illusions about history, as I now recall. Perhaps she was trying to teach me not to have any.

During the Civil War, the War Department, as soon as it conveniently could, told the relatives of the dead in Vermont and Ohio, in Michigan and Maine and Illinois, what had happened. Sometimes it sent back the remains, if any. It must have done so, since there were graves of Union soldiers killed in action, as well as some dead of wounds and of disease, in both Williamstown and Waterbury, Vermont.

Vermont! We did not think it extraordinary to live in that state. A person had to be born somewhere and to live somewhere. But we had some veterans around—and we had faith in those veterans—to remind us that Vermont had won the Civil War. We had the old regimental flags in the State House and we had heard of Stannard's Vermont Brigade coming in on the right flank of Pickett's charge at Gettysburg, and stopping him in his tracks. Gettysburg was about as near as we cared to have Pickett or any other Confederate get. A few Confederates came down from Canada and robbed a bank in St. Albans during the war; but for our ancestors and friends that was not war, it was merely illegal.

My grandmother naturally took no pains to make me fond of martial glory. She thought, I am modestly certain, that I was a good little boy, and she had no wish to see me grow up and get shot. Once, when a brass band from some migratory show that was to appear at the Waterbury Opera House was passing by 27 North Main Street with all its horns blowing and all its drums beating—or both of them, the bass and the snare—she shook her head mournfully. "That is the music," she said, "that has sent many a boy to war."

I was wishing, before she spoke, that there was a war and that I was old enough to be in it. But I couldn't tell her what was in my heart. I didn't dare try to make her understand my martial dreams; I couldn't say I wanted to be a dashing cavalryman, with enough brass buttons to attract whatever girls I admired, and a reasonably quiet and good-natured horse; and if I had to be wounded I did want one of those girls to bend over me and stroke my aching brow, and cry.

My grandmother, I knew even then, might have laughed at this dream of mine, instead of crying. The girls might have laughed too—I'm afraid.

I couldn't explain these things to my grandmother, nor even to my mother, who remembered the day when the news came of Lincoln's death, and how my grandmother, who hated war and violence, who hated hate, had sat down and cried.

Lincoln had been dead thirty-three years in the spring of 1898, but the Civil War wasn't dead, nor most of the veterans who had fought in it. The war came to us very real in many ways. One of my collateral relatives on my mother's side had been a casualty, in a sense; he had enlisted in an infantry regiment, and when his training routine had required him to run eighteen miles on a hot day between Burlington and points south he had suffered a heart attack; he had been unable to kill any Southerners but he got a pension just the same, and I saw him and talked to him.

My mother's sister, my Aunt Alice, had married a man who had really been killed in the Civil War. This was Uncle Lucius, who as a child had twice run away from home to get into the army, and had lied about his age until he did get in. Uncle Lucius came out with the seeds of the tuberculosis from which, almost a generation later, in my birth year, he died. My aunt received a pension; but this was no substitute for my Uncle Lucius, who had been a pioneer salesman of harvesting machinery, and a good one, and I suppose might have become rich if he had stayed out of the Civil War and put his mind to it and kept healthy.

I once asked my Aunt Alice if Uncle Lucius had killed a man every day while he was in the army in the war. She shook her head. She wasn't as bitter about war as was my maternal grandmother, her mother, but she didn't care much for it. Not every day, she said. Certainly not every day. Maybe he hadn't ever killed anybody. I was disappointed. Other boys' uncles and other relatives had killed countless Rebel soldiers, or so their nephews and such said. Why hadn't mine?

But no matter how much you cherished martial glory, you could never get much information about it out of an old soldier. The only visible sight of it I ever had from such a man was provided by a veteran who used to come into J. K. Linton's store. He was a farmer. If you got him in the right mood, which may have been after he had taken a little something for his stomach's sake, he would roll up his pants leg and show you a running sore beside the shin. This, he assured you, was a wound he had received in one of the last battles of the Civil War. The surgeons had wanted to take his leg off. He hadn't permitted them to do so. They said his leg would never heal, and it hadn't; but he still had a leg.

I do not pass judgment on this man's statements. He could have been a liar. The thing he showed may be medically impossible, though it was clear he had an imperfect leg. But I thought I was really seeing a wounded soldier, and I envied that man past all explaining.

I knew a blacksmith in Williamstown, and to this day I can bring back the scorched smell that filled his misty shop when he put a red-hot horseshoe on a hoof; and how he blew at his bellows; and how the fire came up red, and how the world was thrilling and beautiful.

This blacksmith, whose name was Grover Caldwell, had been a soldier. He even had a canteen he had carried in service; if you filled it and drank, the water came out bitter as medicine. He said he had been told during his army days that this purified the water and kept a man from getting fever. It had worked for him; he hadn't got a fever, he was alive. Like most people in those days, and some now, he had faith that if anything tasted bitter, or hurt, or was in some other way unpleasant, it was good for us.

We boys asked this blacksmith one day what was a battle like? He thought a while, nursing a hoof between his knees and paring off some superfluous horny material, and smiled, I now think sadly. You never knew what a battle was like, he said. There was so much smoke you couldn't see anything.

Another veteran came to the schoolhouse, not long before Decoration Day, and made a little speech about his army experiences. I was all set for bloodshed. What he told us was that they put him and his comrades on a ship—there was a thing called "they" in that war, apparently, as in all wars, that disposed of men's bodies and souls—and took them down to Norfolk. The ship ran aground somewhere, I don't recall where, but they got it off and proceeded. But he didn't tell anything at all about the fighting. None of the veterans ever seemed to want to tell us much about the fighting. We may have had men in our town who belonged in Stannard's Brigade and who had come yelling down on Pickett's Confederates on that third day at Gettysburg; but I never heard one of them tell about it. They didn't want to, or so it seemed.

I wondered why. From where I sat at my desk in the grammar school I could look out, left and southeast, to Mr. Ainsworth's pasture, and see the lines of his peaceable, rambling, hill-climbing stone walls. For me, those walls were lines of trenches; I was in one of those trenches, a brave Union soldier, fighting for my country.

If I had been a soldier, I thought, I'd have been proud to tell all about it.

The veterans seemed proud only on Decoration Day, when they were the main figures in the parade and heroes for a few hours. Civil War veterans weren't scarce then.

On this occasion they wore pretty much the same uniforms they had worn in service—blue with brass buttons, and forage caps. There was a color sergeant I much admired, a carpenter, who set the butt of the flagstaff into a socket at his waist supported by a white belt and shoulder rigging. It was a big flag, and a proud one; and a man who had carried the colors in action had a right to be proud, too, for in an attack he stood a fair chance to get shot.

I don't believe we had any lieutenants, captains, or majors, not to mention colonels, in Williamstown. General E. Bass, after whom our house was named, apparently belonged in an earlier war—the Mexican, perhaps.

There was another sergeant, however, and he gave the orders: "Ten-SHUN! Mark TIME! For-war-r-r-r-d MARCH!" And the band, also shining in blue uniforms with brass buttons, but mostly too young to be veterans of the Army of the Potomac, would start tooting and drumming, and away the parade would go to the cemetery.

We school boys would be given small flags and allowed to march at the rear end of the procession; and there would be a marshal, riding up and down, and trying to look military without falling off his horse, which wasn't used to being ridden and wasn't a veteran of the Civil War. The marshal would have a sash over his shoulder, and he would wave everybody to go faster or slower, whichever it was they were not doing at the time; and if I couldn't be a veteran I did wish to be that marshal. But I never was either the one or the other.

The only military glory I achieved at that time—or, I might as well add, at any time—was the rank I held in an unarmed but quite ferocious unit organized among the students of the Williamstown Graded School. I don't recall that we ever did anything to defend our country, or our town, or that our enthusiasm lasted more than a few days.

However, there was something in me at that time that suggested executive ability. I was, in short, made a corporal. I don't suppose General Eisenhower was half so pleased when he was told he would be put in supreme command of the Normandy Landing as I was when I was made a corporal in the Williamstown Graded School Cadets. In fact, I am sure he wasn't; for it was his melancholy duty to become what the Teutonic mythology calls a chooser of the slain. Nobody was slain while I was a corporal of the Williamstown Graded School Cadets. Not by me, at least.

The taste of glory took on a slightly bitter flavor, however, when my parents found a memorandum, in my own square-angled and then quite legible writing, that attempted to define my new responsibilities. I was, it seems, the analytical type. "The duties of a corporal," I had written, not for publication, but for my own guidance, "are to make the men stand in line."

I imagine I had visions of the Williamstown Graded School Cadets not wishing to stand in line, and of the corporal, meaning myself, using some kind of influence to make them do so.

My parents seemed to consider this memorandum funny. I did not agree with them at the time; but it may well be that their attitude changed, though it did not extinguish, my yearning for the military life.

At any rate, I turned from fantasy to, as we might say today, reality. I realized that at the age of ten I did not have the makings of a corporal in the United States Army. I did not, to be candid, really want to fight. What I wanted, as the Spanish-American War overtook us in that extraordinary year, was to be a drummer boy. I wanted to march at the head of my regiment, in some grand, historic charge, beating on my drum and encouraging others to be brave. I believed that the enemy would not bother to shoot a drummer boy.

One of the saddest moments of my early life came when I

learned that drummer boys were no longer desired, because buglers—who, for some absurd reason, had to be grown up—had taken over their functions. You no longer drummed up excitement before a battle, you bugled it up.

I didn't know how to play the bugle. I still don't. Nor would it do me any good if I did. The Army, which still has foolish notions about age, wouldn't hire me. And whatever bugle calls are needed now are recorded on tape in a studio, and opened with a can opener.

2

I spoke of the Spanish-American War overtaking us. This it did by degrees. Its origins and reasons were not clear to me, but I hopefully watched its approach—a war was what a boy wanted; even if he couldn't get into it because of the foolish ideas held in the adult world, still he wanted it.

In the big pantry off the kitchen of our part of the Ainsworth House, my mother had covered the shelves with newspapers. This was a thrifty Vermont habit, although manufactured shelf paper, which cost money, was already in use in some of the wealthier homes. I believe my mother scalloped the edges of the newspapers, which kept them from curling over.

You could go into the pantry, hunting for a doughnut or a mouse—there were more doughnuts than mice, but one of our cats once caught four mice at once in that pantry—and as you ate the doughnut, or waited for the cat to catch the mouse, or both, you could read the shelf paper. So I remember a printed story that said the battleship *Maine* had arrived in Havana Harbor for a courtesy call. At the time all I thought of was how wonderful it would be to be old enough to be a sailor on the battleship *Maine* and visit Havana.

I was lucky not to be such. As the history books say, the *Maine* was blown up on the night of January 25, 1898, with the loss of 260 lives.

The Spaniards said her magazine had exploded; but as prospective enemies we didn't believe anything the Spaniards said. Other persons asserted that the Cuban insurgents had set off a mine under her keel, with the intention of making us think the Spaniards did it and so getting us into a war with Spain— naturally, on the side of the insurgents. Boys in the Williamstown Graded School had no doubt as to what had happened; we knew the Spaniards had done it, and that we ought to reimburse ourselves for one battleship and 260 lives by taking Cuba and anything else that was handy away from Spain.

Right was right and wrong was wrong in the Williamstown Graded School in 1898. This was mighty convenient, as I now realize.

Nobody ever traced the criminal to his lair. Perhaps he had no lair. There was, however, a Spanish-American War, whose history will not be here written except as a ten-year-old boy in Vermont saw it.

I recall a few newspaper headlines which told of our triumphant progress toward a bit of organized slaughter. By this time I wasn't waiting until my mother put the old newspapers on the pantry shelves. I heard talk at the store and around the lamp-lit table after supper at home at night. And there was no subject we talked about so much at school, or so hopefully, as the coming war with Spain.

I gather, from a subsequent reading of wise men's books, that we Americans, not the Spaniards, were the ones who wanted to go to war—as, indeed, from a boy's point of view, why should we not? Some persons, even then, held that we were wrong, morally and otherwise. This did not matter; the Williamstown Graded School believed that the year was ripe for glory.

As the conflict came nearer, Williamstown people in general thought in terms of the Civil War. The veterans of that conflict were too old to be of much use in a war with Spain; but there did exist an organization known as the Sons of Veterans, and the members of this society were quite young enough for battle. It turned out that few of them volunteered. Perhaps they had been bored with war from hearing their fathers talk so much about it. My own father, being a Scot by birth, hadn't been in the Civil War; and being Scottish in his love of argument would sometimes contend that maybe the South had been right, after all. Of course he did not say that the Spaniards were right in 1898. Had he done so he would have horrified his family, his friends, and his neighbors.

I now perceive that it was the wrong persons who volunteered, as would happen in any war conducted under the volunteer system. The idealistic, adventurous types always offer themselves for sacrifice; and these are the very ones who ought to stay home and produce children.

I don't know how many Williamstown boys did volunteer. A number of them did so, and at the start they had fun. First they went down the hill to Barre, six or seven miles away. Later they returned in heavy blue woolen suits with brass buttons, and had a few days of liberty. Young men who had been slow in enlisting nearly died of envy, and a few of them lit out for Barre and the recruiting sergeant without delay. They feared the army might get filled up and not want any more recruits.

The young fellows who hadn't enlisted, and didn't intend to, were not deceived by the brass buttons. They bided their time, figuring, as I now suppose, that the girls would pay attention to them once the soldiers were out of the way.

The Spanish-American War produced no good songs and many bad ones. I recall standing at the parlor organ while my mother played, my father, who had a fine bass voice, sang, and the rest of us did what we could. One song and tune that return to me went something like this:

> You don't belong to the Reg-u-lars,
> You're only a Volunteer,
> You're only one of the rank and file,
> Yet someone holds you dear . . .
> And during the coming year,
> Uncle Sam will take off his hat,
> To you, Mr. Volunteer.

I have not checked this song with the records. I have merely gone into the abysses of my memory and fetched out what was

there. I could sing this piece, even now, but I do not expect
to be asked. If I have misquoted it, and the author is in the
house, I hope he will correct me.

Another tune prevalent at the time—I might even say epidemic
—had a sort of resemblance to this:

> Mid campfires gleaming,
> Mid shot and shell,
> I shall be dreaming
> Of my own Blue Bell.

These words also I have dredged out of memory's depths. Even
at the age of ten I was not sure that a soldier ought to take this
attitude. If he were being fired upon, and if he were expected
to defend his country, he ought not to be dreaming.

However, the real theme song of the Spanish-American War
of 1898 was one not written for it: *There'll Be a Hot Time in the
Old Town Tonight*. This, it turned out, was what our troops
sang when they felt like singing. Usually they did not feel like
singing—and this was not because of the enemy but because of
poor food and various diseases, including typhoid fever and
dysentery, made available to them by a well-meaning Government.

So now my mind turns to the McAndrew brothers, Donald
and Peter. Peter, the younger, was the one who enlisted.

I don't know now why Peter enlisted, what quirk, what rest-
lessness, what fear, what disappointment in love, made him so
eager to take the first opportunity to get away from granite
cutting. But I knew then, in my capacity of boy about town; I
knew it was because he wanted beauty and adventure, the salt
and the glory of life.

Donald and Peter, as it now seems to me, had come directly
to Williamstown from some town in Scotland, perhaps from
Peterhead, where my father was born, or from Aberdeen, where
he had learned to cut granite. They had with them no family, no
relatives whatsoever, and thus they were much thrust in upon

each other. They were big, brawny men, and not sentimental; but there was an attachment between them that made the word brother mean something.

Donald looked after Peter. Everybody said that. If Peter had a cough, as granite cutters often did, Donald worried about it— which was a sensible thing to do, since a cough in a granite cutter might mean death. This much I knew from what my father said, before and after Peter enlisted.

But of course, after Peter enlisted the United States Government looked after him. It not only provided him with food and clothing, and maybe a tent to sleep under when it rained. It also gave him, as I looked at it, martial glory, with a minimum of danger, not to say damage.

I did not think of veterans, on our side, in any war, as being injured in any inconvenient place. Not all my grandmother's sad comments, not all my mother's reticences, could alter this boy attitude. I never dreamed that a soldier on our side could ever have any important part of his face shot off, or his manhood removed by an inconsiderate enemy, or that he could die of tetanus. I realized that he might die; but the death I imagined for him was a bullet through the heart, painless and beautiful. I wouldn't have minded being shot through the heart myself, if only I could have been alive afterward to listen to the kind and admiring things that would be said about me.

So if I had been Peter McAndrew's brother I would not have been uneasy about him after he had enlisted and had started off with his regiment to Tampa, Florida, on his way to wipe out the Spaniards in Cuba. Peter would be all right. Nothing unfortunate happened in a war to our kind of people, to those we knew and loved. Other soldiers often got shot to pieces and died painfully; but not the soldiers we knew best.

As for Donald McAndrew, a boy wouldn't even wonder what went on in his mind when Peter left Barre for the camp in Florida. What was in his mind was expressed in granite, later on. That was his way of talking, which in the end even a boy understood.

3

The soldiers went away to Florida, on their way to Cuba; but glory came to Vermont before they ever reached Cuba. It came in the person of Admiral George Dewey, a Vermonter, who sank a Spanish fleet at what was called the Battle of Manila Bay. Eventually Admiral Dewey came home and had a welcome that must have taken his breath away. Children all over Vermont were named Dewey. So were dogs, streets, and schools.

The heroic admiral's return did not occur in the year of which I am writing; but I cannot refrain from quoting some lines I wrote to be read aloud in school, as that memorable event drew nearer:

> Dewey's coming, Dewey's coming
> And he's coming pretty soon.

Memory yields no more. I am sure there must have been a rhyme further on, because if there was anything my poetry had, it was rhymes. At the moment I believed that Shakespeare couldn't have done much better. But we had something in common; we believed that in time of war it was a good thing to imitate the action of the tiger.

The war moved nearer. Few knew where Manila was, but all of us had heard about Cuba, because it was there that the *Maine* had been sunk. We were on almost familiar ground when Captain Hobson took the *Merrimac* into the narrow entrance channel and sank her, hoping—vainly, as it turned out—thus to bottle up the Spanish fleet commanded by Admiral Cervera.

I associate this episode with George Ainsworth. I met Mr. Ainsworth one afternoon as I was going upstreet. I cannot too strongly underline Mr. Ainsworth's true humanity. He would not have cared to punish my father for the crime of not going to church, and he would have shrunk from the imagined spectacle of a demon poking my father with a pitchfork in some future world for the cosmic offense of being unorthodox. Mr. Ainsworth would have felt sorry for a mouse caught by a cat, just as I would have done. However, as a disciple of Calvin, he would have realized that the cat was in the right and the mouse in the wrong.

Since I was going upstreet, Mr. Ainsworth was coming downstreet. He had been at J. K. Linton's store and had got some news. It wasn't news off the radio or television, because at that time there wasn't any radio or television; this seems odd, but it is true, and I can prove it. Mr. Ainsworth had seen a newspaper, although I do not recall that he flourished it as he spoke.

Mr. Ainsworth halted me as though I were an adult. I suppose he had to speak to somebody about the great news, if such it was. "The paper says," he told me, "that a battleship has been sunk at Santiago." He eyed me like a Hebrew prophet. "We just have to hope," he said, the good, kind man—and this, I repeat, he really was—"that it wasn't one of ours."

In short, if anybody had to be killed, he thought it had better be a Spaniard. This seemed sensible to Mr. Ainsworth, as it did to me, and, as I suppose, to all other loyal people of Williamstown, even the grown-up ones. If a Spanish ship were sunk, and if Spaniards were drowned in the sinking, that would be an advantage for our side. Mr Ainsworth wouldn't stretch his imagination, nor would I, nor would the adult inhabitants of Williamstown, to take in the case of a Spanish sailor who had a wife and children, or perhaps only a sweetheart, in Spain, who would miss him if he were drowned.

Mr. Ainsworth, even if asked to do so by his Government, wouldn't have drowned a Spanish sailor by the simple expedient of holding his nose in a tub of rainwater until the man was no longer interested in breathing; Mr. Ainsworth would have been repelled by the suggestion that he help win the Spanish-American War by sticking a bayonet through a Spaniard; Mr. Ainsworth was a good man, a God-fearing man, and if murder had to be done he would have preferred at all times to have it done by somebody else, duly enlisted and sworn into the service of the United States. Just the same, Mr. Ainsworth would have been pleased if quite a number of Spanish sailors had been destroyed in the sinking of a Spanish ship of war at Santiago; and he would have been sad if American sailors, with just the same number of parents, children, or sweethearts, had given their all for their country.

This did not seem illogical to Mr. Ainsworth. It did not seem illogical to me. I am not even now saying it is illogical; it is just the way things were in Williamstown, Vermont, in 1898.

What had happened was that Captain Hobson had taken a volunteer crew in the collier *Merrimac* into what he thought was the main channel of Santiago Harbor, and had there sunk her. Mr. Hobson was a brave man, and his crew were all brave men. What they lacked was accurate charts of the harbor entrance, and this did not prevent them from being eagerly welcomed when they came home in the fall after our glorious victory. Delegations of beautiful girls—that was what everybody said—met them at the railway stations and kissed them. I did not then see much sense in this.

Mr. Ainsworth would have approved of the Hobson venture if he had known about it. Since he didn't know, he just hoped some Spaniards had been drowned.

Hobson's glory was just part of the glory that went with quite a small war. Almost everybody had some glory. Colonel Theodore Roosevelt led his Rough Riders up San Juan Hill—though later he said he had had to run like hell to keep up. There was a battle called El Canay. General Shafter, weighing three or four hundred pounds, commanded the infantry. The battleship *Oregon* steamed round Cape Horn from San Francisco in time to get into the big sea battle when the Spaniards came out.

As the boys in the Williamstown Graded School used to say, admiring our country and glad to be future citizens, the United States had never lost a war; other nations lost wars, but we did not; and this war with Spain was no exception.

The bugles blew—adults, fortunate adults, blew them, as I have said—the flags waved, and the American arms prevailed. I wondered why we did not go over and conquer Spain, and perhaps annex it, but—luckily, as I now admit—older and wiser heads decided otherwise.

There was one stain on the glory. American soldiers sickened and died of camp diseases in Florida. Those who got to Cuba had the same or worse diseases there. The Army had doctors, but the doctors had forgotten that during the Civil War more soldiers died in camps and hospitals of plain old-fashioned ailments than of wounds received in battle. I knew this, in 1898, at the age of ten. I knew it because I read it in the newspapers. The doctors—at least, the Army doctors—apparently didn't read newspapers.

Yet I still believed in martial glory. I hoped the Philippine Insurrection, which was the name we gave to the efforts of the Filipinos to run their own show without our help, would still be going on when I was old enough to join the Army.

I would have to wait eight years. I had read the recruiting posters, which offered the handsome wage of thirteen dollars a month, plus board, lodging, and clothing, to able-bodied men between the ages of eighteen and thirty-five. I thought I would certainly enlist at eighteen.

When the fighting was over there was an investigation or two. One of these investigations was concerned with what the newspapers called embalmed beef. Our soldiers were said to have sickened and died of this delicacy. I heard much indignant talk of this scandal around J. K. Linton's store. My father and mother talked about it, too.

We had won a glorious victory, but some lives had been needlessly lost. There had to be somebody to punish, as even a boy of ten—especially, a boy of ten in the middle of Vermont, still under John Calvin's baleful glare—had been brought up to expect.

Nobody was ever punished, as far as I know, for selling bad beef to our soldiers. There was, however, a resentment in small rural communities against the packers who were beginning to make a science of turning animals into prepared food. A boy of ten in Williamstown, Vermont, would have heard adults say that the wicked corporations in Chicago were capable of any crime. We preferred, in our family, the meat raised on a Williamstown farm and personally processed by Ben Weaver, our best-known butcher.

Ben was an agreeable man. He used to give big dill pickles to boys who came from families that bought meat from him. I am not sure whether or not he was the butcher who used to come around with a wagon and sell meat directly off the tailboard—steaks, chops and roasts so cheap I couldn't believe it if I knew the prices today; and such trifles as liver, hearts, kidneys, and tripe, not to mention flies, for nothing. Ben also chewed tobacco, and I still remember with real pleasure the two or three times when I was present when he swallowed his quid; this worried him and took his breath away, but he always recovered.

I saw Ben Weaver kill a sheep once, and for a long while I wished I hadn't. He killed gently. He did not hate the sheep. Yet, also, he was not sorry for it. He needed mutton. A sheep was intended by nature to produce mutton. But to me the sheep seemed so alone, so lost, so hopeless and helpless, so cut off from friends. And I went on eating mutton—which was the name we gave to what is now called, in most American meat stores and restaurants, lamb.

I did not connect Ben Weaver killing a sheep with one of our brave soldiers killing a Spaniard. Nobody had ever suggested to me then that all flesh might be designed in brotherhood, and all beloved by an all-pitying God.

I was ten years old. I was not subtle. I had never seen anybody kill a Spaniard, or any other enemy of the United States. Nor had I ever seen a Spaniard kill anybody.

War was wonderful, I thought. I felt that my lot was an unhappy one, in that I had been born too late to be in the Civil War, and not soon enough to be in the Spanish-American War.

4

None of our soldiers from Williamstown died in battle during the Spanish-American War. None of them, so far as I know, ever got out of the country. I don't even know how many of them died at all, except, a long time afterward, of old age, or perhaps of various kinds of accidents.

Once one of the Bean boys was preparing to go hunting but never started; because as he was about to leave the house he blew the top of his head off with a rifle shot. People who had seen the remains spoke interestingly of this at the store. It did not occur to any of us, not to me, certainly, that the Bean boy might have had his head blown off in battle and looked just as unpleasant. Battles were different and less depressing. Everybody said this, except the old Civil War soldiers, who continued to say nothing.

However, Peter McAndrew came back from Florida, after Havana fell. At least, somebody resembling Peter came back. Peter had been a hale, hearty man, full of the physical joy of life. I believe he had played on the town baseball team.

But he came back thin and tired, and he didn't play baseball, and he didn't ask for his old job at the stonesheds. He would have to rest a bit, his brother Donald said; he'd been sick down there in the hot climate of Florida; it would take him a while to get his strength back again.

Donald said this in Peter's hearing. He didn't say much of anything about Peter when Peter wasn't there. Donald looked solemn, but the Scots often did; it was their nature, Mr. Ainsworth said.

Peter himself said almost nothing at all. He just seemed to be waiting for something. He was like a man listening for hoofbeats around the bend, and a messenger coming with news or a summons. He seemed to listen hungrily, and with a liking for silence in which to listen.

If a man at leisure around our town wished to be sociable he would turn to J. K. Linton's store, which was also the postoffice, and be sure of meeting somebody to talk to. Peter didn't go there, not after the first few days, when there had been a small, pathetic flurry of welcome. He wouldn't let anybody be sorry for him; he said he was all right and he'd been lucky; we should have seen some of the boys who had had to be carried off the train at Montpelier and Barre. He could walk, anyhow, he said, and that was something.

But he seemed to want privacy. He seemed to want to think. Somehow people knew this desire of his, and respected it.

Peter took to sitting in the sun in front of Martin's drug store, on the north side of the hotel, not far from the livery stable. He sat there, except as people stopped a moment and spoke and went on, alone. The livery stable boys exchanged jocular greetings with him coming and going, but now there was a kind of tenderness about them.

The year wore on, and after a while, as I remember, Peter buttoned up the blue uniform coat he was still wearing, and then, a few days later, put on his Army overcoat. It wasn't cold enough for an overcoat—we boys knew that.

It wasn't cold enough for an overcoat. Martial glory was a chilly thing while Peter McAndrew sat there, on a chair the druggist put out for him, and tried to get well enough to go back to his old job in the stoneshed.

After a while, and this must have been in the early fall, Donald McAndrew formed the habit of coming by on his way home from work, and the brothers would walk home together, slowly. It wasn't a long walk, just over the bridge by the blacksmith shop and then to the curiously painted red-white-and-blue house, a boarding house at that time, where they lived. Then the days got shorter, as they did then the same as now, and Peter went home early before the closing whistle blew, or, more frequently, as the days grew colder, stayed in his boarding house, where he could sit by the kitchen stove.

I think I remember him in the blacksmith shop one day, near the warmly glowing forge, talking about war with Grover Caldwell. Of course Grover knew all about war, having been in one, whereas Peter had never been under fire. But Grover and Peter could get together on one subject: they agreed that officers were the same in any army, in any war.

I think it was on one of the last days Peter sat out in front of the drugstore, a real sunny day in Indian summer, that Anna Marie Sylvester came by—and I did believe that she and her name were the loveliest feminine things in the world. She was very old, maybe as old as nineteen; but at ten I loved her, purely and all inside myself.

I couldn't ever speak to Anna Marie Sylvester because I loved her so; indeed, if she had been a princess or a queen instead of a hired girl in the Ellsworth house while Mrs. Ellsworth was expecting a baby, I wouldn't have been so much in awe.

She didn't see me that day, but she did see Peter McAndrew, and in a flash I knew, looking from one to the other, that the same thing—a nameless, terrible, and beautiful thing—was in the eyes of both of them. She had a pale complexion at that time, but her cheeks were flushed.

"Hello, Peter," she said.

"Hello," he answered. "Anna Marie."

"You're feeling better?" she said.

Peter nodded. "I'll be all right."

She came a little closer, because his voice was low or maybe because she didn't want me to hear. I drew back, because I was afraid of Anna Marie, and I didn't hear much of what she said.

And it wasn't much she said. I wondered if he, too, were afraid of Anna Marie, because she was so beautiful.

She waved her hand as she turned away. He raised his own hand, and let it fall back on his knee.

"Some night," he said, "when I'm better we'll go dancing."

She turned again, and went on toward J. K. Linton's store. Peter watched her go.

I think I knew what was happening to Peter. I think I knew he would never go dancing. I think I knew he was dying. As he was. As Dr. Watson had known, from the first. As Peter himself had known, perhaps—only, as I knew even then, the way boys know many things they do not know they know, the dying do not speak of death, they consider the subject might embarrass the living.

We boys talked a little, shyly, with Peter McAndrew, while he was still out there, in the waning sun. I don't remember what we said. He didn't answer if he didn't want to, and we knew why. We didn't ask him what it was like to be a soldier. And, in a way, he didn't know. He hadn't charged up San Juan Hill. He hadn't taken Santiago.

So one day Peter was dead. His brother Donald sat stiff and unblinking in a front pew in the Congregational Church while the minister said kind things about Peter, and told us it was a noble thing to be willing to die in the defense of one's country. I wondered about this: Peter hadn't died in the defense of his country, he had died of some disease he had contracted while stationed in a camp in Florida. He hadn't been shot through the heart, like the heroes we had heard about.

It was a good funeral, however. The mourners went up the hill to the cemetery, along the same route the parade followed on Decoration Day—only there was no holiday feeling this time. Donald walked behind the hearse, and he and some of the other Scottish granite cutters were the pall bearers.

Then Donald went home to his boarding house, where now he had only himself to pay for. But he began to stay at the stoneshed overtime, for he had a project.

It seems strange now that Peter McAndrew's death did not, for me, take the romance out of war. This may have been because death among the young was so usual in our time and place. My boyhood friends, Archie Staples and Richard Linton, had had to die because of what I now know was the medical backwardness of the age. Now they wouldn't have to; now Dr. Watson would have a miracle in the little bag he carried, and the great warmth of his heart would not have been so often disappointed. Nowadays, if I am tempted to lament the past, I remember that death among the very young is not considered a natural and inevitable matter any more.

There was Perlie Marlowe, a boy the same as I, except that he may have been a year or two older. Perlie had typhoid fever. Dr. Watson nursed him through the crisis, and Perlie started to get well. Dr. Watson was happy, and so were most of the people of our town, for Perlie was a good boy, of what we called a good family.

Dr. Watson said Perlie must be careful for a while about what he ate. He must take broths and such, and maybe, after a while, ice cream. One afternoon Perlie's parents went off for an hour or so, leaving him safely in bed taking a nap. But Perlie woke up and was hungry. Perlie rose and ate a slice of mince pie that he found on the pantry shelf. It was a good, sustaining pie, for Mrs. Marlowe was an excellent cook.

It was nobody's fault, but Perlie died. In such ways we grew used to death. We didn't think, in spite of what the minister had said, that Peter McAndrew had given his life to his country. He had merely contracted a disease in Florida instead of doing the same thing at home, as he might have done; and as the young men who did not enlist did do in some cases, with less trouble.

I don't believe Donald McAndrew tried to put the blame where the blame might belong, on the United States Army, or on war, on the McKinley Administration, on the condition of medicine, or on God.

Donald carved a granite marker that was put over Peter's grave. It was in the Williamstown cemetery still, the last time I went there. I suppose he got it out of a book of designs; I suppose, in any case, he got it out of his heart. It was a tree trunk, broken a few feet above the earth, as though by a high wind. I saw it, I still remember it.

But I still thought, it would be a fine and glorious thing to be a soldier.

———

I remember an old lady standing just inside a white picket fence, in front of a small, neat white house. She is standing beside a snowball bush, as I suppose it is still called. There are roses, too; but I associate her with the snowball bush because her hair is white, the snowball berries are white, and the small, white house goes with them.

I do not remember whether I spoke to Mrs. Dole, as I think it was, or whether she did more than smile at me. Why do I so remember her across all the years? Why does this picture stay with me, why will it always stay with me until the day I die?

But there it is. I present it in my gallery of portraits, without any story, except that Anna Marie Sylvester indeed lived with Mrs. Dole, and worked in Mrs. Dole's house as long as she could, and died in Mrs. Dole's house when there was nothing else left for her to do, or to hope for.

It is Mrs. Dole, however, that I see. She fingers the snowball berries, without picking them or even marring them, and she smiles—at the whims of nature, or at life, or at the boy who for the moment is halted in front of her picket fence and can think of nothing to answer to her friendliness.

I see her standing there, even now, even after all the years. Did she know her picture was being taken?

CHAPTER ELEVEN

——◄••►——

A Time for Dancing

*M*R. *AINSWORTH*, as I was saying, had shut up the old dance hall in his house that had been used when the place was an inn; really devout people were opposed to any kind of dancing in which anything approaching an embrace was possible. The Catholics were an exception to a certain extent, the Methodists were more strict than the Congregationalists, and for the life of me I cannot remember how the Universalists felt about it.

Still, you couldn't quite kill the dancing impulse, and some young persons who later settled down, married, and raised large families had their wild dancing year or two first.

For me, this dancing was a thin, far-away lilting of violins. I don't even know where it took place. It might have been in a hall over the drygoods section of J. K. Linton's general store. I knew there was such a hall, for one winter I spent quite a few evenings there, in the presence of some of my contemporaries and their parents, trying to avoid learning how to sing. It was possible, too, to drive to Barre if the young man had the use of a horse and buggy; and if the weather were fine, the young man and his girl could have a good time driving back and watching the dawn come, and maybe getting home in time for milking, or sweeping out the store, or going to the stonesheds for a day's work.

Some parents worried not only about the dancing but about letting their daughters stay out so late, or so early; my parents didn't have this worry, for my sister was then about six years old.

As for myself, I never did learn to dance until I was in my last year at college—and maybe not even then.

We had square dances or barn dances when I was going to high school in Waterbury, but I can't recall even these innocent diversions during my days in Williamstown. They permitted at least a few momentary clasps of the hand, the boy's big paw engulfing the girl's smaller one, and a thrill traveling back and forth; and some of the extremely pious citizens had their doubts about them. It has sometimes seemed strange to me, in later years, that really good and careful young persons in our town ever got their courtship to a point where they could be married.

However, some dancing did take place, and among those who danced was Anna Marie Sylvester. I don't know whether she danced more after Peter McAndrew died than she did before; but she did go on dancing. She was so young, so full of the music of life, that she had to.

My love life at this period, if I may call it that, was complicated. In my own age group I deeply loved Millicent Byrnes. It did not matter whether or not Millicent loved me—I didn't ask her and wouldn't have known what to do if she had said either yes or no. I also loved Miss Miller, the teacher who used to tie her apron with a big bow knot in front, and then reverse it.

And I loved Anna Marie Sylvester. I loved Anna Marie Sylvester more than anybody else. This involved no trouble for anybody, for Anna Marie didn't know I existed. I did not have to marry her, or try to marry her, or not marry her, or be faithful to her—such obligations were not laid upon the shoulders of ten-year-old boys. All I had to do was to love her, and I still do not know what kind of love this was—I haven't had time to look it up.

Two pictures of Anna Marie have stayed in my memory all these years. I wish she could have known that those pictures would last so long—I now know that it might have pleased her that even an invisible boy should keep her so long in his heart; and I did want to please her.

The first picture is of a Sunday morning in the Congregational Church. I had almost not got there in time, and when I did arrive I sat in one of the rear pews. There was room enough, for even if the Reverend Silas Blake, our pastor at that time, had had the tongues of men and of angels, he couldn't have found enough Congregationalists to fill the church.

I had been there during the first hymn and a part of the prayer, when Anna Marie Sylvester came in and sat at the other end of the pew. I wish I were still capable of the kind of joyful embarrassment I felt then, I wish I could tell her about it, even though the telling could serve only to amuse her—and myself. I don't know what color her eyes were, I know only that they were beautiful. I never dared look at them. Her hair, I know, was dark, her face beautifully oval, her complexion white and pink, with none of the artificial aid she would have today, her hands demure and soft, in spite of the housework she must have been doing.

I wanted to look closely at her, I wanted to be really invisible and dwell upon her; but what I did was to turn shamefacedly away and pretend I didn't know she was there.

My second picture of Anna Marie Sylvester brings her walking on a summer evening past the crowded porch of J. K. Linton's store. The men from the granite sheds had had their suppers and come downstreet or upstreet; and a few of the farmers had come into town after doing their chores, or were lucky enough to have hired men who could be trusted to do them.

Anna Marie wore a dark silky suit with a white blouse under the jacket, and a dark hat with flowers on it. It may have been an ordeal for her to come past the men on J. K. Linton's porch, for she must have known they were looking at her. What men ever didn't look at you, Anna Marie?

But Anna Marie came on with her head high, her eyes not turning toward the group in front of the store, yet not seeming to keep away by deliberate design. She could have gone into the drygoods part of the store without causing comment. I suppose she could even have gone into the grocery and postoffice part and bought a dozen eggs or a pound of butter, and nobody would have thought the worse of her.

Just the same, J. K. Linton's store was a sort of men's club in the evening, and as a rule women did not go in there then. And on this evening I remember Anna Marie did not go in.

She walked past as though to music that she heard, though other persons did not hear it. Her walking was a kind of dance, as I knew even then. Watching her go by, I had a warm pride in her, as though she were somehow, however distantly, related to me.

Beyond this, I have no picture of Anna Marie Sylvester. I must have seen her many other times, but we do not choose—especially when we are ten-year-old boys—what we are to remember.

I can remember things I was not required to remember, such as a good part of *Horatius at the Bridge,* but I have forgotten a number of the capitals of the states of the United States, though I was ordered by my teachers to memorize them—and for a time did carry them around with me.

But my mind, seeking what was useful to me—and why it was useful I shall never know—ordained that Anna Marie Sylvester, nineteen years old in 1898 and therefore a very grown-up young lady by my standards at that time, should be visible to me forever, sometimes sitting in a pew in the Congregational Church and sometimes walking like a princess, in the glow of a summer evening, past J. K. Linton's store.

Anna Marie was a good girl. Everybody said that when they spoke of her. She was a good girl, they said, though a little reckless. Anna Marie never got into trouble, not in the way they meant it when they spoke of trouble in those days.

What they meant was, Anna Marie never had a baby born out of wedlock. That was what they meant by trouble, those excellent persons living in Vermont villages, and other villages, in that far-off time. Not having enough money wouldn't be trouble in that sense. Being sick wouldn't be trouble in that sense.

2

The advantage of being a boy loving some girl of his own age, and some older girl, such as Anna Marie, and some totally dream girl of no age at all, was that he wasn't aware of this emotion all the time, and didn't have to do a single thing about it.

It wasn't until he was drifting into adolescence that that problem, and many other problems, arose. Being a boy between ten and twelve was as free and easy as being elderly, and it was handier, because a boy had more energy than an old man and could in time become an old man, whereas an old man could never again become a boy.

Anna Marie wasn't in my thoughts, therefore, all day long, or even any part of any specified day, unless I saw her as she passed by. I thought much more about Millicent Byrnes, and pictured myself in various heroic situations which would cause her to admire me rather than to give her entire attention to one of the Linton boys. But Millicent wasn't always present in my daydreams, either. There was so much for a boy to do, be, and become.

My contemporaries and myself were drawn toward girls and at the same time repelled by them. We instinctively knew we would need them later on in life, but we considered them—though I did not then know the word—effeminate. In trying to impress them we tried to be utterly different from them. We wanted to be wild and savage, but we knew they would tame us some day—and even at the age of ten we accepted this, silently, without words, a little sadly, as our fate.

Meanwhile, we were Indians.

Millicent, with her shining red hair—a little like my mother's, as I can now say without fear of startling my psychiatrist—played with dolls and kept her face clean, though it may be she wished for more vigorous amusements. Anna Marie Sylvester walked up and down, in her deep innocence, and her every step was a part of a dance.

As for me, I went fishing once in a while, or out to the combined gristmill and sawmill at Mill Village, or in the fall rode my bicycle with my brother and other boys, or ran wild races in the gathering darkness, whooping to high heaven, as we all felt compelled to do. We tried to extend a small cave above the falls, and, failing that, built a tree house. We got tired of the tree house and built a small log cabin, but never had the persistence to make it high enough to stand up in, and didn't learn how to patch a stone chimney with clay to hold the smoke.

While this was going on I forgot all about Millicent for hours at a time, and never gave a thought to Anna Marie Sylvester. They were like characters in a book I laid down and picked up again. I identified myself with them as I did with the characters in *The Three Musketeers,* except that I was a brave man with a sword and they were ladies who needed a rescuer.

It may have been during this summer—I don't quite know— that I passed long, long hours sitting on the driver's seat of an old meat wagon that Mr. Ainsworth had allowed somebody to abandon in the yard of one of his disused, or only partially used, barns. The canvas top was in good condition, and came far enough forward to keep the sun out of my eyes, or even shut off the rain. When I had climbed up there I was not easy to find, and I had gone a long way. I was running a locomotive on the Central Vermont, blowing the whistle at every crossing, and bound for Montreal and enchanted points beyond. I was driving a covered wagon across the plains, and the Rockies were in sight.

I could do these things without taking my attention off the book I was reading, no matter what the book was about or where the scene was laid. I read not only Dumas but The Duchess and Rider Haggard, Conan Doyle, and a few dozen of the ten-cent, paperbound books that Street and Smith used to put out. I couldn't afford to buy such books, or any books; but we boys had a friend in George Beckett, the town clerk, who was also a harness maker and a philosopher. Mr. Beckett may have procured the Street and Smith books originally with the thought of selling them. When nobody bought them he lent them, free of charge, to us print-hungry youngsters. He was the first free circulating library I ever knew.

Anna Marie Sylvester at that time didn't live too far from Mr. Beckett's shop, which was a hundred feet or less from his square and ugly house. I know she walked by sometimes when I was in the harness shop; but as between Anna Marie, a woman I worshipped but could never have for my very own, and a detective story that I could take home, I chose the book.

I might even have preferred the book to an evening with Millicent; for I didn't have to talk to the book, whereas Millicent would have required conversation of some sort. And I couldn't think of anything to say to girls I adored. It never even occurred to me that they might be interested to learn that I did adore them.

This was the year that Ralph Stevens, who lived with his uncle behind the Universalist Church, broke his collarbone. He was the second boy in town I knew who lived with his uncle. It had its conveniences, because the house rules were not strict. It also had its drawbacks, because we knew even then that an uncle, occupied all day with mending bicycles and doing other mechanical chores, could not give much attention to a boy's troubles. On the other hand, Ralph's uncle had a large collection of Old Sleuth, the detective, and we borrowed these of him just as we borrowed Street and Smith from Mr. Beckett.

Ralph also had a music-box which played *The Blue Bells of Scotland* and several other tunes by a marvelous arrangement of metal spikes on a cylinder. I am not sure how this was done, but I think there was a sort of something that twanged when the proper spike was called upon, and that these twangs made up the melody. I can't see how there could have been any harmony.

At any rate, I do remember sitting in Ralph Stevens' uncle's house on a rainy day, probably along with my brother and one or more of the Linton boys, and listening to the music, and possibly wondering what they would invent next. The best I could do in the way of music was to hum through a sheet of tissue paper wrapped around a comb, although my brother could play *Silvery Waves* and other tunes on our parlor organ.

This makes me think of the organ tuner who came around once while we were living in the Ainsworth house. He would press the foot pedal in order to get the necessary wind, and then he would put his finger on a key to see how far off tune it was. I thought he was a remarkable man to be able to tell whether or not we were out of tune; but what I now remember about him is that he was a little man and that he had hairs growing out of his ears; and I couldn't help speculating as to whether or not these interfered with his sense of pitch.

However, what happened was that Ralph Stevens broke his collarbone by falling out of a butternut tree. My brother and Ralph, and possibly the Linton boys—though I do not mean to involve them in the crime we committed, if that was what it was —had gone butternutting in Mr. Ainsworth's upper pasture, above the falls.

There was an old butternut tree up there (it is a little older now, I am sure) which still bore abundantly. We had had a little plane geometry in school, and we tried to measure the tree's height by the length of its shadow. We did not succeed, but we did conclude it was too high for a boy to climb; and we satisfied ourselves with picking up the sticky green windfalls and knocking down a few others with stones. Then we toasted marshmallows, pretending we were pioneers living off the wilderness.

Mr. Ainsworth's tree yielded too few butternuts to meet the needs of four or five hungry pioneers. Green butternuts weren't good, either, though we would eat a few for luck, just as we would eat chokecherries. They had to be dried out before they were of much interest. So butternut gathering became a game. We wanted to bring home as many as possible.

We moved over from Mr. Ainsworth's pasture, which was on the East Hill, to Jim Beckett's pasture, which was on the lower slopes of the West Hill, and there found other butternut trees. Jim Beckett was the bachelor brother of George Beckett. Jim was, in his small way, a careful business man, which George was not.

Jim would never have learned that we were poaching on his butternuts if Ralph Stevens hadn't broken his collarbone. Ralph, who was an active and fearless young man, had volunteered to climb one of Jim Beckett's butternut trees to shake down some of the nuts. The rest of us lit a fire and began to lay out our lunch. I doubt if we had coffee at the time, but we may well have had frankfurters.

Then there was a thump. Ralph Stevens had fallen as he started to climb down the tree. He lay on the ground moaning. One of us got water from a nearby trickle and poured it over his face. He didn't seem to like this, but waved feebly, and went on groaning.

One of the other boys tore off across the pasture toward town. The rest of us may have looked longingly at our frankfurters— we were, after all, small savages—but we didn't eat any. We thought Ralph was going to die.

Dr. Watson came at last, and a farmer drove a wagon into the field. Ralph was carried home, and it was no more than a day or two before he was up and around with one arm in a sling. I felt some resentment, I must admit. Why couldn't I have been the one to fall out of the butternut tree and be a hero? After the first hurt and scare, it would have been fun. But it had to be Ralph, and for a week or so he was a prominent character around town.

One day I met Jim Beckett in front of J. K. Linton's store. Being a shy boy, I didn't especially wish to converse with him, but he stopped me.

"How is Ralph Stevens?" he asked.

I mumbled that Ralph was all right.

"You were getting butternuts on my land, weren't you?" he asked.

"I guess we were," I confessed.

He rubbed his hands, like a character in a Dickens novel—he really did, though I hadn't read much Dickens at the time and didn't recognize the gesture. "That's fine," he said. "That's fine. Of course you understand those butternuts belong to me."

I nodded, to indicate I did. I knew, but couldn't say, that in the boy world in which I lived, butternuts—and sometimes apples—belonged to whatever boys would take the trouble to get them. If I had been a few years older I would also have known that Jim Beckett had never picked any butternuts on his pasture land, or hired anybody else to pick any.

"That's fine," Jim Beckett repeated. "And I'm not going to be hard on you. I'd like you to pick all the butternuts you want on my land. We'll go into partnership. You can keep half and give me the other half."

"That's fine," I said, picking up Jim's phrase.

"Don't forget," he said, eyeing me sharply.

"Oh, no, Mr. Beckett," I replied.

But somehow or other we did forget. After Ralph got well enough to walk around a lot, though not to climb trees, we picked some more of Mr. Beckett's butternuts—stopping when we had collected what we thought was our own half.

We laid the Duffus share of the butternuts out on an old table in the lumber room upstairs, next to the locked dance hall; and after they had dried out and turned dark brown they were as good as any butternuts I ever ate—better, I think, because we knew that if Jim Beckett had any butternuts that year, he bought them.

We did not mention this item to our parents, and neither did Jim Beckett, to give him credit for a kind of sportsmanship.

The last I heard on the subject from Jim was on another day when I met him on the street. I had been inclined to cross over or go round when I saw him coming, but in a small village such as Williamstown was this was not easy.

"Have you got any butternuts for me?" asked Mr. Beckett.

"Oh, no, Mr. Beckett," I said. This was about all I ever did manage to say to Jim Beckett, though I could talk all day to his brother George.

"Tut! Tut!" replied Jim Beckett.

I slipped past him and did a little running, not because I thought he would pursue me, but because, I suppose, it is a boy's nature to run when he is embarrassed, just as it is a cat's nature to wash.

This was the end of the butternut episode for that year. As for Ralph Stevens, he got over his broken collarbone, and was then no better than the rest of us.

I can still taste the butternut fudge my mother made that fall or early winter. I wouldn't dare eat any now, though; not because my innards would not be able to digest it, but because I would be afraid I wouldn't like it as well.

For one thing, it wouldn't have the remembered tang of those fall days when we went out in the brown hill pastures, and life stirred in us with an energy and joyousness we never felt in spring. Or a different kind of joy.

3

The Ellsworth baby was born about that time; and not long after this event Mrs. Ellsworth decided she didn't need Anna Marie Sylvester any more. In our town pregnancy justified a hired girl, but motherhood didn't. Only the rich, such as the J. K. Lintons, who were supposed to have an income of several thousand dollars a year, over and above expenses—and of course they could get all they wanted from the store, free of charge— could have a hired girl all the time.

The Lintons did, in fact, have a hired girl at about this time. Her name may have been Lydia Brown, and she was quite pretty. I could have talked to her, since I went to the Linton house occasionally, but I don't believe I ever did. Anyhow, it didn't seem worth while—I loved another. Or several others.

I don't know what happened to Anna Marie Sylvester while she was working for the Ellsworths, but I shouldn't wonder if she got her first taste of a life different from existence on a hill farm. I shouldn't wonder if she fell to dreaming and her pulses quickened.

She may have got a few modernistic ideas from Mrs. Ellsworth, who wasn't a woman to worry about conventions. For example, Mrs. Ellsworth kept going to church and to the store and sometimes to church sociables long after it was evident to all who saw her that she was going to have a baby.

This wasn't considered proper in small Vermont towns in 1898. Women who were visibly on the way to reproduce stayed home and sewed. When the baby appeared the mother reappeared; and as near as I can guess, the conventional adult attitude was to be surprised. I must have felt this to be right, because I was shocked when Ralph Stevens said that Mrs. Ellsworth was going to do what she was going to do. Ralph was a little shocked, too, but he enjoyed talking about it.

Village boys knew much less about life, if I may call it that, than farm boys did. Our conversation was sometimes vulgar—I would be worried if I didn't believe this—but at the ages of ten to twelve, we were almost pathetically pure of heart.

At twelve—but that is another story, and not even impersonally a personal one.

At any rate, Mrs. Ellsworth, after flaunting her interesting condition in the face of the town as long as she could, stayed home for a week or two and had her baby—girl or boy, I don't recall. I think Mrs. Ellsworth liked Anna Marie and wanted to do something for her. Maybe she wanted to help her get an education, for this was the thing a Vermonter would think of first for a young and attractive girl. Education was our highest ideal, just as I later learned it was in my father's native Scotland.

So it was Mrs. Ellsworth, I think, possibly with Dr. Watson's help, who got Anna Marie to work for old Mrs. Dole, who lived alone behind a picket fence in a small white house not far from George Beckett's house and office. Mrs. Dole had sold a hill farm after her husband died, and had enough money left over to live in town in a simple way. Now she was a little too old to be alone, and her only daughter had married and gone to California. It seemed a good plan to have Anna Marie work for her for a while. All it cost was board, and maybe three or four dollars a week.

So Anna Marie went in and out of Mrs. Dole's house. I scurried by, on my way upstreet or downstreet, trying not to look, hoping to see her and afraid I might. I wished I could be invisible, like one of those characters in the Arabian Nights, which I had even then read in an abbreviated and purified edition; I would have liked to stand in the dooryard and see her come down past the snowdrops and the faded rose bushes.

I am sure Ann Marie would have been surprised to know this worship that she inspired. I wonder if she would also have been touched. I don't know how my young friends felt about her, for none of them ever mentioned her until later.

We didn't gossip about Anna Marie. Sometimes we looked, or tried to look, wise, and repeated scraps of scandal about other girls, that we had overheard at the store. But none of us, at the ages of ten to twelve, really knew what we were talking about.

So Anna Marie Sylvester walked in innocence and purity, just as she walked in beauty. I am sure of this now, just as I knew it by instinct then.

But Anna Marie did begin to get the dancing fever. Perhaps her parents hadn't allowed her to dance when she was on the farm. Perhaps the joy in life she so clearly had could express itself best in dancing. She might have had a gift for it, for everybody who had ever seen her at a dance—and of course this couldn't include venerable and pious persons such as Mr. Ainsworth—spoke then, and later, of how well she danced.

But she danced. It was said that she bought herself a new red dress out of the small sum that Mrs. Dole paid her, but I never saw her in this dress—all I could do was wonder whether she looked more beautiful in it than when she came to the store or to church in plain black.

I think Mrs. Ellsworth, with her advanced ideas, would have accepted Anna Marie's dancing as natural and good. I don't know what Mrs. Dole thought about it, but I never heard that she complained when Anna Marie, after working faithfully all day, sometimes danced all night.

Mrs. Dole's mind, I think, was gently failing. It was Mrs. Dole who was reported to have said, "You know, I haven't seen Mr. Beasley come by since the day of his funeral."

And Anna Marie was kind to Mrs. Dole, I am certain. Anna Marie couldn't have been unkind to anybody. Everybody said that, especially later.

It was Dr. Watson, I know, who worried most about Anna Marie's dancing. This was not because he was concerned with the proprieties, though he was a good church member and always went to services when he wasn't needed elsewhere. Dr. Watson worried because Anna Marie wasn't in the best of health, and needed sleep if she were to get well again.

I suppose he ordered a diet for her, and I have no doubt he also made her take cod liver oil—a milky substance that you shook well in a big bottle and then shut your eyes and consumed with a big spoon.

But Dr. Watson couldn't make Anna Marie sleep when she

didn't want to sleep; he couldn't make her want to be middle-aged when she was so young; he couldn't make her want to stop dancing. Did I suspect this then? I must have, for the thought is sharp in my memory now. Perhaps it became sharp, with an unforgotten poignancy, because of what happened and the way people talked about it.

Nowadays Anna Marie might not feel that the youth in her, that drove her and tormented her so, was a fragile and passing thing. She might not be so much in rebellion against a fate closing swiftly in upon her.

At any rate, I now know she set out to spend her youth as though it were an inheritance that would turn into dust if not used.

I think it was youth and life she loved, and not any especial person. How she had felt about Peter McAndrew, who came back from his army service in Florida to dwindle and die, I don't know. How could I? All I know is that the last thing I heard him say to her, and also the first thing, was, "Some night, when I'm better, we'll go dancing."

Of course he never was better. It could have happened, though, that she remembered the words. It could have happened, because strange things happened in our peaceful, matter-of-fact town, that she carried in her mind, even against her will, the memory that she had a date to go dancing, some night, with Peter McAndrew.

Meanwhile she had to dance with especial persons, even though she might have danced beautifully alone; might have danced in the mist that rose sometimes over the newly-mowed hayfields in July, might have danced by October moonlight, might have danced—but this I thought of later—on a great stage, with the orchestra playing for her and an audience waiting to rise to her in a thunder of applause.

But in the place where she was, and the years she had, and the time within those years, and the kind of music Vermont could provide for her, there were, of necessity, especial persons. Tony Mantelli and Bill Mansfield were two of these persons. Tony was a granite cutter, one of those exquisite and temperamental workmen who could do the last final touches on a granite angel to perfection. Bill was a hired man for a dairy farmer on the East Hill, which meant that when he spent a night dancing, he spent twenty-four hours without sleep. I didn't know Tony well, but Bill was easier to talk to and understand. Bill said that if he worked for Deacon Bulger at what he was then getting he would be able to buy himself a farm after a while—as near as he could figure it, one hundred and fifty-six years.

He shook his head sadly, and said he didn't believe any girl would be willing to wait for him that long.

But Bill went dancing a few times with Anna Marie Sylvester, and when she went dancing with him she naturally didn't go dancing with Tony, whom she had known longer than she had known Bill. Tony, it seemed, thought Bill had taken Anna Marie away from him just when she might have been on the point of becoming Tony's girl.

One Saturday night, after old Mrs. Dole had had her supper and been put to bed with a hot-water bottle, Anna Marie kissed her good night and walked out to where Bill was waiting for her just outside the picket fence. Bill may have smelled of the Slater barnyard, but this wouldn't have bothered Anna Marie—she knew about barnyards and what went on there, and how hard it was to get the smell of one completely off a man's shoes and from under his fingernails and from behind his ears.

A good, clean barnyard smell meant, very often, a prosperous farm; it meant a land running with milk, if not with honey; and if the milk wasn't always pasteurized and people got typhoid from it nobody worried, for nobody knew there was a connection.

Where the dance was to be held I don't know; but Anna Marie and Bill walked upstreet in the cool fall night, perhaps close together, perhaps with Bill's arm around Anna Marie's waist. Peter wouldn't have minded that, for Peter was where he couldn't mind anything any more, or where he saw things in large and astronomical terms; Peter was where the stars began, Peter was out beyond the full moon, as I might have thought about it then.

Not that I did think about it until the next morning brought the news. There was much for a boy to think about on the night of a full moon in October besides a young woman and a man walking out together.

But the next morning the news was that Tony Mantelli had crept up on Bill and Marie from behind and tried to stab Bill in the back. I have forgotten all the details, except that Bill showed up with his arm in a sling and Tony was arrested by Constable Nichols, bound over to keep the peace, and released on bail. I believe he had to go to Barre to be tried, later on.

Everything then went on as before, as far as a boy could see. Anna Marie kept on working for Mrs. Dole, though somehow she seemed thinner and worried-looking, with a sort of shining in her eyes that wasn't pure happiness or pure youngness. Bill kept on taking Anna Marie to dances, whenever he could get time.

And Tony kept on working in the stoneshed and coming to J. K. Linton's store sometimes in the evening, just as he had always done. I don't know what people said to him or whether they avoided him or just pretended to forget what had happened. I don't know what he said to Anna Marie if he ran across her, as he must have done. I don't know whether he dropped his eyes and hurried past when he met Bill Mansfield, or whether he told Bill he was sorry and let it go at that.

Boys of my age did not speculate on such matters. What we knew was that Tony had been bound over for trial, and whenever we saw him we thought perhaps we were looking at a man who would have to go to jail. We didn't think Tony would be hanged, for though he had done his best to kill Bill Mansfield, he had failed; but we imagined he would have to wear a striped suit and be shut up in a cell and live on bread and water, and perhaps have to tunnel his way out and return after five or ten years, an aged man with a long, white beard.

I don't now recall what eventually happened to Tony Mantelli. My belief is that when he finally came to trial what he had done was so far back, and the cause so completely removed, that it didn't seem to matter any more.

For we were wrong, when we saw Tony Mantelli, black-haired,

black-eyed, with his sensuous Italian face, moving about town, in thinking that it was he who was doomed, he out of the three of them.

4

When people in those days in Williamstown, or similar towns in Vermont, came down with what we called consumption, they usually didn't go to some milder climate—usually they couldn't afford it. They stayed where they were, and fought it out—and generally they expected to lose the fight and did lose it.

One of my male relatives in my grandmother's generation decided to stay alive when he encountered this situation. He shut himself up in an upstairs bedroom, closed all the windows and kept them closed, and went to bed. His wife brought him up whatever he wanted to eat. Some persons said that he got a lot of reading done during this period and was extremely well-informed at the end of it. Others said this was nonsense—he just lay there and thought, or just lay there.

At the end of five years, so the story ran, this male relative got up, put on his clothes and resumed a normal life, dying, of some disease other than consumption, at a ripe old age.

Modern doctors would say, I imagine, that what the man needed was quiet while his lungs healed, and quiet was certainly what he had.

But quiet wasn't what Anna Marie Sylvester wanted, and it wasn't what she had. She wanted life, as I see so clearly now; she wanted all the life there was, years and years of it, and all vibrating like tall grass in the meadows when a late June wind runs over them; she wanted joy and beauty, more of each than the whole state of Vermont could contain.

Dr. Watson was attending Mrs. Dole, and one day he noticed that Anna Marie was thinner and, except for the high color in her cheeks, paler. "Young woman," he probably said, in his gentle, impersonal way, "you mustn't work too hard, you must get more sleep."

He wouldn't have discussed this case, or any case. He knew the secrets of half the families in town, and kept them in his own weary heart. Perhaps it was Mrs. Dole herself who talked a little with persons who came to call on her, and worried out loud about Anna Marie.

I don't remember much of how Anna Marie looked in those days. I suppose I had a furtively stolen image of her in my memory, and that she would always look like that lovely image to me, no matter what happened—and this was, indeed, the case.

But it was said, after a while, that Dr. Watson had told her she had consumption, and that she simply must rest. He may have tried to make arrangements for somebody else to replace her in caring for old Mrs. Dole. I don't know about that. Maybe he thought that Mrs. Dole, having lived through so much, wouldn't take the disease, at her age, from Anna Marie; and maybe he thought, too, that life for Anna Marie would be easier if she stayed with Mrs. Dole than if she went back to her parents' farm.

But Anna Marie wouldn't make life easier for herself, anywhere. She didn't want life to be easy, she wanted it to be exciting. She kept going to dances, sometimes with Bill Mansfield, sometimes with other young men, maybe once, even, with poor Tony Mantelli.

Bill Mansfield loved her, I am sure; but he had a hard decision to make. He wanted her to do what Dr. Watson said, and not go dancing either with him or with anybody else. But Anna Marie, so people said, grew temperamental as the weeks went by. She had been very gentle; but now, they said, she made fun of Dr. Watson and what he had told her, and stamped her foot and blazed up when anybody tried to argue with her.

Even Bill Mansfield. They said she slapped him once when he came to take her out and then, after he looked at her feverish face and kissed her hot lips, argued with her to stay home instead. He had started to get out the backgammon board, and that made her furious and also sent her into a fit of wild laughter. So they came out together, and he tucked her carefully into the seat of the sulky he'd brought. I saw him do that once, though maybe not that time, and I wished I could have helped with just one corner of the robe.

I don't now know whether Anna Marie liked being tucked in or not; I don't know whether or not it made much difference to her, after Peter McAndrew died, who tucked her in; I don't suppose she wanted to be tucked in at all, I suppose she wanted all the winds of heaven to blow around her, and not be shut off from them at all, even in October, even in November, even afterwards; I suppose she wanted to be untucked and receive all that life had to offer, without protection of any kind.

Being tucked in by good, kind, humorous Bill Mansfield may have signified to Anna Marie the life she would lead if she gave in, and got well, and stopped dancing, and was a woman like other women, and didn't love beauty quite so much, nor hanker quite so much for things a woman couldn't have in Vermont at that time. These thoughts, for all the affection she might have had for Bill Mansfield, may have made her seem cold to him.

But he did love her. A boy of ten could know that. I insist, after all these years, he did love her; and somehow this made him an uncle, or elder cousin once removed, of my own. I thought Bill Mansfield ought to have her, and marry her, and see that nothing ever, anywhere, at all, hurt her.

I supposed that if Bill married her, they might produce children. In spite of all that was said about this process by my fellow boys and in conversations of elders overheard, I wasn't yet sure precisely how this was done, nor even that it was right and proper. A son of the Puritan revolution couldn't be sure that anything whatever was proper—except, perhaps, a deacon eating himself into a stupor at a church supper.

If Bill had married her, and had bought himself a farm, with a mortgage to encourage him, Anna Marie would have gone where the other farm women went: into weariness and early aging, and no fresh, venturesome beauty any more. This was the fate that waited for her, and not the worst fate that ever befell a woman. Because, as it is clear to me now, she would always have seemed young and lovely to Bill Mansfield.

But she wanted to dance. It was to dance that she was born. How could Dr. Watson prescribe otherwise for her, or Bill Mansfield persuade her? Tony Mantelli, the knife-wielder, would understand this better than Bill could.

Would Peter McAndrew also have understood? Would they two have found a way together? Peter had the Celtic in him, with all the sadness and all the force of love and joy. If he hadn't died they might have gone dancing together, as they planned, and maybe things would have happened differently. Maybe it would not have been what we spoke of as galloping consumption that would have knocked at her door and started her coughing, in the early morning, when it was rest she needed.

The ten-year-old boy couldn't know these things. He could only sense the sorrow when gradually the whole town seemed to understand that if Anna Marie didn't do what the doctor told her and stop dancing she would surely die—and it was only Anna Marie herself who couldn't, or wouldn't, understand.

Perhaps she wouldn't, knowing all she knew. Perhaps a world without dancing in it seemed of little use to her. Perhaps she also dreamed that if she danced enough, and somebody held her tightly enough in the waltz, and the fiddles kept the rhythm and never played *Home Sweet Home,* then she wouldn't be ill any more.

Because spring would come. I knew about spring, with the snow melting, first, around the tall hemlock tree in the front yard, and the crows swarming back by hundreds, and the flood water coming down over the ice in the little gorge behind the Ainsworth house, and finally the unendurably warm breath from the south, and a great, relaxing sweetness in the land. I knew this, and she must have known it, too, in her different way. She wouldn't have wanted, not in those times, to go tearing through the woods, or to build a tree house, or to fish for trout as I did; she wouldn't have wanted to build a raft and go down Stevens Branch the way Huck Finn went down the Mississippi; she wouldn't have longed to climb trees, half afraid and half in ecstasy; she wouldn't have wanted just to go running and howling nowhere or anywhere at dusk on an early spring night; she wouldn't have wanted to take off her shoes and run barefoot in the dust.

Or would she? How do I know? How do I know, remembering her now and wondering about her, how much she wanted, and what? Because the things she might have been entitled to want, and to expect, today, were not the things of the year of which I am speaking.

Anna Marie waited for spring, but she could not wait long enough. Maybe, if she had shut all her windows tight, as my relative did, maybe if she had shut out Bill Mansfield and Tony Mantelli and all the rest, maybe if she had shut out love and the hope of beauty, maybe then she might have lived well into the spring and might have seen the roses bloom again in Mrs. Dole's front yard.

My maternal grandmother had that wish, many years later, and died, as she had desired, in June. But Anna Marie was young, and what she wished was not to die at all, ever, and never to be old—and of this wish she had one portion, as everyone does of every honest wish.

She stopped dancing when she could no longer get up from her bed; and then, not many days later, she died.

My mother said to me, on the day of her funeral, "Robbie, what have you been crying for?"

I did not think she could have guessed this secret, and I said, first that I had had something in my eye, but it was out now, and, second, that I didn't know.

My mother smiled in her kindly, elderly way, though she was then, as I now realize, still young—much younger than I have been for many years. "That's the worst kind of crying," she said, "and the best."

Then she went to the kitchen and got me an apple and some bread and butter, with sugar sprinkled richly on it. "This will make you feel better," she said—and it did.

I wanted to tell her about it, wanted to tell somebody, but I never did.

During the following night there was an early snow, which I suppose covered the grave of Anna Marie Sylvester, just as it did other portions of the Williamstown earth that were approximately six feet long and three feet wide. It probably made Anna Marie's grave seem like a white mound; but I did not go to look at it.

I went sliding, in Mr. Ainsworth's pasture, on what we called a jumper, which was a sort of one-legged ski; I slid into a strip of wire fence above a stone wall and cut myself somewhat, but such things we never minded much. There was a kind of red glory in the sky when we stopped, the half-dozen wild animals that we were, and scattered to our homes, yelling and hilarious and glad, for no reason we could have given, to be alive.

"Did you have fun?" my mother asked, not inquiring why I was a little late for supper, following my brother home by ten or fifteen minutes.

"Yes, I did," I answered eagerly.

But in the night, when the wind howled around the corners of the General E. Bass House, I seemed to hear violins and the soft, clear shuffle of feet.

Maybe, I thought, she did; maybe she did keep her date with Peter McAndrew; maybe she's dancing with him now, somewhere, out beyond the moon, somewhere in the stars; maybe she's happy and well and beautiful again.

At first I was a little frightened, because I wasn't certain the sounds weren't really coming from the dance hall, almost above my head. But then I wasn't frightened any more—not of Anna Marie Sylvester.

Because, I knew, one isn't frightened of persons one loves, no matter where they go or whatever happens to them.

The mud in the middle of the road had frozen, so that the wheels of passing buggies and wagons clacked and rattled over it, instead of slushing quietly the way they had done only the day before. Where water had collected in the ruts there was ice now. I went up along the side of the road to the Pool Bridge and noticed that the grassy hummocks in the marshy parts of the meadow were white and stiff with frost; and there was a little ice at the very edge of the brook, where the current did not keep the water moving.

There was now the sniff of coming winter in the air, though most of it would be gone by noon, and we might have to wait for three or four weeks, or even longer, before there was ice enough for skating or snow enough for sliding down hill. Now we were sure, as we had not been in September and October, that the great change of the year was coming. We had only to wait.

Even before I had crossed the bridge and come within sight of the schoolhouse yard I could hear the excited yelling of boys who had arrived before me, even before the warning bell had rung. I began to run, almost skidding on the frosty planks of the bridge, as though if I didn't hurry winter would be there before I was.

CHAPTER TWELVE

The Stuff That Dreams Are Made On

*I*F THERE were not so many other witnesses, I should think
I dreamed the town I seem to remember. Surely I dreamed
part of it, and a part of it was real. What my brother and
sister remembered I did not wholly remember. What I remembered, and have been trying to tell, may never have been wholly
in their memories at all.

Each town, each village, is as many communities as there are
persons at any moment living in it.

It is true, however, that the Williamstown we each knew, in
our various ways, in 1898, is not there any more. It was the
stuff that dreams are made on, and it has now been undreamed,
and another sort of morning has come, other than the mornings
we knew.

There was a magic, and a spell, and a curse; but the magic
has been waved away, and the spell broken, and the curse was
a curse of sleep and not of pain.

The town and village as I knew them seemed permanent. I
thought, without ever putting the thought into words, that we
were fixed in time and place, and nothing would ever change
very much, we youngsters would never grow up, our parents
would never grow old and die, the past and future were stories
and make-believe.

2

Merrill Linton told me one day that his father had said, "This town pretty near broke up last year."

I was startled. I asked how a town could break up. I hadn't noticed anything coming loose.

Merrill shook his head wisely. He didn't know the answer. What I now suppose was that this was partly the tail-end of the depression of the 1890's, from which the Spanish-American War and, as we Vermonters, big and little, mostly saw it, the noble and wise policies of the Republican Party, had helped to lift us. It may also have been suspected, even then, that it would be better to haul granite by rail into Barre and Montpelier than to lug it by road or rail into Williamstown.

What made Williamstown the most prosperous as well as the most cosmopolitan of small towns was the granite business and the people it brought. Whatever exists seems natural to a boy, and so it seemed natural to me that our small town in the hills, in Orange County, Vermont, should have three languages —English, French, and Italian, or maybe four if you included the broad Scotch some of the men from Aberdeen spoke. It seemed natural that four distinct races or nationalities should come downtown on Saturday night to hang around J. K. Linton's store, or listen to a band concert, or see an outdoor patent medicine show, or just buzz around.

The Civil War memorial in front of the Congregational Church, on the left as you went in from Main Street, had nothing but English names on it, with maybe a few Irish. But if there had been a monument put up in honor of the soldiers of the war of 1898, English names would not have sufficed.

This was the way it was, however. This was the way it always would be. The hill farms said so. The stonesheds said so. Everything said so, the meadows and the hills, the regular comings and goings of the seasons.

It would snow in January and December, and between those months, about midway, there would be a little warmth—too much, sometimes. But the climate wouldn't change, even though

Mr. Ainsworth did once remark, during a long dry spell, that maybe it was the Lord's will never to let it rain again. Nothing would change. As for myself, even though I had turned ten years old in July, 1898, it was impossible that I should turn eleven in July, 1899, and that this process should go on repeating itself until, let us say, the year 1958 arrived.

No; Williamstown, Vermont, 1898, was a finished product, the way I looked at it, the way all we boys looked at it. Who can ever believe in the future? There isn't any future.

3

We therefore looked at our town, not knowing that much of it was transient; and at the stonesheds, the particular feature of our town in 1898, not knowing that they would pass like the insubstantial cobwebs of a dream.

A boy does not think of capital investments and the returns thereon, or of what makes business in general go. Our view of stonesheds was a material one. There stood the buildings, where our parents would rather we did not go during working hours, except when sometimes we took my father's dinner pail to him. There was, during those working hours, the clickety-clack of hammers on stone—a sound I have never heard outside of the granite towns, and which I will remember to my final day. There was the great strength and beauty of this stone, the cranes that lifted and carried it, the chips that were daily wheeled out to be added to the everlasting terminal moraines around the sheds, the smell of the slush, whatever it was, that was used to polish the granite.

Sometimes we boys would slip over to one of the stonesheds on a day when nobody was working—Sunday, maybe. It was fascinating to wander among the half-worked stones, to inspect the tools abandoned when the closing whistle blew, to see the crane machinery all ready for work, but still and unmanned. We never thought of a day when the tools would be laid down for the last time and the stationary engine and crane would work no more in that place, nor the men who operated them. The tools, the chisels, were the property of the men who used them;

but dead men, or sick men, or men who had turned to some less deadly and less beautiful occupation did not need them.

In the yards outside the sheds, in a wilderness of granite chips, stood the derricks which did the outdoor handling of the stone. Iron rungs ran up the vertical members of this apparatus, for the convenience of the men who had to adjust the rigging. One of us would always dare the others to climb these poles, and, with whatever sinking of the heart, this we had to do. I remember to this moment the first time I tried this, with no previous experience of dizziness on high places. I made the top without hesitating, then I looked down, and everything swam.

"What's the matter, Rob?" asked Merrill Linton when I had lowered myself shakily to the ground. "Scared?"

"What's to be scared about?" I demanded, keeping my voice as steady as I could. "For two cents I'd go back up right away."

Merrill fumbled in his pocket. "All right," he said.

I backed off. "What's the use?" I asked. "I've been up once. If that don't prove it, going up a dozen times wouldn't."

Another thing we did was to climb up, inside the shed, to where the operator of the overhead crane sat. This wasn't so bad, however, because the height was less and there was a kind of enclosed seat that made a boy feel safe.

Handling granite, high or low, was a man's job. I wished I were man enough to do it. Then I was afraid I would grow old enough to have to do it. But I knew I wouldn't. I would be a boy forever.

4

There were, I suppose, three worlds in Williamstown: the world of the stonesheds, the world of the villagers, and the world of the farmers. We boys found mysteries in the worlds of the Italians and the French Canadians, but these worlds were not completely strange. Or they were no more strange than the worlds of all adults, for we boys were a community to ourselves.

At school there were more children of the old stock than of the Italian and French Canadian; but I think this was because the men who worked in the stonesheds were younger than the natives and in many cases hadn't yet married or hadn't yet had children.

As I look at a picture of the children of the Williamstown Graded School taken about 1898, give or take a year, I can detect the Scotch and Welsh blood in boys or girls whose names I remember, one or two with French Canadian names, none that I am sure were Italian, but this doesn't mean there were none, and of course the Irish. There is one boy I have always thought looked like Huck Finn—he still does, in this photograph. There is one girl I thought then, and long afterward, as beautiful as the dawn; I think I can see why I thought so, but I am not quite sure.

This picture was taken on the broad front steps of the school, with the teachers standing at the top. Some of them I remember, but not their names. What would one of them say if she asked me, as she did once, to bound Europe and Asia, naming each body of water, each bay, gulf, and strait, all the way round? She once did ask me and I did. I would like to please her, for she has a pleasant face; but I am not sure I could.

Where now is the Barents Sea? What became of it after 1917? What became of the small, ineffectual-looking boy child who sits fourth from the left on the top steps in the picture? His ears stuck out like wings but his hair was dark and plentiful. The half-frightened look he wears may have been due to his awareness that this was somehow an occasion, a frieze on a Grecian urn, a thing that this child's descendant, as in a manner of speaking is the case, would be studying more than half a century later. He would, I think, view this descendant with suspicion and skepticism. He would be glad he was not that descendant. He would be happy to stay where he is, on the top step of the schoolhouse porch on a warmish day in the late '90's—for warm I judge it must have been, since an unscreened schoolroom window is open and nobody is heavily dressed.

Where is that boy, that immature moon calf? What happened to all of us after the photographer finished his work and school was dismissed? I know what happened to my brother, and also to my sister, though she is not in this picture; as I write both have lived to what would have seemed to us then great old ages.

But the others? Where are the boys I have called Ralph Stevens and Jim Nutting? Where is the little girl I called Millicent Byrnes, and where is her sister Doreen? Can the teachers, all so young and smiling in the picture, be dead or very, very old now?

I try to get back into this picture, and at times and for brief instants I can do so. My brother seems to have a hole in the knee of one of his long stockings; so have I. I believe these must have happened since we left home an hour or so ago, or that we managed to get out without our mother seeing us. Our mother always wanted us to look as well as we could; she was quick with the darning needle and she could tie a flowing bow, of the sort a small boy then wore, as neatly as any woman in town.

There we are; but five minutes later the group must have been broken up. We rose and went away—the teachers to whatever they did at home, the girls, as we thought, to playing with their dolls, the boys to roam and yell.

Such was the youth of Williamstown in 1898: such was that year's here and now, no matter how much it has since become there and then.

The building where this picture was taken was still there when I last visited Williamstown. It was a little bigger, that was all. I think it was bigger, in spite of the decrease in the town's population, because more children now go to school more weeks in the year and more years in their lives. I wish all my long-ago friends in the Williamstown Graded School had had that opportunity.

5

But I am not thinking so much of the passage of time as of the dwindling of a town. For though Williamstown did not break up, as Merrill Linton's father had been afraid it would, it did shrink. What was there in 1898, in that golden year, that could cast such a shadow?

As early as that year there appeared, at rare intervals, a Thing with wheels but no horse, that nevertheless managed to move along our dusty, muddy, and rocky roads. This was a spectacle we wouldn't miss for anything; but we saw it as a free outdoor circus, not as a portent of the future.

We argued over what it should be called. Many persons said it was a horseless carriage—as, indeed, it was. Others called it an automobile, and were rebuked by writers in *The Youth's Companion* and other publications, who said you could not unite a Greek root with a Latin root. This mattered to me, even at the age of ten, after I had heard my father and Mr. Ainsworth argue it.

But the Thing itself, whatever it was called, remained marvelous and incredible. It made a terrific noise. It was always breaking down. Yet it could go from Williamstown to Barre, if all went well, in not much over half an hour; and if it ran at all, it could go when its owner wanted it to.

As far as I know, it did not then occur to our elders, any more than to the intelligent children who listened so carefully to them, that the Thing would do anything to Williamstown. We did not take it that seriously.

This was one of the years, I think, when our rich Uncle Willie, my father's brother from Brooklyn, paid us a visit. I don't suppose Uncle Willie could ever have outspent the elder Morgan; but he did seem to throw dollars around the way we threw pennies, or more so.

And Uncle Willie, a sagacious man if there ever was one, an iron-founder of good repute and some success, never spoke of buying an automobile. Let them have their fun, he seemed to think; he and his family would stick to horses. Uncle Willie had a son, also named Willie, whom he sent to board with us once in order to get some fresher air than Brooklyn's then was —or still is—into his lungs. He also had two pretty daughters, somewhat older than even my brother, but pleasant to have around.

When Uncle Willie and his family arrived—for some reason without Mrs. Willie—it was Uncle Willie's custom to buy a huge bag of candy at J. K. Linton's store and then to hire a horse and rig and take us all riding, or as many of us as could get into the rig. To this day I recall my thrill when I had fallen into disgrace for some reason, or so I thought, and hadn't been invited. Then there suddenly appeared Cousin Joanna, with a buggy, and gaily hailed me. I had been swinging in the hammock by the hemlock tree in our front yard.

Cousin Joanna was wearing some sort of thin summery dress with a silk sash, a large straw hat, and small shoes not made of leather at all, the way shoes were supposed to be, but of some fabric that resembled her sash. I nearly died, first with joy, then with embarrassment at my inability to find something to say. Fortunately, Cousin Joanna had enough to say for two persons, and maybe more. My mother said to my father later, didn't she ever stop talking? But I didn't want her to stop talking. Her talking kept me from having to say anything except yes, no, and uh-huh. And I adored being with her, especially since the others had gone off in J. K. Linton's surrey, and there were just the two of us, a sort of overflow meeting, in the buggy.

Cousin Joanna said I was a poor kid, to be left alone like that when everybody else was out having a good time. I said uh-huh, at which she laughed. She then asked me a little about school, and I told her a little. After a silence she inquired, as so many adults and semi-adults did, what I wanted to be when I grew up, and I told her, as I always told persons who asked this question, that I wanted to be a locomotive engineer. It was my hope, I believe, that some day I would find somebody who would do something to help me become an engineer; maybe somebody who had a locomotive and wanted to train a young man to operate it.

Cousin Joanna, of course, had no locomotive. Few young women had locomotives in those days, any more than they do now, except as the automobile might be called one. But she seemed politely interested.

"Wouldn't you like to be a doctor or a business man or something like that?" she inquired.

I said, more positively than I really intended, no, I wouldn't. She laughed again. "You know what you don't want, anyway," she remarked. "That's something. You're a nice boy, Robbie. I wish you could give me some advice."

I said I wished I could, and waited, but she didn't tell me what kind of advice she wanted.

A buggy and a horse provided good transportation for a young man and his sweetheart, and even for a boy and his adolescent cousin. If this sort of peaceful transportation had continued, Williamstown would still be about as it was in 1898, with some modern improvements—or so I believe.

A horse and buggy did not require the kind of roads the Thing later demanded. The curves could be tight, since a horse and buggy—or an equivalent horse-drawn vehicle—could not pass around any curve fast enough to menace itself or any other conveyance.

Cousin Joanna and I, with Cousin Joanna driving most expertly, as I thought, went up on the West Hill along the road that ultimately led to Berlin Pond. I wanted to stop and steal two of Jake Gilbert's pears from the tree that almost overhung the road—there weren't many pears ripening at any time in our part of Vermont—but I could not suggest this to that refined city dweller, my Cousin Joanna.

In fact, Cousin Joanna had to suggest it herself. We drove on again, each munching a not too juicy pear. The buggy squeaked, the way buggies did, and made a satisfying crunch when we passed over a ridge of rock that the roadmakers hadn't judged it necessary to remove.

This was no way to get anywhere, but it was a satisfactory way to spend an afternoon.

I kept hoping Cousin Joanna would come back to that question of my giving her advice, not because I would know how to do that, but because maybe she would have to tell me about her life in the big city of Brooklyn. "It's quiet up here," she said. "I wish I could stay here and not have to go home again."

I wished so, too; but of course she did go home, when the visit ended a few days later, and I couldn't see that she seemed unhappy about it.

She did say, as Uncle Willie and his family were about to get aboard the train, that she and I would have another buggy ride some day. But we never did.

We never did have another buggy ride, that was the truth. Nobody had buggy rides any more, after a while, except in Bermuda and Central Park, for the quaintness of it.

The Thing with wheels but no horse made buggy rides obsolete, and, without meaning to, killed the Williamstown I knew.

The Thing killed Williamstown, and not out of cussedness, but because it was so demanding. The Thing demanded a different sort of road from the one on which Cousin Joanna and I went riding. The Thing commanded that the bumps be taken out and the curves straightened. The Thing did not like dust or mud. The Thing had no thought of a road taken at leisure, tasted and relished; the Thing had to be somewhere at a given time, anyhow in a great hurry; the Thing wished to hustle and dash, not stroll.

So I recall this gentle ride with Cousin Joanna with a not too melancholy sadness. It was not the last of its kind. Years and years later I could take my future wife buggy riding in California; and even after our marriage I could still hire a rig in Palo Alto and drive her masterfully up into the hills, showing off my horsemanship, if that was what it was, as we proceeded.

But the change hadn't really begun in 1898. Cousin Joanna and I didn't suspect what was about to happen. Uncle Willie didn't suspect it. If he had suspected it, he would have rushed home to Brooklyn, bought himself a Stanley Steamer or whatever it was that could be had in that year, and returned, like a shooting star, to a deeply impressed Williamstown.

So Cousin Joanna and I went jogging through a deep mist of peacefulness, she doing the talking, I doing the listening, but both of us, I imagine, glad to be hearing the slow plop-plop of hoofs and to smell the mingled perfumes of dust, harness, horse sweat, and the vague flowers and grasses of the field.

I was quite happy. This was not a perfect year, I thought. That would come later. But 1898 was not too bad, this afternoon was not bad at all.

6

I don't know what happened to J. K. Linton's store, except that after my time it became a farmers' cooperative, and after that it burned down and was physically replaced by a filling station. If it hadn't been for the Thing there would, of course, have been no need for a filling station.

It is just as easy to explain why the hotel went away as it is to explain why the J. K. Linton store, dissolved into ashes, the smoke of it rising into a clear sky full of images, went away. The hotel burned down. So did the stonesheds. But a store, a hotel, a stoneshed would grow again if the soil were fit for them. In 1898 it was fit for them. Later it wasn't.

If the roads had remained the way they were the afternoon Cousin Joanna and I jogged over them the store, the hotel and the stonesheds would also have remained. I was sure, on that particular afternoon with Cousin Joanna, that they always would. I was so sure that I didn't have to think about it.

The roads were measured by time, and time in 1898 went slowly. Cousin Joanna and I would have needed an hour, at least, to get to Barre by horse-drawn buggy, and perhaps another hour and a half to get back, since getting back was uphill.

Therefore Williamstown could have, and had to have, a hotel, several stores, three churches, and, if business seemed good, two or three granite-cutting sheds. Williamstown was an island in time as time was measured in 1898; and an island must provide itself with the necessities of life.

Williamstown could do this, no matter what it took in from the outside world. It didn't make all its own flour, but it could have; nor process all its own meat, but it could have; nor raise all its own vegetables, but it could have; nor raise much of its fruit, but yet it had apples enough, and berries, and a cherry or two; nor provide all its own lumber, but it came near doing this. Williamstown people could have stayed alive for a long while if the Central Vermont Railway had stopped running and the dirt roads had been blocked. Life would have been Spartan but not impossible.

The stonesheds, in 1898, were one of the facts, the most important fact, that made Williamstown different from most other Vermont towns. They had been built in a rush of enthusiasm; the branch line of the Central Vermont had been brought in under that same magic spell; and there we were.

I am not sure that J. K. Linton and some of the other business men didn't think of Williamstown as a town with a dramatic future—perhaps a coming little city with maybe ten thousand inhabitants instead of just one thousand or so—a rival of Barre and Montpelier.

Certainly somebody with a sense of permanence must have built the newer houses on Construction Hill, at the northwest corner of the village. These houses were ugly boxes, in the square, uncompromising, late nineteenth-century Doric; but somebody must have thought he could get out of them the money he had put into them.

Did he do this? I doubt it. The rents couldn't have been collected long enough before the decline began, and the Italians, Scots, and French Canadians moved away to what they hoped would be greener pastures. For what happened to Williamstown at first was not the ending of its importance as a trading center for the farmers; it was the departure of its cosmopolitan granite workers.

Some of this feeling I must have had, even then. I never liked the houses on Construction Hill. There was a grace that even shabbiness and lack of paint couldn't kill in most of our village dwellings, and in the farmhouses, too. Some of these houses were beautiful. I think the General E. Bass house was such, in the time when I knew it.

But Construction Hill, as I now realize, was like the intrusion of a factory town into a mellow village. It was the worst thing the stonesheds did to Williamstown, just as the mingling of three and more races was the best thing. It would have been better to leave it in pasture, and let the cows graze and enjoy the view across the little valley, over the church steeples, to the near ridges.

(246)

7

How did Williamstown begin to wane from its high position? Was it dying, a little, in my time? What stabbed it harder— some quirk in the granite industry that shifted the movement of stone to Barre and Montpelier; or the weapon that struck at all the small towns from ocean to ocean, from border to border, the gasoline-driven Thing, the smooth highway, the consequent shrinking of the map, so that a market town every thirty miles, say, could take the place of a market town every ten miles or so?

I didn't see anything at all going on, during my time, that suggested the great changes that were to come. A boy of ten wouldn't—boys of ten are almost never philosophers, economists, sociologists, or historians.

I might have suspected an impermanence in the fact that my father sometimes ordered groceries from Ginter Bros. in Boston, and that it was possible to buy shucked oysters in J. K. Linton's store on certain days. These oysters were sold in cardboard containers in pint or larger sizes, and if a boy bought them for his family's supper he carried the container carefully home by its wire bail and hoped for the best. We never ate these oysters raw: they were stewed or fried or scalloped, which may have been just as well considering the state of refrigeration at that time. I never heard of anybody in our town dying of them.

Now, it was plain that when Ginter Bros. and the oyster business came into the picture, Williamstown was no longer self-sufficient. But I didn't see this, and I am not sure that J. K. Linton did, either.

So there was Williamstown, and there was the year 1898. Our family began to disperse a little later, and that is too long a story for the present. I myself left Williamstown in 1901 to go to high school in Waterbury, Vermont, with kindly help from my aunt and maternal grandmother. That, too, is another story— there are so many other stories.

I turn back to that picture of the students of the Williamstown Graded School—sixty-five or seventy children, each one of them eager to live and be happy, each impeded one way or another in the attempt, some doomed to die young, some doomed—if that is the word—to live to a great old age. Well, for each pupil, for each of the smiling and dignified teachers, there is a story, and most of the stories will never be told. I cannot tell them. I wish I could. I can respect the everlasting silences, that is all.

The pains, the sorrows, the gladness, the ecstasies, the fears, the known and secret offenses of a Vermont country town in 1898: these are a part of the long pilgrimage of mankind; they are one with Athens and Rome, with Florence and Paris, with the aborigines of New Zealand and Australia; with all the past, all the present and all the future. But we did not know this then, and especially a boy ten years old did not know it.

Since this is a guided tour of Williamstown as it seemed to a ten-year-old boy in the year 1898, I propose now to explore again, briefly, and finally, this vanished dominion.

This is a high valley among the hills, where the Indians long ago raised corn. It is so wide a valley, by Vermont standards, that we were not crowded in it. But the hills were there, and we were cradled in them.

If I went upstreet from the General E. Bass house, I had the lovely brick building of the Sibley farm on my left, with its attendant barns and the meadows stretching level for I suppose a quarter mile or so. On my right would be Mr. Ainsworth's meadows, not much used at that time except for producing hay. As I neared the Pool Bridge, where the brook crossed the road, I might see marshes on either hand if it were spring or early in a rainy fall. There was a modern house or maybe two such on the Sibley side and a stone wall on the Ainsworth side. Once, on that stone wall, not far from the bridge, I saw a stone covered with light green moss of a strangely lovely shade; but when I bent to admire this stone, it was not a stone at all but a snake that swiftly uncoiled and slid away. I drew back alarmed, but I still recall the beauty as well as the fear.

The Pool Bridge was overhung with willows. The nature of the stream underneath changed from year to year as the sand migrated upstream or downstream; I never knew why. Daice swam in it, and suckers lingered patiently for the baited hook, knowing perhaps that few cared to bother catching them, but hoping to be appreciated and compared with trout, once they were in the frying pan.

The bridge had a sort of bulwark on each side covered with corrugated iron and overhanging a little. I used to cross this bulwark, on the outer side, hanging by my hands. Other boys weren't all courageous enough to do this, and after a while I wasn't, either. Where did all that valor go, I wonder, when I needed it in later years?

After one crossed the bridge, the village began. On the left there was a sort of tenement building, two stories high, with verandas, painted in a dark brown, gloomy in winter but pleasantly cool in summer. Beside this tenement there ran a short road, with two or three houses on it. In one of these houses lived Millicent Byrnes; this was a magic building, but I don't recall what it looked like.

Beyond, on the left, was the schoolhouse, a squared-off structure with no architectural pretensions whatever. Though I welcomed vacations in 1898, I loved this school and most of the teachers who taught there.

Just beyond, still on the left, was the house where Willie Stone had lived and died—and always, for me, after that tragedy, it had a sadness.

On the right, almost opposite, lived Mr. and Mrs. Liberty Jeffords, a respected elderly couple to whom I sometimes spoke when Mrs. Jeffords consented to bake some loaves of bread for the Duffus family. These smelled so good I almost ate them up on my way home.

Further along, and still on the right, was the Linton residence —a happy, comfortable place during J. K.'s good days. I remember it in brown paint, and I suspect it wasn't one of the oldest houses in the village. The last time I saw it the paint was peeling badly, and my heart ached a little.

On my way upstreet I came to many houses and other structures which had meaning for me. There were George Beckett's harness shop and his new house, and the older house on the back of the lot where we lived for a while later on; there was the

Edison Girls' brick house on the left; there were, in succession, on the left, the Town Hall, the Universalist Church, the Congregationalist Church, and the Methodist Church; there were, on the right, the stores, beginning with modest establishment run by Mr. Brockway, an elderly man with a short beard and a quiet disposition. I don't now see how Mr. Brockway made his living; and maybe he didn't, maybe he only thought he did. His stock was crowded higgledy-piggledy into a rather small, dark room; he had a pronounced lack of enthusiasm about everything; and though he was polite in a melancholy sort of way I never saw many persons in his store, or heard the sort of conversation audible in J. K. Linton's establishment which was so educational to young boys.

Maybe what Mr. Brockway lost by not attracting customers who liked to sit around and gab, he saved on the crackers and cheese which such customers were inclined to eat and neglect to pay for.

Anyhow, there was Mr. Brockway. In summer he kept his root-beer cold; and once, I believe, I bought five cents' worth of excellent partially rotten bananas from him and wasn't too ill thereafter.

Beyond Mr. Brockway's store, still on the right, was the meat market, where Ben Weaver would sell you a steak for twenty-five cents, but it would be a good steak; and maybe he would give a boy a slice of bologna free. He would also give away crackling, which was the residue from pork fat tried out to make lard; I didn't like this at all, but it was filling.

Then one came to the Linton store, the Monument House, the Martin drug store—the one Fred Ainsworth didn't own—and Seaver's general store, which I think sold clothes, furniture, and various odds and ends, and must have competed in some respects with J. K. Linton's establishment. And there were the three churches on the left.

By this time one would be about at the bridge, the upper bridge, with I forget what on the right side and the blacksmith shop on the left side. On the far side of the bridge a road led up to the box factory and then into farm country. I think there was a cheese factory, too; perhaps at that time, or a little earlier, they had put the cheese in boxes and shipped it out.

The road, or street, that one followed if one didn't care to visit the box factory or the cheese factory pursued its way between two scattered rows of houses, two of which—Dr. Watson's and the Congregational parsonage—had especially friendly associations for me; and in another lived Jim Nutting, my excellent companion.

On the right was the cemetery, where lay not only the fathers and mothers of our hamlet and some of the soldiers who had been brought home from Civil War battlefields, but also Peter McAndrew and Anna Marie Sylvester, and a few of my own generation, among them Perlie Marlowe, Richard Linton, and Archie Staples.

On such a tour of our village I would avoid the road to Barre, which kept straight ahead, and swing right toward Mill Village. The sawmill and the gristmill might engage me for a few minutes, and then I would swing right some more, past a woodworking shop above the mill dam. This shop was often worth looking into, and smelled better than any perfume except possibly new-mown hay and some scents of cooking.

There were a few modest houses beside the stream; these, I believe, belonged to French Canadian "lumpers" who worked in the stonesheds. I was a little afraid of the French Canadians, I can't recall why. They were, in general, I now realize, the best-natured of men; and when they threatened to kill each other, they never intended to do so. But I hurried by, if I was alone.

Opposite these houses there was a farm, owned by I don't know who; what I remember of it now is the way it looked one fall—maybe the fall of 1898—when the field nearest the road had been planted to corn and pumpkins. I stole an ear of corn, which was hard chewing; but what I remember is the beauty of the yellow pumpkins among the brown stalks.

Our tour would now bring us past the Rattlesnake Tavern and so around to the stonesheds and over another little bridge, whence one could look across the marsh and the meadow and see the General E. Bass house.

Then the railway station; and maybe, even after all this walking, it was still bright morning, and Old Man Webb would be at the throttle ready to take the train down the grade to Barre, and Jim Kennealy, the conductor, would be yelling, "B-o-a-r-r-r-r-r-r-r-r-r-d!" the way an old-fashioned conductor always did, as though two or three thousand people were waiting for the word.

I did not, as I said, leave Williamstown until 1901. Yet now it seems to be time to step aboard. It is time to say goodbye to Millicent Byrnes, whom I loved so purely; to the lovely flitting ghost of Anna Marie Sylvester; to Jim Nutting, Ralph Stevens, and the Linton boys; to Mrs. Linton, most excellent of Sunday school teachers, and to good-natured J. K.; to George Ainsworth, who talked to me man to man, and to the Reverend Silas Blake, who helped stir my ambitions and those of other boys; to Mrs. Frankum, who stands out shining and with middle-aged loveliness among all my teachers; to the Italian woman and to Wilford Niles, for whom somehow, in spite of his feeble wits and his uncouthness, I felt an apologetic fondness; even to the livery stable boys, even to Sheridan Dabney; to Fred Ainsworth, that tragic figure, whose pleasantry about the candy called pig's delight I have remembered while forgetting so many other things; to all these people, to the sinners and the strangers, to all who composed our little town—to these it is time to say goodbye.

It is time, after this tour of 1898, to say goodbye to that year. Jim Kennealy repeats his "B-o-a-r-r-r-r-r-r-r-d!" Old Man Webb pulls his throttle and blows his whistle and the fireman—ah, if only I could have been that fireman on at least one trip!—rings the bell frantically.

We are moving, gathering speed, down the grade to Barre and points north, south, east, and west. We are also headed toward the twentieth century. I look back with homesickness and forward with eagerness. Soon we are out of sight of Williamstown and the year 1898.